# THE CHEEKY GUIDE TO BRIGHTON

*Extremely informative, and the perfect accompaniment to all that is irreverent, fun, left-of-centre, amusing, hyperbolic, and wild in this town."*
**Jeff Hemmings** (editor of The Latest magazine)

*"Informative, fun and anecdotal, the best guide around to Brighton & Hove..."*
**Nigel Berman** (editor of New Insight magazine)

*"Indispensable"*
**Surf FM**

*"Cheeky Guides exist in some improbable universe where guide books are dreamed up by Salvador Dalí, designed by Viz, and written by Billy Connolly."*
Local comedian **Jo Neary**

*"Hip, entertaining and in-depth."*
**Jody Thompson** (NME)

**The Cheeky Guide to Brighton**
Written and researched by David Bramwell
Additional writing and research by Jeremy Plotnikoff

ISBN 0 9536110 2 7

Published in 2001 by
Cheekyguides Ltd
72 Buckingham Rd • Brighton • BN1 3RJ
www.cheekyguides.com
Comments or suggestions: david@cheekyguides.com
Business enquiries: jeremy@cheekyguides.com

©2001 Cheekyguides Ltd
All rights reserved

### Acknowledgements
Thanks to Alex, Andrew Bird, the guys at Hexagon Archive, the Comedy Dairy team for agreeing to dress up in ridiculous garbs for the photo shoot, everyone who sent helpful e-mails (especially Adam), Vince from G-scene, Freddie from Scene 22, Paul Kemp and Harriet...sweet Harriet.
Photographs on pages 135, 136, 137, 140, 142, 144 and 203 by kind permission of Brighton Source Magazine
(special thanks to Judith for letting me rummage through her drawers).

### Thanks to the following contributors:
Dave Mountfield, Brian Mitchell, Lisa Holdcroft (for several club reviews), Andrew Bird, Stephen Drennan, Steve from 'Melting Vinyl' and Martin Johnson.
*A free 'Cheeky key fob' will be in the post soon, as a way of saying thank-you for all your hard work.*

### Artwork
Thanks to Lisa Holdcroft for the cover, maps, games and the innumerable cartoons that appear in this book. She is Brighton's answer to Rolf Harris, and should you wish to employ her talents or make burping noises at her, call (01273) 705658.
Special thanks to Stella Starr for the saucy postcard and nipple tassel guide. And hats off to the dry Northern wit of Brighton miscreant Antony Hodgson for his wonderfully acidic depictions of Brighton and Hove.

### Editing
The inital text was impeccably proofed by Stephie Plotnikoff, despite being days away from having her first baby. Final proofing was done by Brighton's coffee house aficionado and lounge-lizard Michael Keane.

Special thanks to Peter Pavement for helping get it all ship-shape at the end, and for doing a brilliant job with the photo love story, bus-spotting section, and Marina advert.

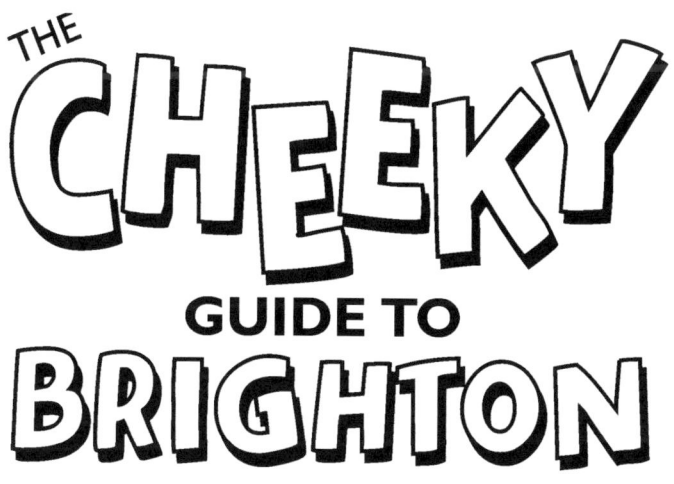

# THE CHEEKY GUIDE TO BRIGHTON

## SECOND EDITION

Written and researched by David Bramwell

Additional writing and research by Jeremy Plotnikoff

Illustrations by Lisa Holdcroft

# About the Creators of this Book

**David Bramwell**

Raised on the wrong side of the tracks, David spent much of his early twenties wrestling with his strict Voodoo upbringing, but after moving to Brighton 10 years ago, he conquered his problems through a yeast-free diet and embroidery therapy, although he does still occasionally stick pins in his wife when she gets on his nerves.

Being the principal writer and researcher of the book, David is, of course, the one who gets all the blame if someone isn't happy with their review, and only recently one disgruntled restaurateur threatened to *'hunt him down like a pig'* for derogatory comments about his Chicken Kiev.

David lives with his wife Alex in the respectable Seven Dials area of Brighton where they are heavily involved in charity work, and only recently raised over £300 when they auctioned off their daughter 'Skegness' for scientific experiments.

**Jeremy Plotnikoff**

Russian in origin, and loved for his naturally furry head and body, Jeremy was found washed up on Brighton beach after a particularly heavy drinking binge in Leningrad. Yet to have grasped any of the English language since his recent arrival in Brighton 10 years ago, he communicates through grunts and strange wheezing noises, but was recently discovered just to have been choking on a biscuit.

Jeremy is responsible for the layout and design of this book as well as fiddling the accounts, lying to publishers and implementing crude torture techniques on any potential competitors. Despite all this he has a nice smile and is a vegetarian, although his recent course of hormone treatment to have his breasts enlarged has raised a few eyebrows.

**Richard Hadfield**

Having chosen to go to Australia for the Olympics during the making of this book, Cheeky's newest but most elusive member contributed precious little, but did keep our spirits elevated with up-to-minute news on the women's badminton.

He currently lives in Oxford with a menagerie of guinea fowl and his fiancée Jane, who smells of gravy.

## ABOUT THIS BOOK

### The making of this book

Back in the good old days, Cheekyguides were cobbled together in an afternoon, using whatever resources were at hand, which was often little more than an old photocopier, some flour, water and a sprig of basil. Nowadays, making a Cheekyguide requires a crack team of experts labouring day and night to bring you the jocular reviews, aesthetically pleasing photographs and exotic spellings that our devoted fan has come to know and love. If you would like to contribute, have an area of expertise about Brighton that you think would benefit this book, or you simply wish to hang out with stylish people who have made something of their lives, contact us and we promise not to laugh at any unsightly deformities you might have.

*We have toiled day and night to be accurate with prices, times of opening etc, but we're only human (except Jeremy who's Canadian) and things change quickly in Brighton, a café today could be an airport tomorrow. If you spot any changes or mistakes, drop us a line and we'll be grateful. Gushing adoration in the form of gifts and money will also be warmly received.*

*Nobody paid to be reviewed in this book and with the exception of a cookie, half a Guinness and a box of truffles, we still haven't had any freebies.*

*I know, I know, what a wasted opportunity.*

### In researching this book we have:

- had ectoplasm thrown at us
- nearly died after an encounter with the world's worst halitosis
- met the ghost of my dead grandfather
- given up trying to review a comic shop when it became apparent that their game of dungeons and dragons stopped for no-one
- auditioned lap-dancing girls
- been fondled in a séance
- found a baby wallaby in the High Street
- had various 'things' pierced just for the sake of reviewing a shop
- been subjected to half an hour of Bavarian oompah music
- witnessed a guy walk in a café, eat a bowl of sugar, shout – 'fuck the lot of you, I'm going home for a wank,' and then walk out again

### And finally, a quick word about adjective abuse

We would like to reassure our more erudite readers that the word 'funky' does not appear in this book and gratuitous uses of the words 'cool', 'groovy' and 'Peacehaven' have been kept to a minimum. Thank you.

Jeremy and David are currently available for village fetes, gala lunches and children's tea parties, though not to host them, just to join in.

# CONTENTS

## INTRODUCTION 8
In the beginning there was only herring • Brighton myths

## PRACTICAL STUFF 13
How to get here • Getting around •

## HERE, THERE, AND EVERYWHERE 18
The Old Lanes • North Laine • The Beach • The Seafront • Kemptown • High Street & West Street • The Marina • Parks & Gardens • Hove

## WEIRD AND WONDERFUL 36
WONDERFUL: Interesting Places • Spotter's guide to Brighton celebrities • Where to take a good stroll • Creatures of the salty depths • Sport
WEIRD: The great outdoors • Where to contact the dead • Palmists and clairvoyants • Stuff that legends are made of • Bus-spotting guide • Have a surreal afternoon in Brighton

## SHOPPING 59
Records • Books • Comics • Videos and movie memorabilia • Groovy things for the home • A good place for buying presents • Musical instruments • Clothes • Oddities • Markets • Auctioneers • Costume rental • Charity shopping

## FOOD 86
Late-night eating • Specialist food shops • Sandwich bars • Cafés and café bars • Top ten greasy spoons • Restaurants • Best chippy • Take-away • Late-night off-licences

## WATERING HOLES 117
Trendy bars • A bit of local colour • Where to go for a natter Cocktail bars • After-hours drinking • A pub crawl in Hanover

## DISCOTHEQUES 134
Clubs • Special club nights • What's on at a glance

## ENTERTAINMENT 146
Cinemas • Theatres • Cult and DIY TV • Comedy • Gambling

# CONTENTS

## MUSIC — 156
Venues • Promoters • Tickets • Local radio • Hall of fame • Local band scene • Getting a gig • Busking • Musicians' wheel of life

## LOCAL HEROES AND ECCENTRICS — 170
Local heroes • Spotter's guide to local eccentrics • Cooper's for haircuts – an appreciation • Adventures with Brighton's most eccentric shopkeeper

## BRIGHTON IN THE MOVIES AND BOOKS — 186
Movies • Books • Literary events

## GAY SCENE — 191
Pubs and clubs • Cafés and food • Cruising areas • Saunas • Gay lingo • Lesbian scene • Special events • Shopping • Magazines and websites • Important information • Support • Hotels

## SEX AND FETISH — 214
Shopping • Tattooists and piercers • Lap-dancing clubs • Saunas

## MIND, BODY AND SPIRIT — 221
Shopping • Yoga and Meditation • Floatation tanks • Astrological charts • Therapists • Where to find out more

## WHAT'S ON — 226
Diary of events • Local press • Websites

## PLACES TO SLEEP — 232
Hotels • B'n'Bs • Guesthouses • Hostels • Camping

## OUTSIDE BRIGHTON — 244

## USEFUL INFORMATION — 246
Local information • Internet Access

## INDEX — 248

## MAP — 254
Map • Street index

## INTRODUCTION

# In the beginning there was only Herring

**1500s**     Brighton starts life as a prosperous fishing village, paying the government 4000 herring a year in taxes.

**1783**     The town becomes a fashionable health resort when a certain Doctor Russell declares that drinking the sea water here would get rid of your boils and put hair on your chest. Not advisable today unless you want to get rid of your hair and have boils on your chest instead.

**1790s**     Brighton's first massage parlour is opened by Sake Deen Mohammed, with the wonderful title of the 'Brighton Shampooing Surgeon'.

**1823**     The Prince Regent has the Royal Pavilion built as somewhere he can bring back a few mates after the pubs have closed.

**1930s**     Torsos start turning up in boxes around the town beginning the reign of the infamous 'trunk murders'. The King's elephant was suspected but nothing was ever proved.

**1960s**     Brighton is host to the 1964 'It's a Knockout', featuring the Mods and Rockers fighting it out on the seafront. The town remains a regular host to holiday battles for the next few years or so, as the beach becomes no man's land, and whoever takes control of the novelty postcard shop is the winner.

**1972**     Sir Laurence Olivier campaigns fiercely for kippers to be returned to the menu on the Brighton Belle railway line.

**1974**     Singer David Lee Roth re-locates to Brighton after quitting his band 'The Red Ball Jets', and opens an unsuccessful sandwich shop called 'Roth and Rolls'. A year later he returns to LA and forms the legendary Van Halen.

**1979**     Quadrophenia is released and Sting has his equity card revoked. Scuffles start up again on the beaches for a while, as all the Mods completely miss the point of the movie.

**1984** Lady Thatcher visits the bathroom and survives the IRA bombing of The Grand Hotel. Others are not so lucky.

**1988** Brighton witnesses its first cannabis famine as infamous ex-resident Howard Marks is arrested.

**1989** Hundreds of packets of cocaine are found washed up on the beach, up the road at Peacehaven. Police cordon off the area when Bobby Gillespie arrives to have a closer look.

**1992** Local cult 'the Temple of Psychic Youth' join hands around the Pavilion and attempt to levitate it, but are stopped at the last minute by the police. Apparently their founder Genesis P.Orridge had dropped 20p and just wanted to check that it hadn't rolled under there.

**1995** The West Pier is declared an independent state by a bunch of squatters, but after two weeks they run out of rizlas and abandon their plans. Inspired by this, only a few months later, Chris Eubank announces in the press that he wants to buy the West Pier, and set up his home there, with a helicopter pad at the end.

**1998** A chip-pan fire causes the famous Albion Hotel on the seafront to burn down. *'Meester Fawlty, is fire is fire....'*

**1999** The Cheeky Guide to Brighton is born, despite several death threats and a kidnap attempt by their arch-enemy, 'The Flaccid Guide to Brighton'.

**2000** Brighton makes a heroic bid to achieve city status by organising a bonanza of unique and exciting events such as...er...erm......er....

# BRIGHTON MYTHS

## Hippy Stuff
New Age legend decrees that a stone circle once stood in the Old Steine, but was smashed up by the Victorians and used to form the base of the big fountain there. This is acclaimed as the magnet of all Brighton's energy and weirdness. It is interesting to note that Old Steine means 'old stone'. Give Julian Cope a ring, he'll put you straight.

## Grave Tales
Brighton seems particularly rich in stories of underground tunnels and burial chambers. One particular myth tells of a house here in Orange Row, which is supposed to have the original entrance to the old Brighton catacombs. Although blocked off with railway girders now, it is still said to be littered with the dead bodies from an ancient flu epidemic.

Also, keep your eyes peeled for the pyramid-shaped grave of a guy called Mad Jack, who insisted on being buried sat upright at an iron table, wearing top hat and tails, a bottle of claret at arm's length, and with his dinner in front of him*.

And where else would the world's most infamous occultist, Aleister Crowley, be cremated, other than our very own Woodvale Cemetery?

## Murder Mystery
Take one of the tours during the festival and you will learn about some of the gruesome murders that happened in the 20s and 30s here. There are many accounts of body parts being left around town in trunks, and a severed head is said to have once been left in a bag by the Horse and Groom bar in Hanover.

One year, Jason, a friend of mine, decided to do the murder tour, and left his house to walk down to Bartholomew Square where it was starting. The guide introduced the tour by saying:
*'We'll commence by visiting the location of probably the most gruesome murder Brighton has ever known'*, and proceeded to walk the group back to Margaret Street, where Jason lived.
*'Hey this is the street where I live!'* he thought with growing alarm.
*'And it was in this house that the body was dismembered and stored in a cupboard for two weeks...'* said the guide pointing at Jason's bedroom window. Jason always sleeps with the light on now and has rekindled his friendship with Mr Floppy his big fluffy bunny.

---

*since last year we discovered this to be true. The pyramid is in Brightling (well it's nearly Brighton) and his real name was John Fuller.

## The Ubiquitous Eubank tale

This short and simple tale comes in many forms but the basis of it goes that Chris (wherever he is) is making a big public display of the fact that he's got a mobile telephone and is making a real show of taking important calls from important people. When, all of a sudden, to his utter embarrassment, the phone starts ringing in his hand.

Now several people I've met lay claim to this one and seem to get a bit annoyed when I suggest it's an urban myth, even though I've heard countless versions, ranging from Chris shopping in the Old Lanes, to Chris jogging along the seafront.

For visitors to Brighton, this story can be adapted and applied to any B-list celebrity from your hometown. Take it away, play with it and make it your own.

## The Hand of Glory

A charm believed to cure lumps on the throat once carried the name of the 'Hand of Glory'. The recipe for this involved a number of gruesome things including the severed hand of a recently hung man, which was rubbed on the offending article or made into a candle. The last hanging to take place in Brighton was at the Steine in 1834 where a woman with a gammy neck was believed to have run from the crowd, taken the dangling hand of the dead man and joyously rubbed it all over her affliction.

For anyone interested, the recipe for the Hand of Glory is still available from local occult archivists 'Hexagon'.

# How to get Here

**PRACTICAL STUFF**

## BY RAIL

Rail Enquiries 0345 484950
or 08457 484950
Connex 0870 603 0505

Trains from London leave Victoria and Kings Cross Thameslink about twice an hour. The Victoria link is usually quicker; about 50 minutes for the fast train. Be careful when returning to London late at night however, check when the last train leaves, it's usually before 12am, even at weekends. There are also direct train services along the coast if you are not coming via London. Rumours abound about a 30-minute service to London starting sometime in the very near future, but nobody in the know seems any the wiser about it.

### At the station

You'll find cash-machines, bureau de change, hotel reservation kiosk and buses and taxis waiting outside. If all that seems too formal, just go straight out, keep walking, and you'll be at the beach in less than 10 minutes.

## SUNDAY TRAINS

*For some reason, there are often repairs to the tracks on a Sunday, which means your inward or outward journey to London may involve three coach journeys via Littlehampton and Barnsley, so check before you travel. I kid you not, I have spent some miserable Sunday evenings dreaming of being at home by the fire sipping fine wines, when instead I'm standing in the rain in the middle of sodding nowhere, waiting for a BR bus driven by some fuckwit who doesn't know where he's taking you. And when he does eventually turn up an hour later and sets off, the bloody bus breaks down. And to top it all off, you don't have a seat. And yes this has happened to me before. Now that's off my chest I feel much better. Ignore this at your peril.*

## PRACTICAL STUFF

### BY PLANE

**From Gatwick** A train and £6.70 out of your pocket will get you to Brighton in 30 minutes. If there are four of you, a taxi will probably cost less because the trains are so damned expensive here. The cheapest option is to get a coach.

**From Heathrow** What a drag, you must really enjoy doing things the hard way. Get a tube to Victoria then a train from there. It'll take two hours at the most.

### BY COACH

**National Express**
Corner of St. James's Street and Old Steine. For enquiries 0990 808080

Tickets can be bought here, but you do have to walk about two blocks to Pool Valley Bus Station in order to catch the bus. The trip to London takes about an hour, and will set you back about £8.

### BY ROAD

Once you've packed your sandwiches, toothbrush, bucket and spade, make your way to the London orbital M25 then take the M23/A23 all the way to Brighton. It shouldn't take more than forty-five minutes once you've left the M25. It's as simple as that. If you travel between 5pm and 7pm through the London rush hour, it's best to take a Travel Scrabble. If you're lucky enough not to be coming via London, you'll probably be taking the coastal route along the A27.

### PARKING

Devilishly tricky and expensive. If you're not parking in a multi-storey you'll need vouchers from newsagents and any other shops with a green 'v' outside for parking in the streets. It's a little confusing because it looks the same as the vegetarian 'v' that you get on Linda McCartney sausages. My advice is, park out of town and walk, or get a bus, it's never that far to anywhere in Brighton. Voucher parking starts at £1 an hour in the town centre and 50p outside. One of the cheapest carparks is near the bottom of Trafalgar Street.

### BY HELICOPTER
(01273) 296900

You'll get as far as Shoreham airport, then it's a 2-hour walk to Brighton along the seafront. What do you mean you haven't got a helicopter? Everyone in Brighton's got one.

# Getting Around

## TAXIS

202020 • 204060 • 747474 • 205205

There are plenty to choose from and all the services are pretty much the same. It shouldn't cost more than a few quid to get across town and I believe all the companies are 24-hour. Incidentally, the taxi-drivers in Brighton are required by law to carry inflatable rings under their seats, so check when you get in. If there isn't one you should be able to blag a free ride.

## BUSES

### Brighton and Hove Bus Company
(01273) 886200

For getting around the town centre there is a flat fare of 80p. Buses are frequent and will take you practically anywhere.

## BUS TOURS

### Open-Topped Bus Tour
(01273) 746205

Brighton for lazy-bones.
Do the lot in one hour for £6.50 (although they are threatening to raise it to £7 very soon).

Look out for a new exciting commentary to be added this year as the tour takes you achingly close to both the West Pier and the Dome.

The tour operates March to October and there are spots all over town where you can catch a bus, the most obvious being outside the Palace Pier. The tour is conducted in over 20 languages including Esperanto.

## BRIGHTON SUBWAY

Closed due to subsidence and water-logging, Brighton's once-famous Metro-line used to stretch as far as Eastbourne, Worthing and London. Nowadays it is home to Brighton's expanding subterranean community and illegal bear-baiting societies.

## FESTIVAL TOURS

During the festival in May, there are a whole host of tours ranging from ghost tours, gay tours, historical tours, literary tours and a tour of the sewers. Some are good, some are awfully dull.

The sewers tour is particularly recommended, and I bet you just won't be able to resist buying something from the souvenir shop.

Some of the ghost tours are fun too as you always get a few good stories to take away, even if they are made up.

In fact, I've always wanted to return to some of the scary places I've been taken on a midnight tour, then, the next evening, dress up and hide in one of the spots and jump out and scare all the tourists at an opportune moment. You're right, I have a juvenile sense of humour.

**PRACTICAL STUFF**

**PRACTICAL STUFF**

## BIKES

It's quite pleasant cycling around parts of Brighton, although the hills can be a bit of a drag at times and the council have only made a half-arsed attempt with proper cycle lanes. Be especially careful cycling down North Street and Western Road, as some of the bus drivers will squeeze you off the road onto the pavement, owing to their careless driving and the lack of a much-needed cycle lane. The seafront is great though; it's long and flat and you can play dodging the dozy gits who always walk in the cycle lanes.

## CYCLE HIRE

**Sunrise Cycle Hire**
Under the West Pier
(01273) 748881
(late March-September)

Three quid an hour, twelve quid a day, ten if you're a student. They also do tandems, which is handy if you're a horse like me needing to make a fast getaway from the scene of a crime. Oh my god, have I said too much.

## LIMOS

**Hannington's Limos**
(01273) 329877
Ask for the Limo service

**Linkline Limos**
(01273) 580500
6-hours around Brighton costs £220

**Lancaster Limos**
0800 7313613

If you want to do the tourist thing you could always take a trip in Brighton's stretch limo, although parading around in a small white whale at £50 an hour isn't my idea of money well spent.

## WALKING

Visitors from LA might be interested to learn that this outdated form of transport is still immensely popular in Brighton.

## SKATEBOARDING

Brighton has one of the largest collections of skateboarders in England. This probably has as much to do with the weather as anything else, but we also have our own skate park and numerous other good spots to skate. These are, however, diminishing rapidly, as lippy young ankle-biters with bad attitude have pissed off the general public so much that £150 fines are starting to be issued against skaters.

### The Skatepark
Located at the Level

The park consists of one halfpipe and numerous other small ramps, and it is a good place to meet other skaters.

There are good displays of local graffiti here, just take a peek on the back of the halfpipe.

## OTHER SKATE SPOTS

**St. George's statue**
(Old Steine)
There are some nice ledges here.
**Cottesmore School**
Couple of good flat banks.
**Woolworths**
Some cool places behind here.
**Seafront**
(Between the piers)
Some good drops and rails.
**Sainsburys**
The car park is a good place to skate if it is raining (only after shop hours). Don't abuse this, they are OK about skating here at night, but they are not cool about it when the shop is open.

# Here There & Everywhere

## THE OLD LANES

A series of wonderfully confusing narrow passages and cobbled streets make up this part of Brighton, which is steeped in history and full of stories of smugglers, ghosts and randy nuns.

The passages are known locally as Twittens (an old smugglers expression meaning 'thin street with over-priced shops') and are enclosed by West Street, East Street and the seafront.

You should enjoy simply wandering around here, but don't worry if you get lost; I still do and I used to work here. To find the centre of the maze, try and locate the dolphin statues in the fountain at Brighton Square. It is customary to throw your shoes into the fountain here and make a wish. If you head off past Rounder Records, have a look at their back wall to see which album they have spray-painted on it. As a reference point, you'll be on your way back to East Street.

This is an area renowned for its jewellery and antiques shops, there is also an abundance of cafés, restaurants and clothes boutiques.

It's much more antiquated compared to the fashionable North Laine, but at night-time the busy restaurants give it a new lease of life.

The best time to visit the Old Lanes is at dawn, when the noise of the seagulls and the strange light of early morning pierce through the empty alleyways. At times like this, eerie folklore tales about ghosts and ghoulish fishermen no longer seem like a load of old cobblers.

If you haven't got long in Brighton, I'd recommend a mooch around here. Try Food For Friends for lunch, and make sure you poke your head in at Fabrica (opposite the post office on Ship St) to see which dazzling art installation they have in this beautiful building.

If it's summer, this is a busy area for busking. Look out for the old guy who busks with a rabbit. Once I even saw a girl busking with a rat here. She kept it on her shoulder whilst playing her guitar, and now and again she let it drink out of her mouth. Eurrrgghh!

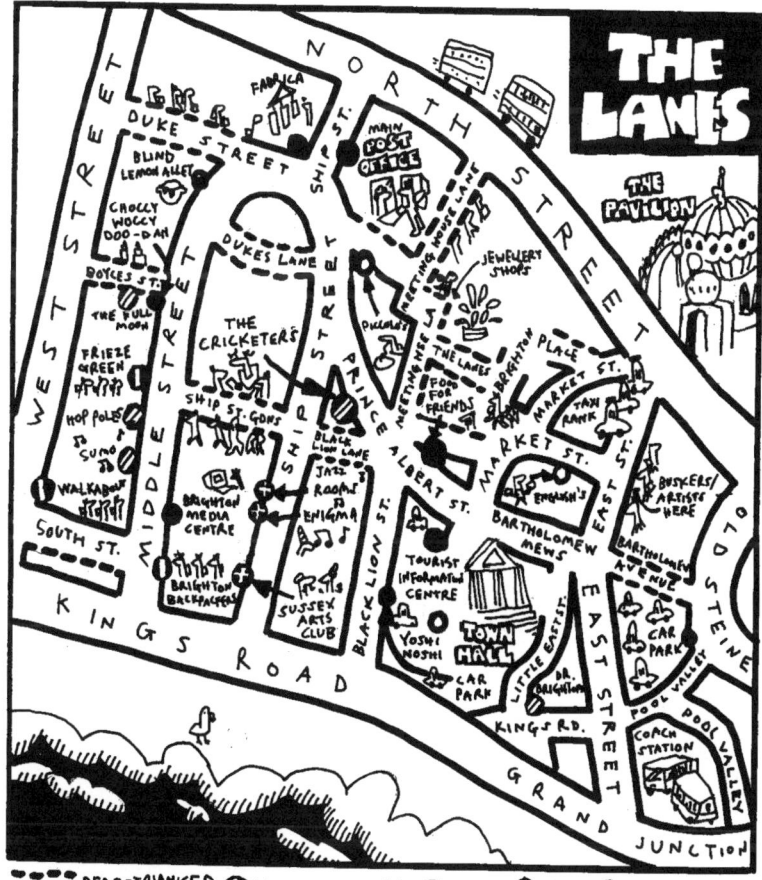

**HERE, THERE AND EVERYWHERE**

## NORTH LAINE

Known as Brighton's bohemian quarter, this unmissable area has some of the best shops, pubs and cafés in town. Glamorous, young, posey, vibrant and pretentious it may be, but Cleethorpes High Street it is not. In fact, the North Laine does its best to be Haight Ashbury, Carnaby Street and Greenwich Village, all rolled into a handful of streets.

This locality prides itself on its café culture, which blossoms during the summer months. Balconies heave with milkshakes and suntanned legs, and tables and chairs start to sprawl out onto the roads. It's a pleasure just to hang out on some of the café balconies and watch the world and its dog go by. The Bamboo Bar and Kensingtons are notably good haunts for this. On Saturdays, Gardner Street is pedestrianised, and becomes one enormous mass of cappuccinos and sunglasses.

The North Laine is, of course, posers' paradise, and from 60s kitsch to 90s chic, every fashion gets a look in. Walk down Kensington Gardens in full 'KISS' make-up with cream crackers stuck to you, and still few heads will turn.

### Three unique features about the North Laine

1) Smoking is compulsory in most bars and cafés in the North Laine.
2) Everyone who lives here will, at some point in their life, buy a drink for a man known as Dave Suit.
3) If your parents turn up wearing Pringle jumpers, somebody will see it as an important fashion statement.

Many of the shops here are unique and shamelessly glitzy. Pussy, Borderline and Re-Vamp are just a few worth seeking out, where you will find everything from silver platforms, CDs by the Chocolate Watch Band, and fetish kitchenware. This area has a fabulous collection of record shops and clothes shops too, not to mention kitsch and retro gear from the likes of Cissy-Mo. And don't be afraid to stray off the beaten track at times, Acme Art with its surreal sculptures and eccentric owner is well worth seeking out.

The shops are also a good starting point for checking out what's going on in the clubs and venues, as the streets visibly sag under the weight of posters and fliers in every window. In fact, it can be information overload as they are handed to you on street corners, and thrown at you from the tops of buildings. You'll even find them taped to the pavement at weekends.

If you stand around in the same spot for too long in Sydney Street, someone will stick a poster on you.

In the North Laine anything goes, the more flamboyant the better. Fashions and sub-cultures fight for space along these busy streets, so don't be surprised if you end up going home with an exotic tattoo and your genitals pierced; it will simply have been a Brighton experience.

### Three things to look out for in the North Laine
1) Big Ian standing outside Immediate Clothing on Sydney Street having a fag.
2) The busker who plays Bright Eyes on the penny whistle over and over again at the bottom of Trafalgar street.
3) The UFO fairy lights at Xmas.

Snoopers, in the North Laine

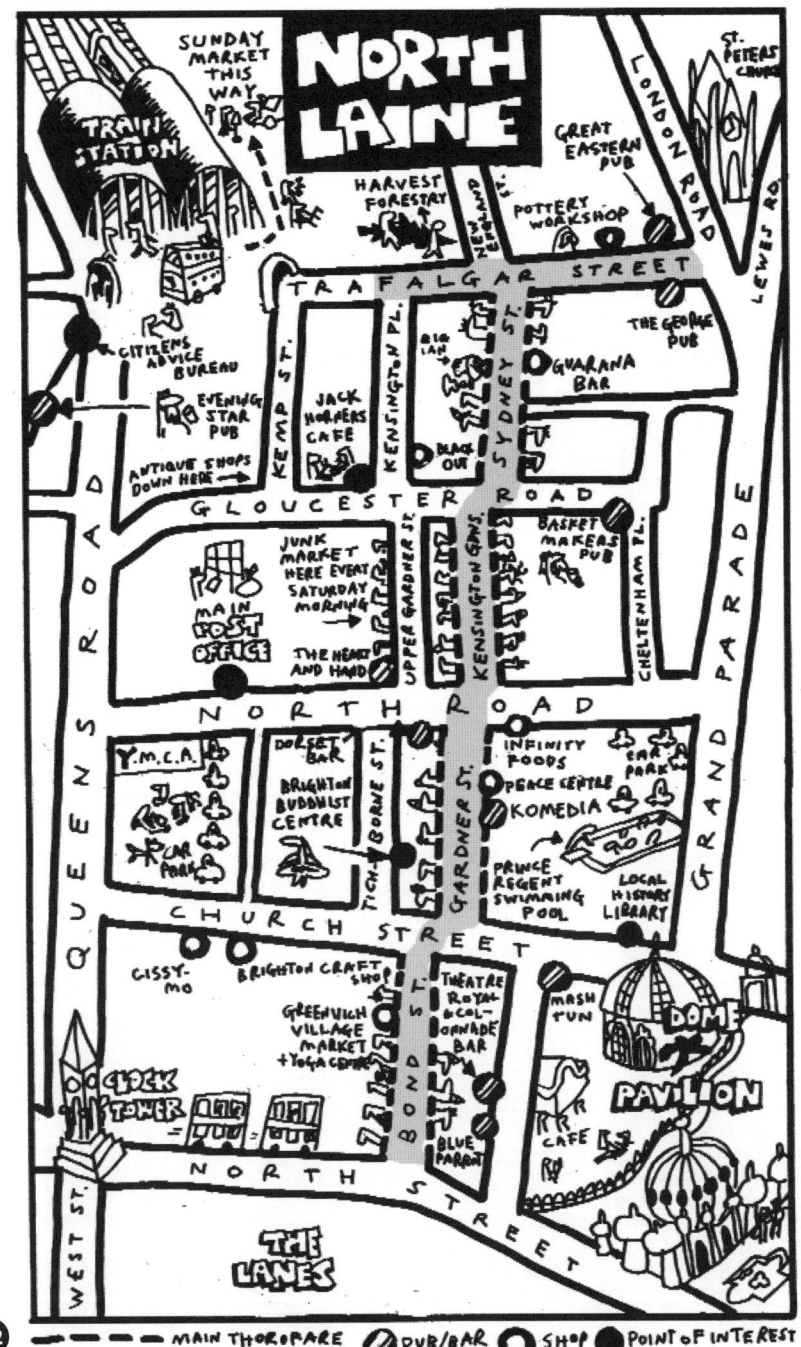

## THE BEACH

*'The beach washes away the ills of mankind.'*
**Dr Richard Russell**

Stretching from the nudist beach near the Marina, across to Hove and beyond, this is one of the main inspirations behind all that is Brighton. In summer, it's always littered with life; from families with kids to groups of bright young things, and the obligatory loony with a metal detector.

'Hey, I found another ring-pull.'

When the sun is out, most likely you'll want to join the crowds down there and brave the sea for a swim, or just hang out and be a sun-lizard. There's also a new volleyball area if you like to do it Baywatch-style, or for the more adventurous, the banana boat ride is definitely worth trying.

At night, between the two piers, the beach is usually crowded with over-spill from The Fortune of War and other bars down there, and there's usually a good buzz about the place. This is also a hot-spot for many of Brighton's best-known clubs, such as the Zap, The Honeyclub and The Beach, so expect the clubbing crowd to be out in force. It's definitely a good place to hang out and chat, and if you feel like doing a little wooing, it can be a lot more conducive outside than in, where you'll have to shout and slobber in someone's ear just to tell them you like their friend.

Sometimes though, when it's a warm night and you're in the mood, it's good to by-pass the busy bars and clubs. Just find a quiet spot, get some beers and food, and come here with friends and watch the sun going down.

If you're still around after all the clubs have cleared, it eventually gets pretty empty, although there's always the odd clubber who's crashed out after too many pills, and a guy still looking for his contact lens. In fact, even in the cruellest winters you will find little pockets of life here, like penguins on an iceberg. What better than a walk by the sea for a little thinking and introspection?

And finally, it's time to come clean. Yes, it's true I'm afraid, it is all stones and not sand. But as a small compensation, when you take your picnic down the beach, and the wind whips up, you will not be crunching your way through a cheese sandwich. Saying that, over 4 billion stones and not a decent one for skimming…

### A Cheeky Tale

I have it on good authority from one of the guys down at the Artists Quarters that the unsightly CCTV camera, which lies between the two piers, only spies on the pathway and ignores the beach altogether. The reason being that when organising its location with the police, one local councilor allegedly refused to let the camera overlook the beach, declaring to the Police:
*'I don't want you guys seeing what I came to Brighton to do 25 years ago.'* So...birds do it, bees do it and now we know that even local councillors do it...

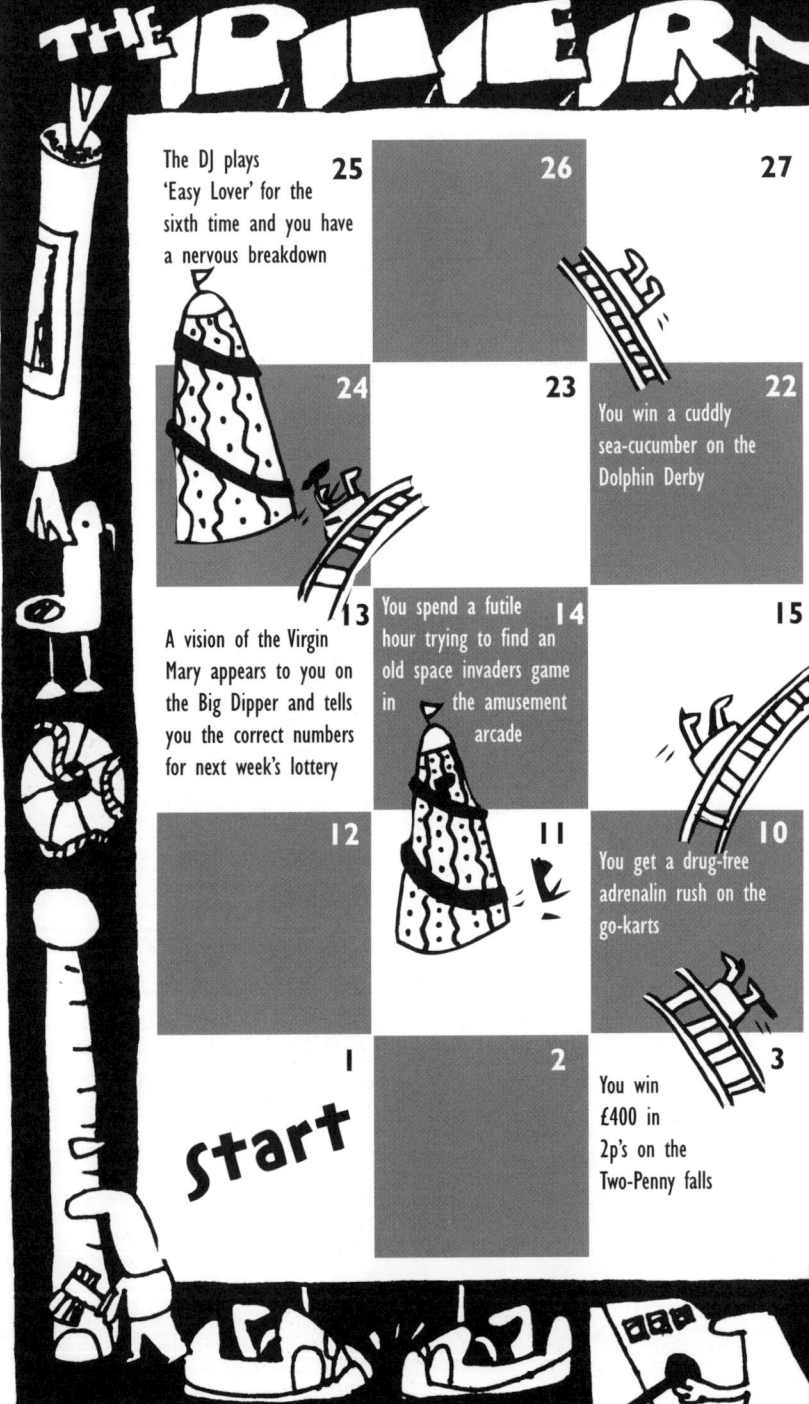

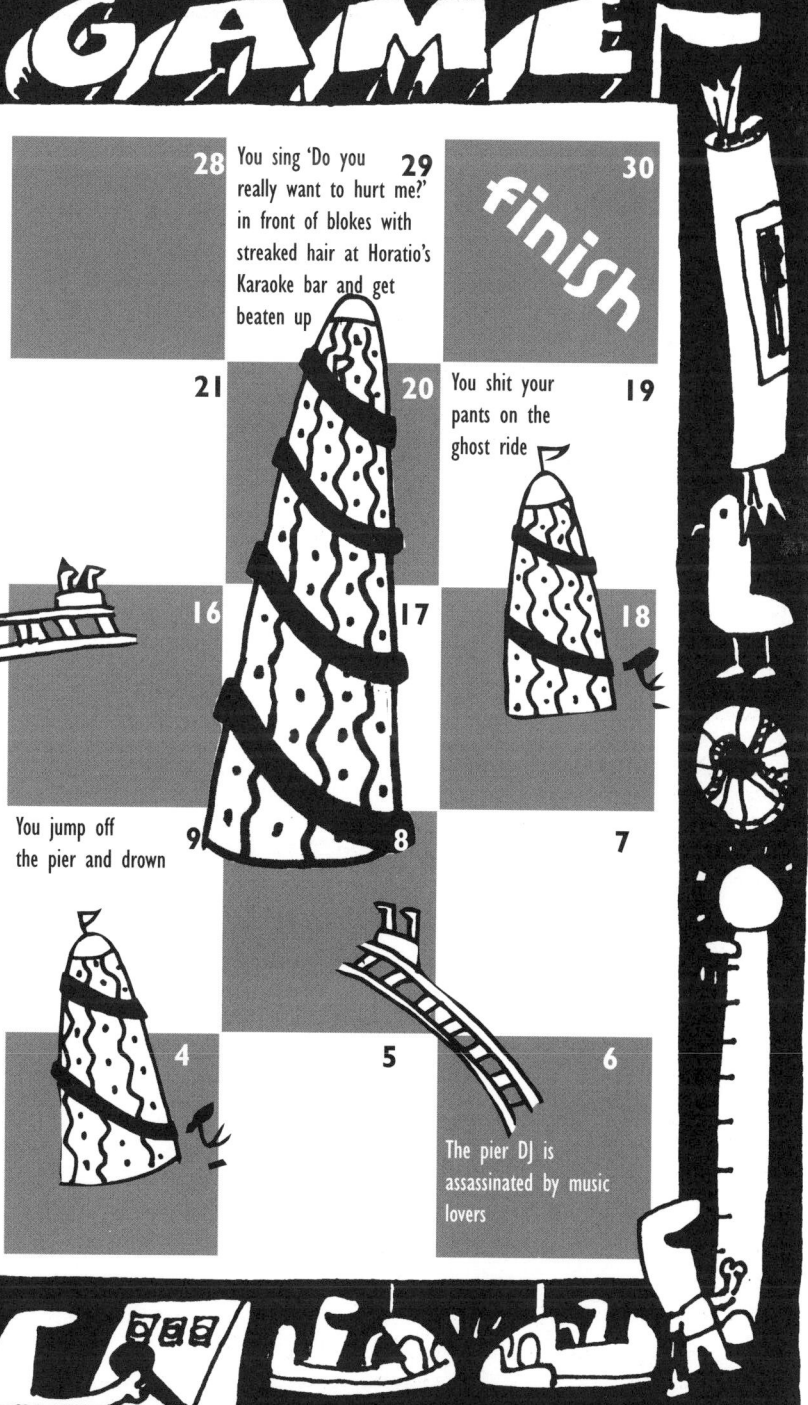

The West Pier

## THE SEAFRONT

### WEST OF THE PALACE PIER

If you don't have a lot of time to spend in Brighton, make a priority of visiting the seafront between the Palace Pier and The West Pier. Here you'll find café-bars, plenty of clubs, amusement arcades, café-bars, the Fishing Museum, the Artists' Quarters, palmists, café-bars, sculptures on the beach and usually an assortment of outdoor entertainment during summer. When it's warm, the beach here just packs out, and you can sit outside the bars or bring your own food and beer and find your own spot on the beach. If you want a good walk however, follow the seafront path all the way to the multi-coloured beach huts in Hove.

As you've probably gathered, there are dozens of places to stop for food and most of the clubs do refreshments in the afternoons, which gives you a chance to check out what they're like inside. If you want to leave some of the crowds behind though, and go somewhere more relaxed, keep walking until you reach the Meeting Place Café (near the angel statue) where plastic chairs and motorway café food await you with open arms.

### Things To Look Out For
### The Victorian Penny Arcades

There are two between the piers, where for 50p you get 5 old Victorian pennies to use on all the old machines. I particularly like the 'What The Butler Saw' machines, look out for 'Two Lovely Ladies' and 'Easy Chair Frolics'. Then there's the 'Win A Fag' machine, 'the Electric Tickler' which gives you a pleasant electric shock, and the fortune telling machines that will massage your ego.

### The Artists' Quarters
(see Wonderful Things to Do)

## The Big Green Bagel

This sculpture arrived about 4 years ago as a gift from the Mayor of Naples after we donated his town a large bronze herring.

Officially entitled 'Il Grande Bagel Verde', but known locally as the 'Seasick Doughnut', it survived last year's storm and several assassination attempts by local art puritans.

## The West Pier

Closed until 2002 when, after extensive renovation, it will finally be re-opened to the public. But for now they're running regular tours.

## EAST OF THE PALACE PIER

The miniature Volks Railway runs along this stretch of the seafront all the way to the Marina, a reminder of how much smaller people were in the old days.

There isn't much in the way of entertainment along this stretch, unless you count two crazy golf courses and the rather shabby Peter Pan's Amusements half way down, although the arrival of the Concorde 2 (the home to the Big Beat Boutique) may herald the start of a re-development program. Just beyond here, however, lies the strange old house, set into the promenade before Duke's Mound.

The story goes that before the promenade was built, all the houses along the front were sold and demolished apart from one, whose stubborn owner refused to sell. The council couldn't move him, so in desperation they built the promenade over his house and it still remains there today. Clarence Palmer who owns the Volks Railway lives there now.

Further on from here is the once controversial nudist beach, which is now mainly used by the gay community.

Look out Blackpool

While this whole area of the seafront is in need of re-juvenation* it does come alive when there are car and motorbike rallies, or at events like the dance day, when it fills with floats and music, and 1000s of hardcore clubbers get to see daylight for one day of the year.

And finally our thought for the day: Why does the train on the Volks Railway have a steering wheel ?

*but please God, not **more** café-bars...

# HERE, THERE AND EVERYWHERE

A couple of happy poofs

## KEMPTOWN

Cross over the Old Steine from the bottom of North Street and you'll find yourself in Kemptown, a haven of B&Bs, some good shops, and home to much of Brighton's flourishing gay and lesbian community.

Bristling with life, day and night, Kemptown's energy seems to come from a celebratory and ever-growing gay scene, mixed with the overspill of all the life and vitality emanating from the seafront.

This is also a place where many of Brighton's eccentrics seem to congregate and make up for lost time. Buy your strawberries next to a drag queen in Safeway or stumble across the guy in St. James's Street who always dresses immaculately in tails and white gloves. Kemptown may not be a part of Brighton that has been dressed up for visitors, but it is precisely the rough edges that provide the appeal.

To explore Kemptown simply take a walk up St. James's Street. The side streets that run down to the sea from here are mostly home to countless B&Bs, while the streets on the opposite side are often worth investigating, especially George Street, with its film memorabilia shop and other curiosities.

St. James's Street is also host to health food shops, barbers, second hand shops, a few good pubs and plenty of gay haunts and cruising spots.

Follow it for long enough and it eventually becomes St. George's Road. Here Kemptown begins to feel more like a village. With a great flea market painted in garish pink, the Beatles memorabilia shop, gift shops and record shops, this area is quickly taking shape as a colourful new shopping area.

Continue far enough and, at the end, you'll reach Sussex Square and Lewes Crescent. These stunning white Regency flats are occupied by some of Brighton's affluent bohemians, and have had their fair share of well-known residents, Lewis Carroll, Gaz Coombs, Stephen Berkoff and Howard Marks being just a few.

And your final Kemptown destination must surely be the first floor balcony flat of number 10 Lewes Crescent. Still regularly photographed by Metal fans, this is said to be the actual room where living legend Ozzy Ozborne wrote the rock anthem 'Paranoid'.

## HIGH STREET

Starting as North Street (down at the Old Steine) the main road stretches up and beyond the Clock Tower, where it becomes Western Road, and when it transforms again into Church Street, you're well into Hove.

With the exception of Ann Summers, the Pound Shop and some good bookshops, it's just a regular high street with all the usual chains and a big indoor Shopping Centre. Past Waitrose you get to see the big Regency squares, which are beautiful, though the view is much better still from the seafront.

Continue for another half a mile and you will soon be deep into Hove. Tattoos and piercings start to thin out and begin to be replaced by blue rinse hair. From here it all descends into a wilderness of restaurants, cafés, and estate agents.

## WEST STREET

*'A collage of Ralph Lauren'*
Kieran Long

Follow the trail of strong aftershave and blue-legged girls as you enter the world of amusement arcades, nightclubs, theme pubs and burger bars. One man's meat is another man's poison. Known by the police as 'little Beirut'.

Lewes Crescent in Kemptown

# ENTER THE CRAZY & EXCITING
# BRIGHTON

**Feast on top nosh from the American restaurant chain Tatty Carbuncle's**

**Marvel at the American-style bowling alley**

**See the stunning Asda car-park**

**Enjoy an American-style in-car meal from the drive-through McDonald's**

# WORLD OF THE MARINA

**Brighton's architectural masterpiece**

**All the latest American movies at our Multiplex cinema. Over 300 screens***

**Factory outlet shopping offering: a pet pampering service, knitwear for rugged men and polo shirts in over 400 shades of pink**

**Concrete galore!!!**

**Coming soon – the Brighton Marina American-style football stadium**

*And guaranteed no subtitled foreign shit.

## PARKS & GARDENS

### Queen's Park
Between Kemptown and Hanover

If you're coming from Kemptown, head up Egremont Place, go through the arch and the park is immediately on your right.

This is the closest park to the town centre and is the kind of place where football games and Tai Chi lessons exist side by side. It has a small café, toilets, tennis courts, kids play area and a fairly typical small lake (which used to be a roller skating rink in the 60s).

What I particularly like is the way it's landscaped with gentle hills and these strange old monuments that are littered around. Best of all, it has great climbing trees and a small death slide for kids. Be sure to come back early evening when the families have gone and treat yourself to a few goes.

### Preston Park

This is the largest park in Brighton located a little way down Preston Road. For starters it's a great spot for cycling, you can use their professional track at the top of the park and then race back down over the bumpy road or simply cycle around the park's perimeter. There's also a café in the middle and loads of space for big sports games.

Whilst it's a good place for a picnic, the ever-present noise of cars from the main road can sometimes spoil a tranquil afternoon.

Look out for the goatee beard brigade taking Ultimate Frisbee very seriously and try and find the Steve Ovett statue at the bottom of the park, facing the road. Remember the Alan Partridge sketch where he 'pops out' of his skimpy satin shorts? You're seconds away, Steve…

### The Rock Garden

Cross over the road from Preston Park and enter this beautifully sculpted garden through a small gate. Follow the twisting paths up and around past the pond all the way to the top. Leave the path and carry on up and you can see the half-deserted railway far below. It's a nice spot for a secluded smoke or maybe 1-2-3 rescue at dusk for the big kid in you.

### St. Ann's Well Gardens

This small park in Hove has a scent garden and a few intimate picnic areas. Tennis fans might like to know that if you want a free game, they don't start charging here before 10am.

My favourite feature is the strange clock on a pole that overlooks the courts and bowling green; it's straight out of the cult TV series, The Prisoner.

### The Level

Found just behind St. Peter's church, this is more of a place for hanging out in summer really.

Come and give your dog some exercise whilst watching teenage boys endanger their gonads doing BMX tricks in the skateboarding park. There's a nice bit by the paddling pool area with its trellises, little kiosks and surreal bridges, but don't get too excited. It's best as a place for a game of footie or rounders.

Don't miss the fair when it comes here for two weeks at the end of April and August.

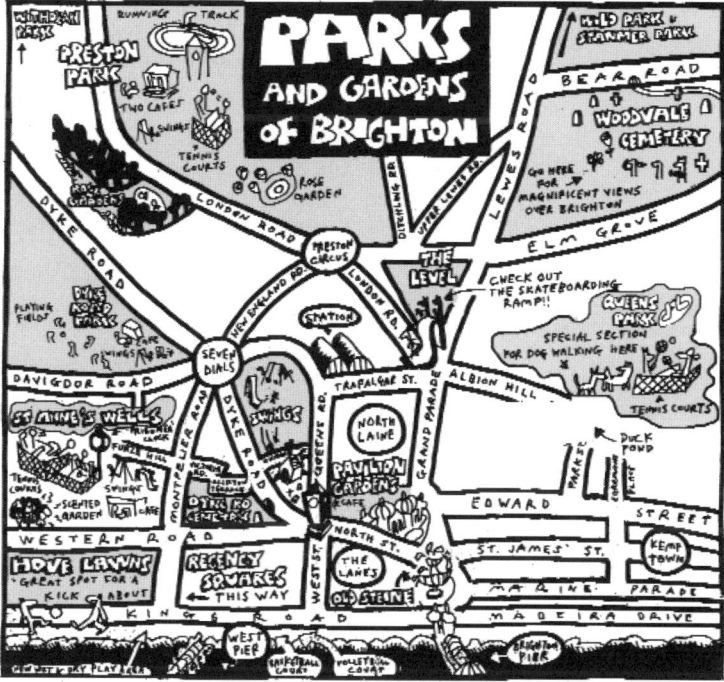

## Dyke Road Cemetery
*Dyke Road opposite
St. Nicholas' Church*

From the Clock Tower go up Dyke Rd and you'll find this place on your left just after the traffic lights.

Part cemetery, part park and relatively unknown, this is a perfect spot to come and flop about, read a book, bring a picnic or do some meditation. I love it here. It's never busy and it does the job if you want to feel like you've left the rat race behind. Look out for Gandhi's grave.

## The Pavilion Gardens

After a morning's shopping in the North Laine, these gardens behind the Pavilion are perfect for a spot of lolling about. There's usually a ton of people about when it's warm, but it can be a pleasant alternative to the overcrowded beach and is one of the rare spots in the town centre with a bit of decent greenery.

If you're in need of refreshments the café does drinks and is famous for its rock cakes. Look for the photos on the café history notice board on the side of the hut. They sure had big ears in those days.

## Brunswick Square Gardens

The large expanse of lawns and gardens in this stunning square are open to the public, and make a beautiful spot for a picnic close to the seafront.

# HERE, THERE AND EVERYWHERE

Postcard courtesy of Antony Hodgson

## Hove, An Apology

Last year I offended tens of people by not including Hove in the title of this book (as officially Brighton and Hove come as a package these days). But, as there's little in the way of entertainment in Hove, except for eating and drinking, it didn't seem to merit the inclusion. Hove begins at Boundary Passage (the longest alleyway in Brighton, opposite Little Western Street) and continues all the way to Devon. Although it has nearly succeeded in throwing off its old image of being a home for retired Tories, Hove is still primarily a residential area with a few good pubs, restaurants and a (rather incongruous) lap-dancing club.

What does need to be said though, is that some of the town's most beautiful buildings can be found here; Brunswick Square and Palmeira Square being particularly fine examples of Regency architecture.

There is an age-old joke that Hove should be re-named 'Hove Actually', due to the countless times its residents, when asked if they live in Brighton, reply with snooty indignation — *'No, Hove actually'*.

HERE, THERE AND EVERYWHERE

Welcome to Hove

**WEIRD AND WONDERFUL**

# Wonderful Things To Do

## INTERESTING PLACES

### The Pavilion
Old Steine (01273) 290900
Open 10am-5pm Oct-May, 10am-6pm
June-September £4.90 adults, £3 children,
£3.55 concessions

If, like me, you have a pathological hatred for those dreary tours of stately homes, I still recommend a visit to the Pavilion. True, it's the familiar set-up with those awful little rope chains, and hordes of American tourists giving 'oohs' and 'aaahs' in every room, but you can't escape the simple fact that the Pavilion is just stunning. With the exception of the Pier, this is Brighton's most famous landmark. Could you really visit Paris and not go up the Eiffel Tower?

Built as a weekend retreat for the Prince Regent in 1823, this extravagant palace is home to some flamboyant architecture and even more flamboyant interior design. Despite the Moorish look from the outside, the interior actually has a predominant Chinese theme. Inside it's a labyrinth of colour, bamboo, dragon sculptures and some of the most fabulous rooms I've ever set eyes on, especially the Music room.

It is well documented that the Prince was renowned for his love of women and food. In the bedroom, look for the two secret doors for his midnight rendezvous with Mrs Fitzherbert and the bloke selling seafood in a basket. The door for food is in a corner, the other right next to the bed. Some nights they'd both go in the wrong doors and...well you can guess the rest, but it is Brighton after all.

Don't miss the most outrageous chandelier in the Universe, bamboo trees in the kitchen, a fire-breathing dragon, and if you watch the TV documentary they show upstairs, you won't have to waste your money on a guide book.

Dreamed-up and partly designed by the Prince Regent, this oriental pleasure palace helped establish Brighton as a fashionable place to be seen. One hundred and eighty years later, the Prince's devotions to art, music, extravagance and indiscretion have still left an indelible impression on the town.

Holiday cottages do not come more exotic than this.

# WEIRD AND WONDERFUL

The Pavilion

## The Booth Museum Of Natural History
194 Dyke Road (01273) 292777
Free Entry Open Mon-Sat 10am-5pm
Sun 2pm-5pm, Closed Thurs

This curiosity is the home to hundreds of creatures, skeletons and strange things in specimen jars. When you enter you'll be struck immediately by the smell of mothballs and how gloomy it all is. Towers of stuffed birds line the walls of the room, while in the centre lie two incongruous stained-glass windows. At this point, if you're in a group, I recommend splitting up and going it alone for maximum effect. Walk down the aisles at the side and enter Hitchcock's terrifying world of 'The Birds'. Down the centre you'll find jars with strange creatures in, and at the back, some impressive skeletons. If you're very lucky you might get here for a live taxidermy demonstration.

Look out for: the sheep that looks like Daisy in the Woody Allen movie, the charred remains of a (half-eaten) dodo and the rather strange 'toad in the hole'. I bet you won't find the warthog's head though.

To find the museum, follow Dyke Road from the Clock Tower and just keep walking. It'll take a good twenty minutes, so I'd only recommend it if you are near-by or cycling, as it's really only a half-hour curiosity.

Warning – check first for children's visits, they will utterly spoil your experience.

Could you spend the night here on your own though? I swear they all come to life then.

## The Brighton Museum and The Dome Theatre
Church Street

Closed until late 2001 when both promise to be re-wallpapered. The gallery upstairs in the museum will however, open specially for the May festival.

Fabrica, in the Old Lanes

*THE DOME* ↙

## Hove Museum
*19 New Church Road. (01273) 290200*
*Open Tues-Sat 10am-5pm*

Situated way, way down Church Street in deepest, darkest Hove, the museum is surprisingly interesting for its size. A curiosity of memorabilia from Hove's old days of film pioneering, it also houses local artwork, a children's section and a rather nifty teashop.

The children's room is truly magical, little fairy lights click on as you enter and the exhibits range from old zeotropes and magic lanterns to a hidden cupboard with a periscope inside. For kids it's wonderful, with lots of secret drawers and cupboards for them to discover, but don't worry, adults are allowed to play in here too.

Little-known to your average B&H resident is that Hove was actually the birthplace of British cinema, and the history of cinema section provides a mini cinema where you can watch some of Hove's comic movie masterpieces filmed in someone's back garden. The rather risqué 'Lady's ankles seen through a telescope' must have been the 1898 equivalent of 'Deep Throat'.

And once you've seen all this, the pumpkin teapot, the cardboard cut-out Ringo Starr and the psychedelic carpets, you'll probably want to finish with a cup of tea in their historic tea-room, rescued from Scarborough in the early 80s.

## St. Bartholomew's Church
*Ann Street (01273) 620491*

Located behind Trafalgar Street and London Road. I wouldn't go miles out of your way to come here, but if you're in the area you should pop your head around because it's kind of unusual. This is the biggest brick church in Europe and is impressively decorated with oil paintings, Italian mosaics and marble archways. It could well be the setting of a Peter Greenaway film. They also put on a lot of concerts here, if you go in for big classical events.

## Fabrica
40 Duke Street (01273) 778646 Free
Open Wed-Sat 11.30am-5pm Sun 2-5pm
Closed Dec-April due to a lack of heating

Essential drop-in spot when visiting the Old Lanes, even if it's only for a few minutes. Opposite the main post office on Ship Street, this converted church is now a gallery space for installations and contemporary art.

## The Phoenix Gallery
10-14 Waterloo Place
(01273) 603700
Open Mon-Sat 11am-6pm
Sun 12noon-4pm

This small gallery space is often home to some unusual and unique art from local and visiting artists. Why not combine your visit with a perusal of the strange music stall that's always here at the weekend?

Also look out for the occasional gig, special event and workshops.

## The Artists' Quarters
King's Road Arches

Tucked away down on the seafront, between the two piers and below the kissing statue, this small area has been home for over five years now to a colourful and flamboyant collection of local artists, whose workshops and galleries are permanently on display to the public. Originally owned by fishermen, these little rooms would once have been used for de-scaling fish (to be sold where the carousel now stands) which still accounts for the occasional odd smell.

Far more in keeping with Brighton's bohemian nature than the plethora of tacky café-bars found on the seafront, the Artists' Quarters perfectly capture the creative and communal spirit of the town. Open all year round, even in the most improbable gales, this is London gallery work at half the price, with work ranging from cards and paintings to exotic furniture. Keep your eyes peeled for Sugarglider, with its the weird ceramic sculptures and wiggly worms, try and have a natter with Dave the puppeteer, marvel at Darren Wallace's elegant cartoonish Brighton scenes and look out for Bill's lifetime collection of jars of Marmite. A visit to Brighton would not be complete without coming here.

**WEIRD AND WONDERFUL**

**WEIRD AND WONDERFUL**

# A SPOTTER'S GUIDE TO BRIGHTON CELEBRITIES

*What better way to spend your afternoon than going all gooey-eyed and weak-kneed at having stumbled across your favourite snooker player? Brighton is home to an eclectic bunch of celebrities and I wish you every success with your sleuthing.*

## CHRIS EUBANK
Easy to spot, owing to the fact that most of his waking hours seem to be spent driving his jeep, motorbike or tractor around the Old Lanes and waving at bemused strangers.
**5 points**

## NICK BERRY
The shiny nosed superstar can often be seen walking his four Scottie dogs on the beach in the morning. Don't start singing 'Every Loser Wins' as he is known to get aggressive and recently hurled one of his dogs at a journalist from The Argus, just for saying, *'Hello, hello, hello, what's all this then?'*
**15 points**

## FATBOYSLIM
From Quentin to Norman to Freakpower and a host of other pseudonyms, local hero Fatboyslim can be found DJing at the Concorde 2, supporting Brighton and Hove Albion, or nosing around Mothercare in town. Norman won the hearts of local footie fans recently when, inspired by Cliff's infamous Wimbledon singalong, he led the crowd in a half-hour rousing chorus of the 'Rockafeller Skank', after a match was delayed, owing to the Goalkeeper's bar mitzvah.
**15 points**

## JOE MCGANN
TV heartthrob Joe McGann lives near the Seven Dials and recently made the local headlines when he was spotted in the Tin Drum pulling the legs off a daddy-long-legs and feeding them to his two-year-old son.
**12 points**

## JULIE BURCHILL
Diminutive journalist with a silly voice, renowned for her opinionated codswallop. Keep her away from your washing powder, she'll only try and snort it.
**4 points**

## MARK LITTLE
You'll find him in the Old Lanes making documentaries about vegetarian cafés, hosting the odd event down on the beach or wandering round town in his caveman outfit. It's been a few years now but it's still best not to mention Bouncer.
**15 points**

**EL DIABLITO**

## PATSY ROWLAND
Better known as the frustrated secretary in many of the Carry On movies, whose main role seemed to be pursuing Kenneth Williams around the office desk for a snog and a grope.
Usually spotted chasing thin, blond, gay men down St. James's Street in Kemptown…
**17 points**

## HERBIE FLOWERS
Played with every rock god from Bowie and T-Rex to Lou Reed, and got paid a measly £12 for writing the bass-line to 'Walk On The Wild Side'. Probably best loved however, for writing the classic pop ballad 'Grandad'. See him down the Komedia doing his double bass thing. If you want a good rock'n'roll story, ask him about the time he was in The Wombles on Top Of The Pops.
**10 points**

# WEIRD AND WONDERFUL

## WEIRD AND WONDERFUL

### GAZ FROM SUPERGRASS
The shy popster with the hairy face has moved to Kemptown. He can often be seen down St. James's Street with his chopper out.*
**15 points**

### MRS McCLUSKY FROM GRANGE HILL
Better remembered as Bridget the Midget. I first spotted her at a Ken Campbell performance years ago and occasionally still see her at some of the more unusual theatre events.
**25 points**

### DAVID THOMAS FROM PERE UBU
Strictly for the music lovers this one. Look for him striding around Hove like some crazy Ignatious Reilly from Confederacy of Dunces. Hmmm I feel I've lost a few of you here, never mind, read on.
**12 points (20 if wearing his infamous red plastic bib)**

### STEVE COOGAN
Hangs out in the Hanover pubs, the Nelson on Trafalgar Street and just about anywhere that sells alcohol. If you're an attractive female it's best to wear heavily protective armour when he's around, although he has recently started carrying a tin-opener.
**10 points (25 if he doesn't try and mate with you)**

### THE LEVELLERS
You'll find them in deepest Kemptown, hanging around their studio and making a racket.
**10 points**

*I'm sorry I couldn't resist the chopper joke.

## MARK WILLIAMS FROM THE FAST SHOW

Found at Kambi's grabbing a take-away kebab or hanging around pubs like the Lion and Lobster. Remember the Father Ted episode with Victor Meldrew before you go up to him and say 'Suits you Sir'.
**15 points**

## DEREK JAMESON

The retired Argus columnist and Radio 2 DJ lives the life of luxury in Millionaires Mile along the Hove seafront next door to Norman Cook and Nick Berry. In fact this trio can often be seen out hunting along the seafront, on the three-seater bicycle once owned by the Goodies, with Derek at the helm holding a whaling harpoon shouting: '*do they mean meat, they surely do*' before spearing a fat, juicy seagull for the three of them to take home and devour.
**20 points**

If you've been missed out of our spotter's guide and feel that you ought to be included, please write to us finishing the following sentence.

***I think I'm famous enough to be in your guide because*** ........................
................................................................................................................................

Please enclose £10 and a signed photo. If you are a local celebrity or just have been in The Bill a couple of times this will not be sufficient.

**WEIRD AND WONDERFUL**

## WHERE TO TAKE A GOOD STROLL

### The Marina Breakwater

Down near the Marina is a breakwater that extends for about a quarter of a mile out to sea. Take a walk there at sunset and you won't regret it. If you go when the sea is a bit rough it can be wonderfully hairy. It'll take you about 20 minutes to walk there from the pier so try and time it well for sunset. Then you could stick around in the Marina for a drink (bad idea) or walk back into town and flop around at The Basketmakers (good idea).

### The Undercliff Walk to Rottingdean

From the Palace Pier head left past the Marina and you'll reach Rottingdean in about one hour. Most of the path from the Marina onwards has been carved out of the imposing, chalky cliffs and this, together with the magnificent views of the sea, makes this walk fairly spectacular. And it's good by bike too as it's completely flat. As you get closer to the village you'll start to come across rock-pools and little coves where people go winkle picking and crab fishing.

Rottingdean is, in contrast to Brighton, one of those classic old seaside villages with local shops and boutiques like Hair Talk, Ralph's Cornucopia and, until recently Sally's Tip-Top Tea Shop. Once you've had a nose around, if you don't feel like walking back again, the buses run regularly back to Brighton from here.

This really is one of the best and most accessible walks in Brighton and is the perfect all-season walk. In summer, as well as rock-pooling, there's a café half-way, (usually serving coke and a piece of shortbread wrapped up in cling-film), while in winter you may have your head blown off but if you wrap up warm you won't regret it. Finish off with mulled wine and a cigar in The White Horse at Rottingdean and you'll be in heaven.

### Glynde to Lewes

Although I've never done this walk, friends have recommended it and we even got a lovely e-mail from a bloke called Adam urging us to include it this year. Directions are simple; take the train to Glynde and there is a stunning, and straightforward, walk back over Mount Caborn to Lewes. You won't see a soul, the scenery is said to be spectacular and when you drop down the hill into Lewes, you are only a short walk from the excellent Snow Drop pub.

CHEEKY NEWSPAPER OF THE YEAR

# Evening Anus

NIGHT FINAL

www.cheekyguides.com

**Bubonic plague** reaching epidemic levels in Shoreham See page 19

30p

# MAYOR SHOWS CRACK IN UNDERCLIFF WALK

## Volks Railway to be turned into mobile nightclub

Residents today expressed their CONCERN over the council's decision to close down one of Brighton's best-loved features, the Volks Railway, and turn it into yet another seafront club. Built in 1886, this miniature railway line played a pivotal role in preventing the German forces from invading Britain in the Second World War and up until recently was used for taking visitors to the Brighton Marina to educate them in the horrors of town planning.

### SPEWING

When confronted with the notion that another club in Brighton is going to attract yet more moronic stag parties and pissed up Londoners at the weekend, a council spokesman said:

'maybe so, but it'll be Brighton kebabs they'll have bought to spew on the pavement not London ones, and that's what matters.'

## THE SPUNKY CAVERN

DEAFENING TECHNO MUSIC, ALL DAY, EVERY DAY!!

DECORATED WITH LURID COLOURS AND ORIGINAL ARTWORK FROM DISTURBED LOCALS!!

GASSY PISS AT £4 A BOTTLE!!

ANOTHER OUTPOST FROM (H)E L

**GIANT METEOR CRASHES INTO THE MARINA CAUSING OVER £4,000,000,000 OF IMPROVEMENTS!**

FOR FULL STORY SEE PAGES 12-13

## SAI BABA
Read his new gossip column on page 22

**EUBANKS'S FACE APPEARED IN MY SKIDMARKED UNDIES pages 4,5,6,7,8, and 27**

## The Indian Chatri on the Downs

(01273) 710000 for more information (although when I called it I got an answering machine message from Britney Spears!)

High up on a hill overlooking Brighton is one the town's most curious but least-known memorials, built to commemorate the thousands of Indians who died in Brighton during the First World War, when the Royal Pavilion was used as a hospital for wounded Indian soldiers.

The Pavilion was chosen on the grounds that they'd feel more at home there, but despite these rather misplaced good intentions the wounded men were more than a little bemused at having been placed inside what looked like a Chinese Palace, and of course having Sikhs and Hindus from every cast all under one roof meant that they did not get on famously. The 4000 who died here had their ashes scattered into the sea and the Chatri was built as a memorial to them in 1921, and every year there is still an annual pilgrimage organised by the Royal British Legion and the High Commissioner for India.

### Directions

Take the A23 out of Brighton, follow the A273 to Hassocks and go through Pyecombe. Take a right down Mill Lane and follow until you reach the windmill carpark.

From here go past the Old Barn Farm and golf course, and keep following the path until you reach a signpost. Go through the gate, keep the large clump of trees on your right and keep following the South Downs way. (It's probably best to take an OS map however, as these directions come from some illegible notes I scribbled a year ago and it's easy to miss the Chatri since it is hidden by trees until the last minute).

## CREATURES OF THE SALTY DEPTHS

### The Sealife Centre
Marine Parade, opposite the
Palace Pier (01273) 604234
Open 10am-5pm Mon-Sun
Adults £6.25 Children £3.99

A couple of kippers and a dead dog floating in the shark tank. OK, I'm only kidding, but realistically if you've ever been to one of these places abroad it will probably seem a bit disappointing. Let's face it, with the exception of crabs, fish and toilet paper, there's not a lot else in the English Channel these days.

In its favour, the Sea Life Centre is housed inside a beautiful old Victorian building, the underwater tunnels are pretty good and two new features this year have included seadragons (seahorses fed on chili) and a Captain Pugwash play area. Overall however, the place still needs updating, with better facilities and more interactive features, to justify the expense.

> **Imaginary conversation between father and son Edible Crab:**
> *Son?*
>   Yes dad?
> *Sit down son, there's something I'd like to tell you.*
>   Yes, dad?
> *You know how all these years your mother and I told you that 'edible' meant found under big stones...*

### Rockpooling

Past the Marina on the way to Rottingdean there are some fabulous rockpools where you can find edible spider and shore crabs, sea anemones*, little fish and the occasional beached giant squid. If you're in the car, drive to Rottingdean (just follow the coastal road heading towards Eastbourne) head to the seafront and turn right. From the Palace Pier it'll take 10 minutes to cycle and 30 minutes to walk.

Two locals on the lookout for lunch

### Dolphin Spotting
Stephen Savage
(01273) 424339/ 0777 3610036

There has been an increase in the sightings of dolphins along the coast, in particular Bottlenose dolphins. I must stress that to spot one is rare, but the best time to see them is high tide between May and September. Between the two piers and around the Marina are your best viewing spots.

If you do see one, phone this chap above and make him very happy, he's currently tracking all dolphin and whale activity along the South coast.

*I have searched high and low for the right spelling for this and to no avail. Can someone please put me out of my misery so at least I'll know if it's right for the third edition of this book?

## SPORT

Norman Cook's three-a-side football team

## SWIMMING
### Saltdean Lido
Saltdean Park Road,
Saltdean (01273) 880616
Open 10am-6pm every day £3 adults,
£2 kids

Original open-air Art-Déco swimming pool, 15 minute drive from Brighton. It looks stunning, has plenty of chairs and tables outside and is well worth a visit for those of you who love to swim in style. Opens from May to the end of September every year.

### Pells Pool At Lewes
North Street, Lewes (01273) 472334
Open 12-6pm term-time
Weekend and school holidays
12noon-7.30pm

Open-air swimming pool with a claim to being the oldest of its kind in the country. Plenty of space for lounging if you don't mind being surrounded by snogging teenagers.

### Prince Regent
Church Street (01273) 685692
£2.60 adult, £1.35 child, £1.75 student

Across the road from the Pavilion, this large pool has plenty of space, some good diving boards and a big slide.

At weekends, splashing around time is between 10am and 12.30pm, the rest of the time is for lane swimming. The boards are also in use for most of the day during the weekend and early evenings during the week. It's still best to phone as timetables change quarterly.

My only gripe with the place is their insistence on playing Southern FM all day every day. I swim here regularly to try and get away from it all, not to listen to Phil Collins and adverts for double-glazing. I did once complain but was rudely informed that the radio was not for the swimmers, but to keep the lifeguards from getting bored. You just can't beat good old English customer service.

### The Sea
It's free and there's lots of it. A visit to any seaside is not complete without at least getting your feet wet. It's tradition to swim twice around the West Pier before breakfast here, but for newcomers a quick splash around will suffice.

Be careful when the tides are strong, every year someone gets swept away by a surprising freak tide.

### Water Quality

The quality of the sea-water varies daily, but the good news is that it is at its highest in summer when the suns UV rays kill off most of the harmful bacteria in the water. If you have any concerns, contact Surfers Against Sewage for a more truthful account of the quality of our coastal waters than the souped-up crap the water authorities tell you.

Tel. 01872 553001
www.scip.org.uk/surfers.

## LOCAL SPORTS CENTRES

### Stanley Deason
Wilson Avenue (01273) 694281
Open weekdays 8am-10.30pm
Weekends 9am-8.30pm

Squash, table tennis, badminton, basketball, volleyball, gym, astro-turf pitches, circuit training and aerobics.

### Portslade Sports Centre
Chalky Road, Portslade
(01273) 411100

Squash, fitness, badminton, snooker.

### King Alfred Centre
Kingsway, Hove (01273) 290290

Tropical style pools, badminton, table tennis, martial arts classes and gymnasium. Crèche available, phone for details.

The Leisure Centre is most probably being redeveloped some time in 2001 but at time of going to print, all details were still a mystery to all concerned. Whatever happens, the pool will definitely remain.

### Moulsecoomb Leisure Centre
Moulsecoomb Way (01273) 622266

Badminton, table tennis, squash, basketball, roller-skating, gymnasium, sauna and aerobics.

## WATERSPORTS / SKATE HIRE

### Sunhire Watersports Rental
185 Kings Road Arches (01273) 323160

Open May to September and found under the promenade between the two piers. Choose from windsurfing, canoeing or hiring a catamaran or sailing dinghy. Rental prices range from £6 for the banana-boat ride and £8 per hour for the canoes, all the way to £80 per hour for water-skiing, with tuition (strictly for the stinking rich this one).

### Hove Lagoon
Western end of Hove promenade
(01273) 424842 www.hovelagoon.co.uk

Windsurfing, sailing and canoeing come at around £35 with an instructor for a two-hour lesson. Check the website for more details.

### Pulse Station (Rollerblading)
23-25 Kings Road Arches
Open 10.30am until no one wants any more boots. Open June-Sept.

Solomon semi-soft boot skates for hire. £3.50 p.h.
£50 deposit required or a passport.

**WEIRD AND WONDERFUL**

# Weird Things To Do

## THE GREAT OUTDOORS

### Country and Western Weekends
For info (01273) 701152

Spend a weekend on a ranch in Horsham where you'll meet Red Indians in tepees, gamblers, cowgirls and cowboys. You can also expect rodeo, live bands, fishing and err… owls.

Why spend your time in a sweaty club drinking your money away when you could wear a raccoon on your head and be a Wild West hero? Contact Colin on the number above for more details.

(Next big event 12th May 2001 at Wild Park in Brighton)

### Llama Trekking
For info (01273) 835656
Running Wed-Sun April-Oct
Llama for one £35. Share a Llama with a friend? (Ooh, suits you sir!) £45

Just you, the rolling hills, the sun beating down…and your faithful llama by your side. From April to October, this group organises 5-mile rambles over the Downs, which include food and a llama. You can't ride these magnificent creatures but a packed lunch is included and will be carried by your hairy friend. It may be expensive, but when would you ever get the opportunity again?

### Adventures Unlimited
64 Edward Street
(01273) 681058
adventure.unlimited@virgin.net
www.aultd.org

I once spent a brilliant Saturday with a load of friends playing British bulldogs, hide and seek, lateral thinking games and clambering over assault courses thanks to these guys. Not only was it fun and fairly cheap, but we were also entertained by some shameless flirting between my friend Stilly and the organiser.

Needless to say, I thoroughly recommend them, and you should know that they also do loads of other outdoor pursuit days like canoeing, climbing and abseiling.

All events take place outside Brighton, and transport is provided, should you need it. Book well in advance for summer events.

## Adventure Activities
With Keith Fleming
Blackland Farm Mid Sussex
(01444) 235258
www.mtn-activites.co.uk
keith@mtn-activites.co.uk

No relation to Bob, he won't be coughing all over you. Instead, expect a full packed day or weekend that could include rock climbing, canoeing, orienteering, high ropes, mountain biking, abseiling, archery, and the best zip wire I've ever been on.

The farm is set in the middle of really beautiful woodland and is the perfect setting for your weekend adventures. For what you get, it's fantastic value. Ah, the great outdoors.

£150 per day for a minimum of 4 people, rising by £35 per extra adult. All tents are provided for camping and are self-catering. £280 for a weekend, rising by £30 per extra adult. £5 each extra for bike-hire.

*Whenever you're getting demoralised with your job, just think of this guy*

## The Rabbit Roundabout
Follow the London Road out of Brighton, past Preston Park, and eventually you'll get to a big roundabout with a petrol station on your left. Look carefully, any time of day or night, and you'll see the roundabout is home to hundreds of rabbits. Occasionally you might spot a huge pile of carrots in the middle that some kind soul has expertly flung from their car, or perhaps they are placed there by a nearby resident, risking life and limb for these loveable floppy-eared creatures. Marooned indefinitely, it'll only be a matter of time before in-breeding gets the better of them and we'll be seeing misshapen, idiot rabbits living there instead. The question is- how did they get there in the first place?

## The Dolphin Derby*
End of the pier

Complete with its own catchy theme tune, the Dolphin Derby is probably the greatest game ever invented, and more importantly, a chance to earn some beer money for those of you on the bread line. Spend a week on your hands and knees practicing rolling golf balls into paper cups and reap the rewards.

*\*Well it is outdoors I suppose.*

**WEIRD AND WONDERFUL**

## WHERE TO CONTACT THE DEAD
### Brighton National Spiritualist Church
Edward Street opposite Devonshire Pl (01273) 683088

It all starts off surprisingly similar to a Christian service (not least because the hymns are the typical tuneless mumbling affairs) except instead of God, you give praise to 'the greater vibration'. Expect a bit more chat and another hymn, then it all picks up when the guest clairvoyant comes on.

Most of these guys are commanding speakers and come across in an American preacher style. There's a prep talk, some fabulous shaky hands business, then, through the preacher, the dead will start to communicate with a few members of the congregation.

Don't always expect to get chosen, but if you are fortunate enough, they'll ask you to speak, so that the spirits pick up on your vibrations. What follows are nuggets of advice and information for you from the spirit world, which are channelled through the clairvoyant's voice, and all done to the accompaniment of the shaky hands (whether it works without this spectacle, I don't know). The time I was picked, I apparently met my Granddad, whose message was 'stop worrying about your ears sticking out'.

Having never given much thought to the orientation of my ears, I did wonder what that was all about, but then he always was a bit of a joker. Afterwards it's cheese, biscuits and a chat, a flick through Psychic News, and then a well-earned breakfast at the Hand in Hand, over the road.
Sunday services are at 11am and 6.30pm.

## SEANCES

If you are serious about wanting to be involved with a séance group you can e-mail the Cheeky Guide with your name and phone number. We will pass it on to the group, and they will explain what is required. Unless you are staying in Brighton for some time though, this will not be possible. If invited you will be expected to take the evening seriously, but I can guarantee you will have plenty of fun. It's all in the pitch dark and starts with singing stuff like 'Roll Out The Barrel' and 'Daisy, Daisy' to get the energy going. Then, once the spirits have manifested through the medium, watch out for stuff moving around the room and hope that you don't spend the night with a chair on your head as one lady did.

Also expect to get covered in ectoplasm and have some questions ready for when you meet some of the fantastic characters such as James the Victorian transvestite comedian. And if you ask, the ghosts will tell you who your spirit guide is. Do I get a Buddhist monk or Native American Indian chief like everyone else? No, I get a chicken called Cyril.

**At the end of the night not everyone will necessarily believe what they have seen, but it is, of course, something to tell the grandchildren.**

# WEIRD AND WONDERFUL

## PALMISTS & CLAIRVOYANTS

### Margaret
64 Elm Grove (01273) 683623
Open Tues-Sat 10am-3.45pm
Closed 12noon-1pm

When you step in here, be ready to take a time warp back thirty years or more. The walls are littered with fading newspaper articles and curling black and white photos showing Margaret on old TV shows. You feel like you're in a Rita Tushingham movie and Margaret looks and plays the part magnificently.

The readings take around twenty minutes in a tiny room at the back of the shop where she will read your palm or tell your fortune from a pack of cards. Along with the usual stuff like *'you know someone who reads The Daily Mail'*, Margaret also said some pretty accurate and insightful things the last time I visited. The readings range from £11 to £15. Go on, treat yourself to a seaside speciality from a true professional.

### Professor Mirza
On the seafront between the piers

There's a quote from Jimmy Greaves outside, which is obviously a mark of quality, but unfortunately the professor didn't want to be in our guide unless we paid him!

### Paul Hughes-Barlow
295 Kings Road Arches, under the Palace Pier (01273) 677206
Open Mon-Sun 12noon-6pm

The only palmist in Brighton I met whose room was full of interesting books rather than gypsy tat and the usual mystical paraphernalia. Friendly

Pets get their paws read for free every other Saturday at Margaret's

# WEIRD AND WONDERFUL

and honest about his profession and with a good knowledge of the occult sciences, I warmed to him and his reassuringly boyish laugh. Probably a good choice if you're looking for something beyond the usual nonsense. First sittings are a standard £15.

## STUFF THAT LEGENDS ARE MADE OF

### Kappa
Bottom of Trafalgar Street
Opening times defy logic

Run by Peter Grant, this is not only home to the world's largest collection of valves, but also a graveyard to all of Brighton's dead TVs. Despite looking derelict inside, the place is sometimes open, and hidden away behind all the TV carcasses sits Peter, a man who can bring a 1950s Ukrainian radio to life with just the wave of his magic wand. When not doing implausible feats on old electronic equipment, Peter is invariably out and about setting up pirate radio stations, or saving another Russian nuclear power station from going under. If it's old and knackered, bring it here and Pete will fix it.

### D & K Rosen Clothiers
Top of Church Street
Open Mon-Sat 10am-5.30pm

You don't have a look around here, you have an adventure. The owner is one of Brighton's most eccentric characters, well-known for his bizarre banter, and the shop is a haven for second-hand suits, fez and other gentlemen's attire. Rumour has it that this is the place that inspired the 'Suits You' sketch from The Fast Show. Legends don't come much better than this.

### Tony Young Autographs
138 Edward Street (01273) 732418
Open Mon-Fri 10am-12pm, 1pm-3pm
Sat 10am-12.30pm

This tumble-down shop rescued from the 1950s has a surreal and curling collection of autographed photos and bizarre oddities. Where else could you get a copy of the homicide report of the JFK assassination and a broken banjo? Worth a visit for fans of The Twilight Zone but treat the owner with respect, he's an old man and dislikes rowdy people in the shop.

# The spotter's guide to

Last year, when the Brighton and Hove buses got the idea of sticking the names of over 50 famous people with local connections on their buses, it meant that celebrity spotting in this town took a whole new twist.

No longer are you obliged to spend two hours in the rain outside the Brighton Centre just to catch a glimpse of Robbie Williams' flabby bottom. Instead, all you need is a pencil, a copy of the guide and a rudimentary knowledge of public transport. Just 5 minutes on Western Road and you could see Norman Cook, Winston Churchill or even Leo Sayer streak by, and nearly knock you over.

We've only included our favourite 15 here, but serious spotters can find the rest listed at the website www.buses.co.uk.

When you've spotted all 15, send in the completed sheet and the first 5 we receive will win a special Cheeky cagoule.

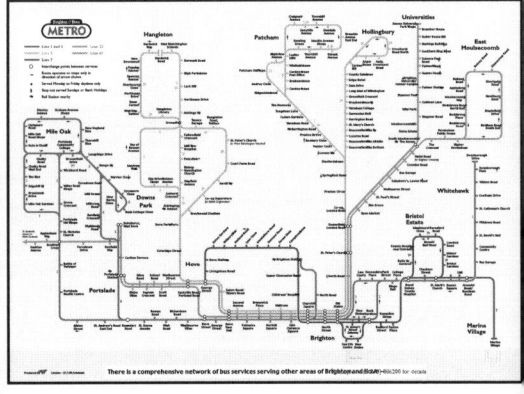

The territory of the Brighton & Hove bus

# Brighton & Hove buses

- **Lord Attenborough** (Bus number 1) – starred in *Brighton Rock* and that thing with the gorillas.
- **Norman Cook** (3) – aka Fatboyslim but once the bassist in Blancmange.
- **Chris Eubank** (4) – star of coffee adverts and celebrated dandy.
- **Derek Jameson** (14) – having once been editor of the *Daily Express* and *News of the World*, Derek is of course only one notch above Peter Stringfellow in the ladder of celebrity fools.
- **Des Lynam** (15) – TV celebrity chef.
- **Annie Nightingale** (16) – Radio One DJ, celebrated for keeping the off-licenses of Hove solvent for the last 20 years.
- **Leo Sayer** (17) pint-sized singer shaped like a Bonsai tree.
- **The Who** (19) hugely successful Mod band whose singer Roger Daltrey once famously sang – 'Hope I die before I get old...', but then changed his mind and settled down into a life of fish-farming instead.
- **Sir Norman Wisdom** (20) – veteran comedian with a bad case of the DTs.
- **Prince Regent** (803) – a swimming pool.*
- **Charles Busby** (824) – small yellow man who spent much of his time hanging precariously from telegraph wires.
- **John Nash** (811) – celebrated country and western singer whose hit 'A cowboy from Whitehawk buggered up my patio', made him a superstar.
- **Stanley Deason** (827) – one-time maverick mayor, who in the early 70s famously elected Frank Zappa as the King of Hove.
- **Carl Vincent** (845) – known locally as 'Vinegar Vincent', Carl is best remembered as having supplied the voice of Pig in the children's program 'Pipkins'.
- **Charles Dickens** (828) – had a mate who knew someone in Brighton.

The male and female of the species

### AMAZING BUS FACTS

- Often seen gathering in flocks at Churchill Square or North St.

- Predators: trucks and taxis.

- Prey: Cyclists, dozy tourists and prams.

*not sure why this one is here.

## HAVE A SURREAL AFTERNOON IN BRIGHTON

Put on your silliest hat, pack up some sandwiches and head off to Baker Street for your first destination, a compulsory crew-cut at Coopers for 120p. The less adventurous among you may simply want to enjoy the window display.

From here, head past the Level to the Lewes Road and take a first right at the big traffic lights. Number 64 Elm Grove is your next port of call, where you will need to part with £15 to discover what the future holds from mystic Margaret. Try not to be frightened by her make-up and listen carefully to what nuggets of wisdom she imparts to you.

At the very top of Elm Grove have a quick cuppa at Beckie's café where you can buy fake designer perfume or maybe just fondle the gnomes. Next cross over and follow Tenantry Down Road for a stunning view as you pass through Brighton's shanty town. The curve of houses you can see in front of you is Roundhill Crescent where Genesis P. Orridge used to live. The strange little huts on either side of you are occupied by Brighton's flourishing Amish community. Keep your walkmans well hidden at this point or you may have a bloodbath on your hands. At the end of the road take a left and look for the entrance to Woodvale Crematorium, as infamous occultist Aleister Crowley chose this as his resting-place. This vast graveyard is remote and enchanting, and should make you feel like you've left Brighton behind.

Leave by the main exit at the bottom, and now start heading into town. On your way back, buy yourself a CD from the strange music stall in the Phoenix Gallery, and to round off your afternoon, find the Basketmakers Pub, tucked away at the bottom of the North Laine. Search the tins on the wall to see who can find the strangest message inside, and then leave one of your own. The best messages that I find will appear in next year's guide.

# Shopping

Brighton can be a shopaholic's paradise, especially if you're a lover of antiques, fashion, jewellery, music, kitsch and all things retro. And with over 700 independent shops in the town centre alone, it boasts more of these per square mile than anywhere else in the UK. The most colourful areas with the best shops are definitely the North Laine, Kemptown and the Old Lanes. For the less adventurous, Western Road and the Churchill Square Shopping Centre have everything that you'd expect to find in a high street (except perhaps for the Ann Summers shop).

The North Laine area is particularly good, not only for its wide selection of clothes and record shops but also for its more unique offerings, like the 70s glam of Revamp or the stylish wares found at Pussy. Get into the mood here and you'll find yourself going home with a wrestling mask, a Mod suit, a tie dye candle and a pair of fetish shoes. And you only popped out for a loaf of bread.

The Old Lanes, on the other hand, are renowned for jewellery, antiques, loads of cafés, and a fairly dull selection of clothes shops. Think of it this way: if the North Laine were Eric Morcambe, the Old Lanes would be Ernie Wise.

And finally, before you rush off with your credit cards, don't get up too early! Shops here can open notoriously late (especially in the North Laine) and not always at the same time every morning. So, do yourself a favour, have a long night out and get up at the same time as nearly everyone else here; around 11am.

## RECORD SHOPS

*Unless your idea of a good record shop is Woolworths, you owe it to yourself to buy a few ultra cool and unusual records while you're here. For a town of its size, the choice is superb and many friends' bank accounts have come a cropper whilst visiting. How could you resist that old Howard Jones 12inch on original clear vinyl? The North Laine is a good starting point for second-hand and unusual records, while Essential Music in the Old Lanes is ideal for re-issued CDs.*

### Borderline

41 Gardener Street
Open Mon-Sat 10am-5.30pm
Sun 12noon-4pm

This colourful place has consistently stocked an amazing range of music ever since I've known it. The shop is small, but avoiding chart music and the obvious mainstream fodder means they have an incredible selection of re-issued Jazz, Soul, Psychedelia, Exotica and Soundtracks, mixed with modern Electronica, Post-Rock and Indie. Most is on CD but there is a smaller selection on vinyl. If you can find a bad record here I'll change my name to Barbara.

### CD, Record and Video Classics

28a Tidy Street (01273) 694229
Open Tues-Sat 10.15am-5.30pm

You'll find a large selection of classical music on vinyl and CD here, together with an assortment of second-hand videos. Lovers of the more exotic might find some Stockhausen and Varese albums if really lucky. Most of the videos are fairly typical stuff but they often have a good selection of sci-fi like Dr Who, The Prisoner and Star Trek.

### Charlie's Orbit

95 St George's Road Kemptown
(01273) 571010 Open Tues-Sat 10.30am-6pm, Thurs 'til 7pm

Nestling in some improbable No Man's Land between the Wire magazine and a charity shop, Charlie's Orbit is a fantastic second-hand CD and vinyl shop on the outer limits of Kemptown, run by a man with a shock of curly hair that would put Tom Baker to shame. Having moved to Brighton from Scotland with an incurable passion for buying records, Charlie's girlfriend decided the only solution was for him to open a record shop and the rest, of course, is history. You'll find Abba and the Carpenters sandwiched between weird Electronica, Post-Rock gods and even old Shimmy Disc records, all of which show Charlie's rather eclectic tastes.

At around £8 a purchase, for a huge selection of rare gems, this is really worth making the trek into Kemptown for. You'll be made to feel welcome, and no doubt go home with a much sought-after bargain.

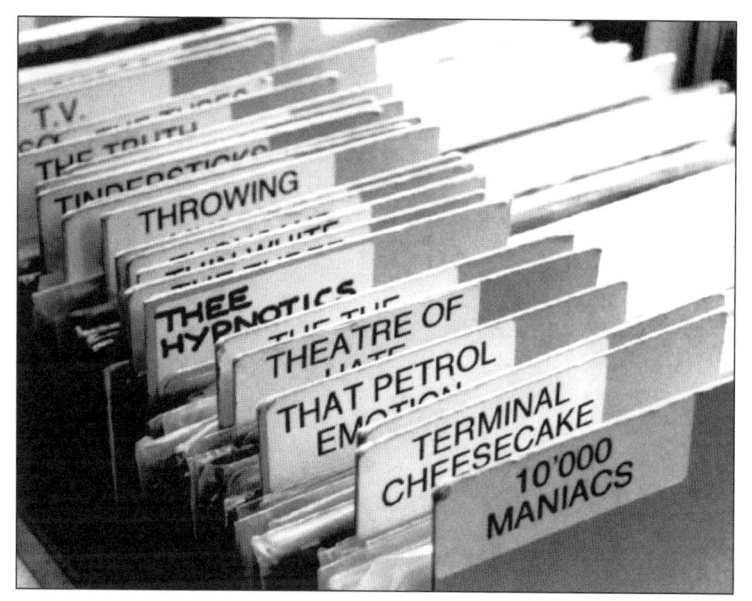

### Edgeworld
Above Hive, Kensington Gdns
Open Mon-Sat 10.30am-6pm

Easy to miss, which would be a real shame, especially for hunters of obscure and underground vinyl. The shop specialises in Lo-Fi, Mellow-Country, Post-Rock, Electronica and Ska-Punk among others. Plus it's a good place to find out where some of the more low-key gigs are happening too. Don't be afraid to ask for a listen before you buy, the staff are refreshingly unpretentious. They'll even stock your own CDs as well if packaged properly. Mine's been sat there for years.

### Essential Music
15-16 Brighton Square
(01273) 202695
Open10am-6pm Mon-Sat,
Sun12noon-5pm

I buy a lot of CDs here, mainly because most of the stock is under £7. Great selection of Jazz, Soundtracks and Easy Listening together with all your pop favourites from the 60s to present day. Having expanded last year the choice here just gets better and better and you'd be hard-pushed to find better bargains in Brighton, even from most of the second-hand places.

### HD2
92a St James's St (07939) 333781
Open 10am-5pm Mon-Sat
(provided the owner doesn't oversleep)

Second hand CD and video shop in Kemptown with a slant towards Sci-fi. The music selection ranges from the truly appalling (is there anyone in the world still wanting to buy the T'Pau video collection?) to some really excellent bargains if you sniff around. I saw Midnight Cowboy and Bullit for £6, which I would have bought had I not spent my cash on the Joe Jackson video for an old friend. I know, I know, I should keep better company.

## SHOPPING

### Little Gems
Phoenix Gallery 10-14 Waterloo Place
Open every Fri-Sat 11am-6pm
(Possibly Wed/Thurs but it varies)

Run by a succession of men with interesting goatees, this is a stall set up in the Phoenix Gallery and run by two music lovers whose ad simply reads – 'Records and CDs that are rather strange'. It is indeed a very eclectic and modest selection of (mainly) instrumental stuff ranging from the very heavy to the very silly. Definitely one for The Wire readers. If that's not enough, most of the stuff is under £10 and you can listen to as much as you want before you purchase. Dress code- goatee beards optional, record bag essential.

### The Record Album
8 Terminus Road
(01273) 323853
Open Mon-Sat 11am-5pm

Tucked away up the hill, just round the corner from Brighton Station, this is the oldest record shop in the country and is a must for vinyl junkies.

The shop specialises in all types of deleted recordings and rare one-offs, especially soundtrack albums, most of which are new or in excellent condition. Don't expect to find a bargain; prices start around £10 and go up to £75 or more for that ultra-rare electronic 50s sci-fi B-movie soundtrack. Owner George also supplies records to the BBC, theatre and radio and has an extensive mail order service. When asked by Mojo magazine why he doesn't stock CDs, George just shuddered and said, *'uh, those ghastly little frisbees'*.

### Recordland
40 Trafalgar Street (01273) 672512
Open Mon-Sat 10am-5pm

This place has been here for nearly 20 years and stocks an impressive range of CD and vinyl from the 50s to 70s. They specialise in Jazz, Big Band, Easy Listening and Soundtracks.

They are a friendly bunch and owner Geoff was once nice enough to play me a whole selection of Jazz records one afternoon when I couldn't decide what I wanted. Don't forget to have a look upstairs too, there's a good selection of old comedy records, from Woody Allen to Bernard Cribbins, tucked away somewhere.

## Rounder Records
19 Brighton Square
(01273) 325440
Open Mon-Sat 9.30am-6pm
Sunday 10.30am-6pm

Having recently undergone a change of management, Rounder is quickly becoming a first class record shop. As well as the usual big range of CDs, they now stock lots of vinyl too – new and second hand all mixed together, which means you're always likely to unearth a nice surprise. There's a 50-50 split of excellent dance and indie pop, and it's often the cheapest in town, especially for vinyl.

## Urban Records
24 Gardner Street
(01273) 620567
Open 10am-6pm

House, Garage, Rare-Groove, Funk, Jazz and more. Two decades of dance music on new and used vinyl.

## Wax Factor
Trafalgar Street (01273) 673744
al@wax-factor.demon.co.uk
Open Mon-Fri 10am-5.30pm
Sat 9.30am-5.30pm

Sensational collection of second-hand CDs and vinyl and a meaty stock of cult and music literature. (See Bookshops for more detail)

# SHOPPING

## BOOKSHOPS

## BIG GUYS
### Borders
Churchill Square Shopping Centre,
Western Road
(01273) 731122 Open Mon-Sat 8am-9pm, Sun 10.30am-5pm
www.borders.com

When all the rest of us are dragging ourselves out of bed, making strong coffee, lighting cigarettes and smearing Marmite on the cat, these guys are up and open. Didn't anyone tell them that in Brighton no one even thinks about getting out of bed before 10am, never mind shopping? Still, that's crazy Americans for you. They do, however, have a fine collection of books, stock one of the best selections of magazines in Brighton, definitely the best collection of story tapes, and some good CDs, if we forgive the MOR monstrosities (does anyone still buy records from the likes of Pat Benatar, Asia and Uriah Heep?). Good place also for small music performances and book readings.

### Waterstones
71-74 North Street (01273) 206017
Open 9am-7pm (except Tues and Thurs open 9.30am) Sat 9am-6pm,
Sun 11am-5pm
www.waterstones.co.uk

Waterstones boast an incredible choice from the bestsellers right the way to the most obscure underground stuff and local writers. Particularly good stockists of cult and art books and occasionally prone to visits by the likes of Will Self and other literary luminaries. Friendly staff give it a local feel and seem to have their finger on the pulse of what Brighton readers are looking for.

### Sussex Stationers
37 London Rd
114 St James's St
55 Western Rd
Open Mon-Sat 9am-5.30pm
Sun 9.45am-5.15pm

Stocking the most popular books of the moment and somehow managing to offer them at a pretty good discount.

## LITTLE GUYS
### Bookmarks
Dyke Rd

Off the beaten track somewhat yet worth finding if you're an avid collector of second-hand literature as they have an enticing collection of books in the window ranging from stuff on alternative health to cult fiction. Last year they had a fabulous collection of really old Christmas books including these 1950s children's pop-up books which unfortunately dismantled themselves when I opened them, and I went home covered in little cut-outs of Father Christmas and his elves.

## City Books
23 Western Rd (01273) 725306

Established now for 14 years, this is Brighton's biggest independent bookshop and favourite haunt of Nigel Richardson (author of *Breakfast in Brighton*). A proper local bookshop, it's the kind of place you find yourself leaving after an hour because you fell into a conversation with the owner about the merits of having Chris Eubank made into sandwiches. Having missed them out last year, they swore never to forgive us and taunted us by hiding our books underneath unsold copies of the 1985 Michelin Guide to Yugoslavia. Despite this, we still urge you to support them, as independent bookshops are a dying breed and it's places like this that give a town its personality, rather than the homogenised corporates.

## Practical Books
14/14a Western Road
(01273) 734602

Specialising in foreign language books ranging from Arabic to Lithuanian, with an impressive selection of literature in countless languages too. They also sell quite a lot of personal development and guitar music.

## Rainbow Books
28 Trafalgar Street (01273) 605101
Open Mon-Sat 10.30am-6pm
(except Thursdays which are until 7pm for some reason)

There is a good range of cheap and cheerful second-hand books here. If you're not sure what books you want just buy a cup of coffee, sit down by the window and browse through a few of them. Alternatively, sink yourself into the sofa downstairs and thumb through the

**SHOPPING**

More storeys than any other bookshop.

Brighton's biggest bookshop
5 floors high

W
Waterstones

The Clocktower
71-74 North Street
Brighton BN1 1ZA
Tel 01273 206017
Fax 01273 205616
www.waterstones.co.uk

thousands of 30p bargains. Everything is cheap and the books are colour-coded for the different prices. There's also a selection of old sheet music in the basement if you're interested.

### Sancho Panza
2 Surrey Street (01273) 773054
Open Mon-Sat 11am-6pm
Closed Tuesdays except term time when you'll catch him at the Sussex Uni market.

Head to Brighton Station, turn left at the top into Surrey Street and you'll find this place at the end, opposite The Evening Star. The choice of stock is impressive and if you're looking for cult classics and underground stuff I guarantee you'll walk out with some goodies. If you're a fan of 60s American literature, you should get a copy of the Richard Brautigan tape here, which features the ultra-rare album the author did for Apple records, and features a great documentary.

It's always worth poking your nose in here, if only to sample that delightful smell that is unique to second hand books shops; the smell of nostalgia and dusty old stories. Ah, I'm an old romantic at heart.

### Tall Storeys Bookshop
88 St. James's Street (01273) 697381
Open Mon-Sat 10am-5.30pm
Sun 2-5.30pm

Five floors of second-hand books and specialising in art and cinema. Narrow staircases and intriguing cubby holes make it a pleasure to look around. But be careful of the stairs; last time I was here I fell down them and felt a real plonker. So don't expect to see me in there until the beard has fully grown.

### Two Way Books
54 Gardner Street (01273) 687729

Frozen in time since 1982, this singular bookshop must be the only place in England still selling Paul Young and Van Halen annuals. If pictures of David Lee Roth in spandex pants aren't your bag, they also do a nifty selection of old comics ranging from Dr Who and Marvel to Karate and Tractor Weekly. Mix that with more bizarre stuff like shelves of Mills and Boon, Giles cartoon books and several discreet piles of porn and you'll probably wonder how they make a living. Barbara Cartland or back issues of Razzle, I wonder?

### Wax Factor
Trafalgar Street (01273) 673744
e-mail al@wax-factor.demon.co.uk
Open Mon-Fri 10am-5.30pm
Sat 9.30am-5.30pm

If second-hand books on the Occult, drugs, Philosophy, Science Fiction, Eastern Mysticism and music are your style, then this is the place for you. The window display should be enough to pull you in as you drool over all the Crowley, Philip K Dick and Burroughs books. They have a pretty good selection of fiction here too, which is just on your right as you walk in. If that's not enough, they also stock one of the best collections of second hand CDs and vinyl in Brighton at reasonable prices. The basement stocks a meaty selection of 7inches and CD singles too.

Be prepared for a good half an hour in this place and if they haven't got what you were looking for, you'll probably end up leaving with what you didn't know you were looking for.

## SHOPPING

### West Pier Books
Down by the West Pier (obviously)

Every day of the week when the weather is good you'll find these guys down on the seafront by the West Pier. Run alternatively by Mark and the guy from local band Polak, both their stalls hold a great collection of second-hand books. As well as running the bookstall, Mark is a local film-maker with a passion for concrete, and has to date made over 30 short films about cement mixers and carparks. Last I heard, he was making a feature film about Crazy Paving. If you get him onto the subject you'll never get away and it's best to avoid picking up a copy of The Cement Garden as that's bound to set him off.

### 124 Queen's Road
124 Queen's Road
(01273) 323105
Open Mon-Sat 10am-5pm

This place doesn't seem to have a name and if you visit you'll see why. The window display defies explanation and the whole shop looks as if the owner got a huge truck full of books and just emptied them into the shop and said:
*'OK, we're open.'*
In fact he always reminds me of Michael Caine in 'Educating Rita', after he's had a few. But ask for any title and if he's got it, he'll rummage through a pile and somehow find it. Deserves a visit just to witness this.

## COMICS

### David's Comic Shop
5 Sydney Street (01273) 691012
Open Mon-Fri 9.30am-5.45pm
Sat 9am-6pm

Independent comics, graphic novels, Star Wars and Buffy The Vampire Slayer related stuff. The staff are friendly, even towards a bumbling novice like me.

### Hive
6 Kensington Gdns (01273) 687802
Open Mon-Sat 11am-6pm
Sun 11am-5.30pm

Two floors of comics, Star Wars figures, gothic gizmos and records (see review of Edgeworld Records in music section). Noisy, busy and definitely worth a browse around. They also stock some unusual magazines, including quite a good selection of fetish, tattoo, graffiti and drug related stuff. Something for all the family.

## SHOPPING

## VIDEOS, FILM & MOVIE MEMORABILIA

### Movie Mania
George Street
Open Mon-Sat 10.30am-5.30pm,
Sun 1pm-6pm

Original posters, photo stills from films, books, old magazines and two terrapins, Geek and Merlin who live in the middle of the shop.

### Enterprise Video
49 London Road (01273) 670052
Open Mon-Sat 9am-6pm

There's some good stuff in here. It's all second-hand videos but some of it is a cut above the usual collections of Brat Pack tosh and cheap thrillers. They have a modest selection of Blaxploitation, Horror, Cult, etc and some deleted stuff and if you can't find what you're looking for there's also a free finder service. Prices range from £2 to £30 for the rare stuff and half price for exchange. Expect a purchase if you drop by. I got a copy of 'Freaks' from here for £7.

### Watch This Space
Kensington Gardens, North Laine
(07790) 956929 Open Mon-Sat 10am-5.30pm, Sundays during summer

Steering well away from mainstream, big budget and blockbusters, owner Mick has instead gone for an excellent range of old classics (Hitchcock, James Stewart etc), cult movies and modern world cinema. And with prices all loitering around the £5/6 mark, anyone with good taste in films is going to find something to take home and cherish.

## GROOVY THINGS FOR THE HOME

### Anatolia
98 Gloucester Road
Open Mon-Sat 10.30am-5.30pm

Specialists in all things Turkish, from earthenware to rugs. Do they still sell the Mosque alarm clocks that will wake you every morning with prayers? You'll have to pay them a visit to find out.

### Pussy Home Boutique
3a Kensington Gardens
(01273) 604861
Open 10(ish)-5.30pm
Summer Sun 12noon-4.30pm
www.pussyhomeboutique.co.uk

Imagine Betty Page meeting Frank Lloyd Wright at a Stereolab gig, and you're beginning to get an idea of Pussy. Often imitated in Brighton but never equalled, this is definitely one of my favourite places to shop. This very stylish and saucy boutique boasts a wonderful selection of cool furniture, chic and erotic books, fetish china, jewellery, exclusive Paul Frank monkey stuff, T-shirts and other oddities. Run by Nicki and her faithful sidekick Gwen, they seem to spend most of the day nattering with half of Brighton over a cup of tea and a fag, yet still manage unfailingly to have the best window displays in town.

### Pyramid
9a Kensington Gardens (01273) 607791
Open Mon-Fri 10am-5.30pm,
Sun 11am-5.30pm

From exotic toilet seats to Simpsons chess sets and furry lamps. They also do a nice line in chrome fans and lava lamps.

### Rin*Tin*Tin
34 North Road
(01273) 672424
Open Mon-Sat 11am-5.30pm

Interesting collection of pre-70s memorabilia, ranging from magazines, toys, games, radios and posters. You know that petrol globe bedside light you've always wanted, well bugger me if they don't have them here.

### TAB
7 Kings Road (01273) 821448
Open Mon-Sun 10.30am-5.30pm
(best to phone though)
Haggle-friendly

Covering everything from the Forties to the Seventies, Tab is a gold mine of retro chic, with furniture, magazines and sunglasses to a vast array of clothes, which, with the exception of some dazzling ties and a few shirts, are definitely more for the ladies.

Upstairs you'll find owner Catherine's 'babies'; an immense collection of retro wallpaper, jealously guarded by Lulu the shop dummy, who reclines in a swivel chair and comes alive when you pop Black Magic chocolates in her mouth. (I'm showing my age here). Last time I was in, Catherine had an original Herald Tribune from 1963 on the day of the Kennedy assassination, a big pile of Look-in magazines (complete with David Cassidy pin-up and Ed Stewpot's column) and a load of 'Robin Day' chairs. If the place is closed don't be afraid to ring; Catherine lives upstairs and chances are she'll just be reading an old copy of Oz and having a fag.

## SHOPPING

### A GOOD PLACE FOR BUYING PRESENTS

### The Brighton Pottery Workshop
94 Trafalgar Street
Open Tues-Sat 9.30am-5.30pm
www.workshoppottery.co.uk

Run by Peter Stocker (the only straight man in Brighton to sport a walrus moustache) his shop has been here now for an incredible 21 years, and Peter still remembers the days when the North Laine was an area that just sold stuff like work boots and maids' outfits, while scruffy urchins would roam the streets shouting: 'Coo ta mister' when you threw them a tangerine.

Of course nowadays the boots are a fashion statement, the maids outfits are sold for kinky purposes, and the scruffy urchins all now play in local band Cheetah. But I digress. The shop sells modestly priced and beautiful earthenware ceramics, all made on the premises, ranging from bowls and plates to more creative figurines.

### Blackout
53 Kensington Place
Open Mon-Sat 10am-6pm

The shop's angle is kind of fashion-folk-art mixed with kitsch religious imagery. They do a great selection of their own designer T-shirts and have some of the best original style jewellery in town. If you're a Goth keep away, they have a policy of selling nothing black here, colour is in (hence the name). Typical stock in the past has included a Tibetan baby carrier for £28, fluorescent loo brushes, Virgin Mary ashtrays and plastic Hindu Gods.

### EM-Space
20 Sydney Street (01273) 683400
Open 10am-6pm Mon-Sat

Run by Kathy and Janine now for a couple of years, EM-space specialise in design-led gifts with a slant towards cards and books.

From the sublime to the ridiculous, stock ranges from artists' sketchbooks and beautiful traditional photo albums (the ones where you

More masterpieces created at Glazed Expressions

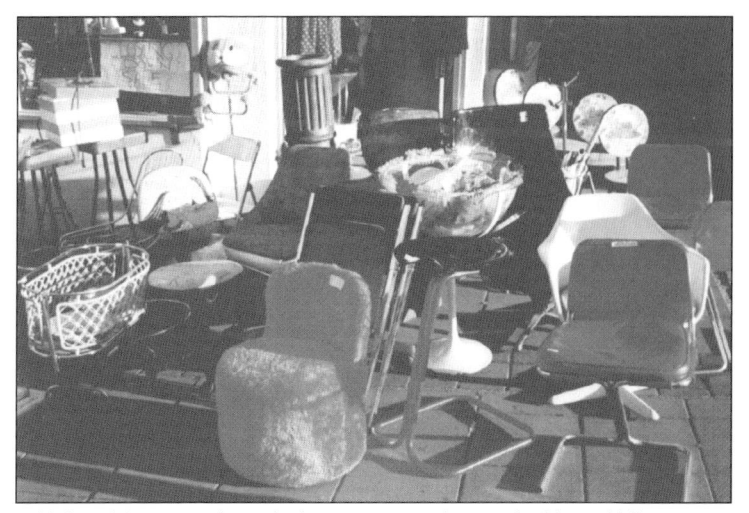

add the sticky corners) to nipple shine soap and nightshirts for your computer mouse (one of their best sellers).

Don't miss the gallery at the back, it contains lots of very reasonably priced work from local artists, including that of resident artist Jim Sanders whose art has recently transformed into completely new directions, after he discovered the joys of absinthe.

### Fossil 2000
3 Kensington Place
(01273) 622000
Open Tues-Sat 10am-5.30pm
Sun-Mon 11am-4pm
www.brightonpages.co.uk/fossil2000

Run by Caroline and Denise, this lovely shop just off the beaten track in the North Laine has an incredible collection of ammonites, trilobites, fossil plates, crystal growing kits for kids and lots of other pre-historic relics. Denise mentioned to me that if you want something specific it's worth asking, as they can *'get their hands on most things'*, which made me wonder whether they had a spare key to the Natural History Museum or something.

Prices range from shark's teeth for £10 to £2000 for a dinosaur head. More unusual perhaps is their collection of flies in amber, beetles in treacle and a wooly mammoth in a tar pit.

### Glazed Expressions
31 North Road
(01273) 628952
Open Mon-Sat 11am-7pm
Sun 12pm-5pm, Thurs late night
www.paintingpotterycafé.co.uk

Prices for the ceramics start around £3 for tiles and eggcups.

Working under the philosophy that everyone is a painter, Glazed Expressions is a painting and pottery café where for a £4 studio fee you can come and try your hand at decorating plates, mugs, eggcups and tiles. Popular with families and children, they will ply you with coffee, hot chocolate and teas for as long as you want and also glaze and fire your finished masterpieces. The late-night Thursday sessions are especially worth coming to, as food is laid on and you can bring your own booze. So men don't be surprised if, after 14 cans of Special Brew, you wake the next morning to find 8 new eggcups sitting on your kitchen table, each badly decorated with pictures of your own genitalia.

### The Old Postcard Shop
38 Beaconsfield Road
Open 10am-4pm Tues-Sat
(01273) 600035

Mercifully you won't find the usual Brighton Pavilion and West Pier pictures here, but instead Keith's shop sells postcards on every theme from Elvis to London Transport. Stock ranges from 50p to £50 and he even stocks those old saucy Donald McGill postcards. If you don't know what I mean think of a cartoon of a man clutching a golf club looking over a hedge at a buxom beauty in a nudist colony whilst uttering some double-entendre about his balls.

He also stocks ephemera like ration books, theatre programmes and old magazines. 5 points if you can spot Kermit the frog in here.

### Silverado
3 Kensington Gardens & 30 Meeting House Lane (01273) 326756
Open 10am-5.30pm Mon-Sat

Owned by Andrew Bird, former keyboard player from Men at Work, Silverado offers beautiful and stylish silver jewellery, including rings, pendants and ear-rings. Look out for Andrew in his cork hat, wandering the Lanes whistling 'Down Under' with a nostalgic look in his eyes.

### Wallis Macfarlane
14 St George's Road Kemptown
(01273) 297088
Open Mon-Sat 10am-6pm

Now in its third year, this gift shop deep in Kemptown sells a variety of exquisite and unusual gifts, including a wide range of aromatherapy oils, soaps of the world (scented with everything from coffee to prawn cocktail) and original pots and cushions by local artists. Describing Kemptown as a cross between Coronation Street and the Left Bank, its two owners Jonathan and Roland are firm believers in strengthening the Kemptown community, and it'll warm the cockles of your heart to see the genuine friendship they have with many of the shopkeepers in the area.

Unhappy teachers take note, they both gave it up several years ago and seem utterly content.

*'The only paperwork I do any more,'* said one of them gleefully, whilst wrapping a bar of chocolate soap.

## MUSICAL INSTRUMENT SHOPS

### Adaptatrap
26 Trafalgar Street (01273) 672722
Open Mon-Sat 10am-6pm

A cut above the usual collection of ethnic instruments, this place sells a whole range of drums, koras, xylophones, singing bowls, old gongs, horns and many other exotic and strange instruments from all over the world. What's more, they don't mind you coming in and playing with them. Owner Les is helpful and will smoke an entire roll-up without taking it out of his mouth whilst giving you advice on what to do if you've damaged your congas (ooh missus). The shop is littered with ads for music lessons and if you're sticking around Brighton and need to find that all-essential sitar teacher, this is the place to look. You'll also find out about workshops and gigs here, ranging from Zither recitals to Shamanic drumming weekends.

### The Guitar, Amp and Keyboard Centre
79-80 North Road (01273) 672977
Open Mon-Sat 9.30am-5.30pm
Sun 11am-4pm
www.gak.co.uk

Created from the barrow-boy charm of its haggle-friendly owner. Gary turned up in Brighton ten years ago with just a broken banjo and the gift of the gab, and slowly built an empire. The shop now has everything you could possibly need in terms of acoustic and electronic instruments and equipment, and, despite not having any competition worth speaking of, still do some terrific deals. More importantly, they've also proved that music shops do not have to be run by metal morons who are more interested in their own talents than actually selling you a guitar.

Will accept body parts as down-payment.

## Music Exchange
2 Trafalgar Street (01273) 239356
Open Mon-Sat 10ish-5.30pm

Cheap and cheerful selection of second-hand guitars, amps and effects.

If you can stand the smell of stale beer, these guys will burp their way through a friendly haggle.

## Mamba
96 St. James's Street (01273) 600160
Open Mon-Sat 10.30am-6pm

Lots of second-hand equipment and a friendly haggle with owner Terry. A good place for someone who's starting into music and doesn't want to spend much. There are some cheap drums in the basement too but they do get snapped up fairly quickly. For a few rock and roll anecdotes ask Terry about his days drumming with Van Morrison.

## CLOTHES SHOPS

*From safari suits for him to rubber cat-suits for her, Brighton boasts a huge collection of retro, exotic and club-fashion clothes shops. Most are located in the North Laine so if you want to get kitted out in something especially slinky for a club night or just want something new for the wardrobe, here's a selection of where to go.*

## Glitzy Tartz
26 Sydney Street (01273) 674477
www.glitzytartz.com
Open Mon-Sat 10am-6pm

Exotic club-wear for girls and adventurous boys, including quality but pricey rubber-wear. One of the most flamboyant and colourful clothes shops I have ever come across and the window display alone makes Topshop look like Hastings in February.

## Jump The Gun
36 Gardner Street
(01273) 626333
Open Mon-Sat 10am-6pm

Probably the only guys in the country praying for a Parklife revival. Brighton's only exclusive Mod shop boasts a handsome collection of suits, shirts and coats for the dapper gentlemen.

Not exactly cheap but Weller drops by every now and again, so I guess it has the stamp of approval.

With everything from the usual Ben Sherman and parkas to their own shirts and a wide and cool range of suits.

### Mambo
37 West Street
(01273) 323505
Open Mon-Sat 10am-6pm
Sun 12noon-6pm

Hip surf and skateboarding fashion items and a range of outrageous Hawaiian shirts all at painful prices.

### Route One
3 Bond Street
(01273) 323633

The guys in here are friendly, sell mainly shoes and clothes and have a decent selection of boards, wheels, trucks etc, and always seem to have some sort of good skate video on the box. They are also pretty knowledgeable on what the current scene is like and can tell you some of the better places to skate in Brighton.

### Yamama
92 Trafalgar Street
(01273) 689931
Open Mon-Sat 11am-6pm

Colourful range of interesting and fair priced clothing with a modern hippy slant. They sell great baggy trousers, hemp-style clothing, shirts and skirts for the bohemian traveller types and the obligatory henna tattoos. If the clothes don't appeal, why not try crocheted slippers or that essential travel backgammon set for those long winter evenings in Tibet or when you're next stuck in a Welsh service station?

### Ghita Schuy
17 St George's Road
(01273) 885275
Open Mon-Fri 12noon-5pm,
Sat 12noon-6pm

Hand made shoes, made to order.

### X To Z
27 Western Road
Open Mon-Sat 10am-6pm,
Sun 11.30am-5.30pm

A rather wild collection of boots and shoes adorns this shop, even if it does feel a bit 80s Goth at times. Expect anything from thigh-high boots to glittery DMs. They also do a rather odd collection of faded punk and metal band T-shirts. Where else could you still buy an Exploited T-shirt?

---

**Yamama**
clothes and jewellery

Design, Manufacture, Retail, Wholesale - we do it all. So what you get are dynamic, innovative clothes and jewellery from a group of talented designers.

Inspired by culture and colour, our clothes reflect the vibrant visual diversities that make up this crazy world we live in.

**Yamama**
92 Trafalgar Street
(01273) 689931

## SECOND-HAND CLOTHES

### Camden Traders
Church Street
(01273) 697464
Opening times- a mystery

Stocking a cheap but nifty selection of second-hand sixties and glam-wear.

I got an e-mail last year from someone who swore blind that on at least two occasions they'd spotted a naked man in here but when I asked the staff they denied all knowledge. Can anyone shed any light on this??

### Circe's Island
22 Trafalgar Street

Decorated with plastic birds, palm trees and fishing netting hanging from the ceiling, this place sells second hand quality clothes, shoes and err...fireplaces. Most of the stuff is for women, and my girlfriend says they have a good selection of coats. They've been two fake furs less since she last went in. Be prepared for Mr. Miserable who sometimes works here. Opening times – *'When we feel like it.'* – Tell him to cheer up.

### Cutie
33 Kensington Gardens
Open Mon-Sat 10.30am-5.30pm
Sun 12noon-5pm

Run by Deborah, once renowned for her wild antics in local band 'Sexlovebusterbaby', her shop sells a wide range of new and used clothes. Of particular interest are her own unique glittery knitwear items, from wristbands to tutus.

### Cushy B
56 Sillwood Street (01273) 774888
Open Tues-Sat 12noon-6pm

Fabulous collection of vintage and period women's clothes from Victorian nightwear and sexy slips to dresses, gowns and accessories.

Expect friendly advice on personal grooming (!) from owner Katy, and a nice hot cuppa if you ask nicely.

## Rokit
23 Kensington Gardens
(01273) 672053
Open Mon-Sat 9.30am-6pm

Well-established and good quality selection of second hand gear, especially their own range of jeans, Hawaiian and Cuban shirts, flares and track wear. The shop looks really cool and the staff dress to impress.

## To Be Worn Again
51 Providence Place
(01273) 277686
Open Mon-Sat 11am-7pm,
Sun 12noon-4pm

Tucked away just off Trafalgar Street opposite St. Bartholomew's church, this is the biggest second-hand clothing warehouse in Brighton. The choice of stuff is the usual 70s shirts, leather and suede jackets and paisley dresses but as there's more of everything you're more likely to find something suitable for a night at Dynamite Boogaloo. Don't miss the backroom with a great selection of coats including three quarter and full length fake fur coats.

### High Street Shops
*If you're looking for the likes of TopShop and Warehouse, you'll find them up by Churchill Square where many of the high street clothes shops for women are concentrated. East Street, Duke Street and Ship Street in the Old Lanes are also good places to start if you're into shops like Kookai, Jigsaw and Next.*

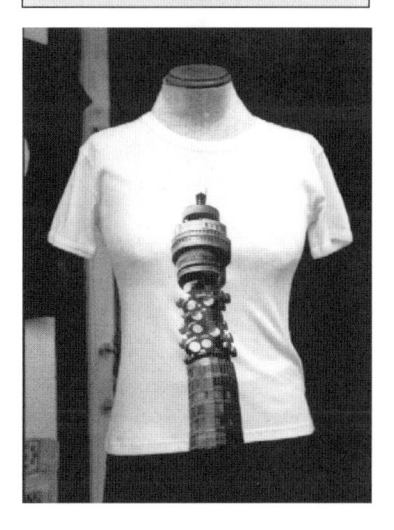

## SHOPPING

## ODDITIES

### Acme Art
41 Gloucester Road
(01273) 601639
Best to phone for opening times as they seem erratic at the best of times
www.acmeartshop.com

The world would be a duller place if there weren't people like Chris MacDonald around. This retired teacher found happiness making strange sculptures from original wood and metal objects and has been established in Brighton for several years now.

There's something very cartoonish and surreal about his work; it's the kind of art you'd expect to find in Terry Gilliam's house. The sculptures make perfect unusual birthday presents but don't be surprised if they end up sitting on your mantlepiece instead.

### Arkham
89 Trafalgar Street
(01273) 628440
Mon-Sun 11am-6pm, closed Wed
www.arkham-darkart.co.uk

Celebrating the darker side of life, this place stocks an odd assortment of things such as clothes, jewellery, ornaments, sculptures and books. The shop is littered with gargoyle sculptures, Edward Gorey books, Gothic videos Giger artwork (from the first Alien film), Skin Two books and Klimt postcards. It's kind of interesting even if you don't feel part of their vision. Imagine Jules Verne meets cyberpunk.

### Paul Bruton Army Surplus
Viaduct Road
Open 10am-1pm and 2pm-4.30pm
Wed-Sat

The two masked dummies that stand guard outside this shop must be one of the most famous sights in Brighton. Both creatures have posed with innumerable tourists and even appear on an album cover by some obscure Scottish band. The stock in here is immense, and you can get kitted out in just about any uniform you fancy, from the pith helmet and khaki shorts style of 'It 'Aint Half Hot Mum', to the German guards in 'Escape from Colditz'. Plus over 30 styles of army trousers, tops and hats at very reasonable prices. And the dressing booth is fantastic!

Another Acme Art masterpiece

## Burchell's

103 Gloucester Road
Open Mon-Sat 9.30am-5pm but phone just to be sure

Wholesalers of religious artefacts and icons. Whilst a three foot oak crucifix would set you back £235, opposite the counter there's always a couple of boxes on the floor of miscellaneous items that you can haggle for, or if you're lucky they'll give you for free. I found a fantastic wooden wallscroll with very kitschy painting on it and parts of a crib set last time I was in and there's usually a few damaged crucifixes in there too.

If you're into religious imagery or need something to spice up your latest junk sculpture, this is the place to come.

## ChoccyWoccyDooDah

27 Middle Street
(01273) 329462
Open Mon-Fri 10am-6pm
Sat 12pm-4pm Sun 10am-5pm
www.choccywoccydoodah.co.uk

You'll forgive the ludicrous name the second you walk in here and take in that sweet smell of Belgian chocolate. The display area is like a Doctor's waiting room full of the most outrageous, over the top chocolate cakes you've ever seen. I saw a spiky fetish chocolate cake recently and one covered in realistic looking chocolate vegetables including carrots and cabbage (!!). Be prepared to pay up to £3000 for some of the top notch wedding cakes though. If that's out of your budget they might still do chocolate action men for £10, which are well worth becoming a total fatty for.

## Hocus Pocus

38 Gardner Street (01273) 572202
Open Mon-Sat 10-6pm, Sun 12-4pm

A particularly odd assortment of stuff here from New Age to drug culture. There's a mixture of new age books and accessories and you can have tarot readings and clairvoyance upstairs.

What is special is their comprehensive stock of drug paraphernalia together with a good collection of herbal highs from hallucinogenics to ecstasy substitutes. The shop has a similar feel to Amsterdam's smart shops if ever you've been.

My favourite item here is the chocolate maggots and the most-ridiculous-thing-in-the-shop award goes to the socks with names on. What kind of person who smokes pot and reads books on Buddhism wears socks with their name on? *'Dont laugh'* said the owner with embarrassment, *'they are our best sellers'*. I think Brighton is starting to get to me now.

## The Lanes Armoury

27 Meeting House Lane
(01273) 321357
Open Mon-Sat 10am-5.15pm
www.thelanesarmoury.co.uk

Souvenir firearms and armour from all periods of history. Get your granny that old Vickers submachine gun she always wanted, or maybe a Luger for young cousin Donald. They also have Kentucky rifles, Zulu war shields, Napoleonic swords and even a helmet from the Iraqi war. A Japanese suit of armour would set you back around £14,000, though for the less affluent you can buy a cap badge for only £3. If the Ronnie Reagan picture isn't up then nag them to get it back on display as there's a good story behind it.

## The Olde Rock Shop

West Pier, Kingsway, opposite Regency Square (01273) 207610
Open winter 9am-5pm Mon-Sun
Summer 8.30am-late Mon-Sun

Of the dozens of gift shops that litter the seafront, this one alone deserves a mention as the building is a period piece and has stood on the same spot for over 126 years and can be spotted in the many films made here from 'Carry On Girls' to 'Oh, what a lovely war!'.

They sell all the typical tourist stuff from sticks of rock to snowstorms, postcards and fridge magnets with mottos like 'send more tourists, the last ones were delicious', and the Geordie lady who works here is good for a natter. As a tip, 'seagull poo chocolates' makes good presents for kids.

## The Pound Shop

North Street near Barclays bank
Open Mon-Sat 9am-5.30pm

A veritable bonanza of bargains. Stock up on food, Xmas presents and condiments. Brighton is not a town of money snobs, hardly anyone has much of the stuff so we're not too proud to come here. Besides, some of the stock is top quality bargain material. If you're a biscuit or chocolate fan like me, go with an empty suitcase…

## Penny Lane Gallery
35 Upper St James's Street
(01273) 686869
www.yellow-sub.com
www.artbeat.co.uk

Currently the only one of its kind in the world, this is a shrine for Beatles fans, stocking original merchandise ranging from a vast collection of vintage animation to memorabilia and old vinyl.

For anyone with even a passing interest in the loveable moptops, the shop is well worth a visit and is beautifully decorated with original Yellow Submarine artwork, models, mugs, posters, a one-armed bandit, and a menacing cardboard cut-out of Paul standing guard in the corner as a deterrent to burglars. Of course authentic Beatles stuff doesn't come cheap, you could pay thousands for original Yellow Submarine artwork but the less affluent fan can purchase individual slides from the American cartoon series for less than a tenner.

### Pathé News just in -
*-The mustachioed Policeman who stopped the infamous rooftop gig in 1969 recently visited Penny Lane Gallery. Apparently he was looking for a copy of the Let it Be video to show to his son.*
*-A rival Rutles memorabilia shop is said to be opening in Hove soon, and will be stocking copies of the video for 'Let it Rot'.**

## Taylor's (Tobacconist)
19 Bond Street
(01273) 606110
Open 9.30am-6pm

A 'THANK YOU FOR SMOKING' sign welcomes you as you enter, and the selection of flavoured tobacco (including chocolate) and Cuban cigars reminds me why it took 10 years to kick such a pleasurable habit. Go on, have a fag.

*this joke is sponsored by the Anoraked Musicians Society

## SHOPPING

## MARKETS

### The Sunday Market
Behind Brighton Station
Open 6am-12pm

As much a part of Brighton as the Pavilion, a Brighton weekend is not complete without visiting the Sunday car-boot at the station. The serious bargain hunters arrive before 7am but if you've had a bender on Saturday night, 11am is a more realistic time to come and you'll still get to see it all. It's the perfect thing for walking up an appetite for late breakfast or early Sunday lunch.

Expect to find record stalls, videos, antiques, clothes, food, weird stuff and loads and loads of crap. One of the strangest stalls is the guy selling manky limbs from Victorian dolls. He's always there, so logic dictates that there must be a regular stream of people who need them. WHO ARE YOU??? Another regular is the CD stall on the far right-hand side which always plays these awful records by 70s Irish comedians. I've yet to see someone walk past, hear it, laugh and then make an impulse buy. And thinking about it, I've never seen the owner laugh either.

One tip- don't be afraid to haggle, and if something seems too expensive, say so. If the stall owner won't take your generous offer of 50p for the Rolf Harris stylophone, take satisfaction in rolling your eyes, huffing, then walk off. If it was a bluff on their behalf they'll run after you and beg forgiveness. At this point, offer 10% less and secure the deal by spitting into your palm and then shaking on it.

To find the market, go into the station, head right and continue until you get to the car-park. Keep walking and it's just behind there.

*Once at the Sunday market, I found this old tin with a goofy looking vicar sticking out the top. If you turn the handle the head moves up and down. It might have cost 15 quid, but you just don't come across stuff like this every day.*

### North Laine Market
Upper Gardner Street
Saturdays only 10am-2pm

Nothing to get too excited about, unless your idea of a bargain is a broken cine camera for £30. But you might find a good book or a cheap shirt, and besides, it's pleasant to wander down, and can be a good alternative to being squashed in Kensington Gardens on a hot, busy Saturday afternoon.

### Fruit and Veg Market
Open Mon 7am-1pm, Tues-Thurs 7am-5pm, Fri-Sat 7am-6pm

Your cheapest option for fresh fruit, veg, fish and other food. There are also plenty of stalls selling things like cut-price tins and dairy products. Perfect for students or if you're doing Brighton on the cheap. Don't buy in bulk though, the stuff here won't last as long as the fruit and veg you buy in Sainsbury's. Do like everyone else; take it home, buy a pizza and watch it rot.

## The West Pier Market
Weekends only

If you slept through the alarm at 11am for the station car-boot sale then don't fret. A leisurely stroll between the piers after lunch should help compensate. Here you will find a modest range of stalls selling clothes, books, sunglasses and other stuff. And don't forget to visit the Artists' Quarters nearby, if you haven't already been.

# FLEA MARKETS
## Snoopers Paradise
7-8 Kensington Gardens
(01273) 602558 Open
Mon-Sat 9.30am-5.15pm

Brighton's largest indoor flea market. There are two floors of stock and a particularly good collection of unusual 60s clothes, but be prepared to pay through the nose. Don't visit if you have a heart condition – you may find yourself saying things like *'I threw mine away last year and they're selling it here for £200!!!!'* or *'sixty quid for that piece of crap?'*.

# WEST PIER MARKET DEBATE RAGES ON

**There was some considerable doubt as to the future of the West Pier market last summer owing to grumblings in the council but it seems like it's staying put, at least for now, which is good news**
What's frustrating is that while the council has allowed the seafront to turn into one long ghastly expanse of naff cafébars and nightclubs, it's things like the West Pier market that uphold the true personality of Brighton seafront. Do we really want this area to devolve completely into nothing more than a clichéd haunt of hen parties, stag nights and weekend clubbers? It's William Burroughs and Kurt Vonnegut vs a fight and a flab-o-gram. WHOSE SIDE ARE **YOU** ON??

EUBANK'S FACE SHOWS UP IN PORTSLADE CLOUD FORMATION PAGE 7 & 8

### Baby for Cheeky Sibling

**In a desperate last minute attention grabbing ploy**, the evil sister of Cheeky Jeremy deliberately gave birth to a bouncing baby boy. The sinister plan managed to derail the completion of the most recent Cheeky guide to Brighton for almost two hours on Saturday morning. The elaborate plan is rumoured to have been conceived more than nine months ago.
**BRUISED BUM**
The Young Kai Lobo Plotnikoff came bum-first into the world kicking and screaming (like his mother) at a healthy weight of 6lb 14oz. Despite the obvious attempt to steal the headlines, the gang at cheekyguides wish mother, father and baby all the best.

## Kemptown Flea Market
31a Upper St. James's Street
(01273) 624006 Open Mon-Sat 9.30am-5.30pm, Sun 10.30am-5pm

Keep going up St. James's Street and you'll find this garish, pink, two-storey building just after the road bends. I somehow prefer it to Snoopers. Sure, there's still a lot of overpriced tat but you can find some really unusual objects and dare I say it, the odd bargain? There isn't much in the way of clothes but there's usually a good stock of cool things for the house, like 60s lamps. And the Gendarme's hat I bought my mum for Xmas was only a fiver!

## AUCTIONEERS

### Raymond P Inman
Fine Art Auctioneers
35 Temple Street
Mondays only

Make sure not to pick your nose or you may find yourself going home with a Picasso.

## COSTUME RENTAL

*If like me you like to ham it up as Father Christmas and Wonder Woman every now and again, it's good to know where to get those all- essential items for a night out at Vavavavoom! or Wild Fruit.*

### Masquerade
26 Preston Road (01273) 673381
Mon-Sat 10am-5.30pm

Masquerade stock the more traditional fancy dress gear and boast an almost inexhaustible range of costumes, much more than is just on display.

With everything from Vampires to Bart Simpson, the costumes do however vary wildly in quality, so try on a few before choosing. A word of advice: be wary of the latex masks, they might look good on, but can spoil your chances of making a good impression on someone when you pull it off to reveal your hair has gone into a flat centre parting and your top lip is all sweaty. This is also a good place for picking up novelty facial hair and wigs. I don't know if these things are important to you but I always feel secure in a new town, knowing where I can buy a false moustache.

### Revamp
11 Sydney Street (01273) 623288
Open Mon-Fri 10am-5.30pm,
Sat 10am-6pm
www.revampfancydress.co.uk

One of the few shops in Sydney Street to have lasted longer than 3 months, Revamp go in more for the glam stuff than Masquerade, and you can hire anything from thigh-high boots to Las Vegas style Elvis gear. They have a really wide range of exotic 70s wear, especially platforms, and if it's fluffy and feathery you'll find it here. There are plenty of clothes for sale here too, as well as joke shop gags and other oddities like vibrators and body paint.

## Stephen Drennan's Guide to Charity Shopping

The first rule of charity shopping: grab it and hold on for dear life, for in Brighton every greedy bug and their monkey's uncle are clued up as to what's cool and what's not.

Brighton itself has three distinct charity shop areas:
The London Road (plus offshoots Baker Street and Oxford Street), Western Road and Kemptown.

Add to these George Street and Blatchington Road in Hove and a couple of gems in Church Street and Sydney Street, and you've got yourself a mighty long day if you're planning a comprehensive look-see.

It's a double-edged thing, however, charity shopping in switched-on Brighton. The place may be swarming with hip kids and dealers, yet the law of averages dictates that this is the place where William Burroughs softbacks might well sing out your name from those PDSA shelves.

**www.friday-ad.co.uk**
The on-line version of Friday's magazine of bargains. The site isn't pretty, but is an effective and worthwhile way to find a good deal on that red velour couch you have been dreaming of. My favourite part (as if you'd be surprised) is the Bizarre Bazaar, which has an enormous section all to itself. Now you can spend hours trawling through strange adverts, looking for that all-essential collection of broken marmalade jars or underpants from the Crimean war, and believe me, you'll find them.

## Fancy Dress Party
Stunning Fancy Dress, Masks, Wigs, Boots & Accessories

### For Sale or Hire

Disposable Helium Tanks
Balloon Decorating
Shimmer Curtains
Party Poppers
Streamers
Souvenirs
Balloons
Bunting
Hats

*All This & Lots More - Have Fun at:*

### REVAMP
11 SYDNEY STREET BRIGHTON
Tel: (01273) 623288
Fax: (01273) 570852

# FOOD

*With over 400 restaurants to choose from, more cafés per square mile than any other town its size and a whole range of exotic food shops, I'll be very annoyed if you end up in McDonald's after all this hard work.*

## LATE-NIGHT EATING

### Grubbs
27 York Place and 89a St. James's Street
(01273) 688111
Open Mon-Wed 12noon-1am, Thurs 12noon-2am,
Fri-Sat 12noon-3am, Sun 12pm-12am

They do a wide range of vegetarian and meat burgers, starting at £1.63 for a regular, but why do that when for twenty pence more you can have Barbecue, Malaysian, Tropical or Hawaiian?

You can sample a bit of Brighton nightlife here most evenings if you want to stick around and eat, but I can't say it's particularly pleasant inside. Be prepared for a bit of a wait though, even when it's empty I've waited up to 15 minutes just for one burger. Is it my imagination or do half the staff always seem to be nursing outrageous hangovers? Maybe you should ask them which parties they go to.

### The Market Diner
19-21 Circus Street (01273) 608273
Open Mon-Sun 9.30pm-11am,
Fri 9.30pm-9am

Found on Circus Street, just around the corner from the Art Block, and one of the most famous landmarks in Brighton's nightlife. This is your typical greasy fry-up café with ashtrays made from the foil base of Mr. Kipling apple pies. It is, however a must for that post-club hunger and a place to meet and socialise with deranged and dangerous people. Their breakfast gut-buster is near-legendary and will satisfy the greediest of pigs, as they certainly don't economise on the lard (although they do a veggie/vegan version, too).

My friend Duncan recommends that you ask for a cup of tea without a fag end in it.

### The Brighton Bystander
1 Terminus Road (01273) 329364
Open Mon-Sat 8am-12Midnight
Sun 8am-12Midnight

Opposite the station, this greasy spoon café will deliver the goods if your taste buds are none too discerning. Quite a chilled atmosphere if you get a table, but don't let them rope you into giving a hand behind the till, an act I've witnessed here on at least two occasions.

Good place for posters and fliers and a perfect opportunity to impress the staff by cracking the joke, *'Waiter, there's a flier in my soup'*.

Also part of the same Brighton chain: the (much cleaner) Innocent Bystander, 54 Preston Street (01273) 728131, where they also do cocktails.

### Subs to Go
146 North Street
(01273) 276551
Mon-Sat 8am-3am

Strip-neon lights and Happy Shopper-style baguettes.

### Kebab Express
39 Queen's Road, Brighton
(01273) 725939

The home to one of the best chicken kebabs in town. The owner Hussein is a little bit on the odd side, and doesn't seem to hear anything other than- *'I want my Kebab with everything'*. If ordering the chicken kebab, make sure to ask for a little Jiggy Jiggy on the side.

Hussein from Kebab Express

## 24 HOUR SUPERMARKETS
**B2**
Queen's Road (by the station)
Western Road (by Lansdowne Place, Hove)

A far cry from the days of old when you'd pop to the 24-hour garage for a loaf of floppy bread and some rizlas, although they do have the obligatory bags of charcoal by the door.

Expect fairly fresh bread, croissants, a meat counter and even Häagen Dazs ice cream. So there is life after Happy Shopper after all.

## SPECIALIST FOOD SHOPS

### Yum Yum Oriental Market
22-23 Sydney Street (01273) 606777
Open Mon-Sat 10am-6pm Friday open late upstairs

A great selection of oriental food. Along with fresh herbs and vegetables there are some excellent Chinese cooking sauces and utensils. And where else could you get tinned squid and tai chi slippers? (By that I don't mean both in the same tin). See our restaurant guide for their noodle bar upstairs.

### The Cheese Shop
17 Kensington Gardens
(01273) 601129
Open Mon-Sat 10am-5pm

Always smelling of pongy feet but with a superb selection of the finest cheeses. Look out for 'cheese of the week', some of the best sarnies in town, Italian bread, olives, French cider and a good range of wines. I asked the woman behind the counter how many times a day someone walked in and quoted The Monty

**FOOD**

Python cheese shop sketch to her, and she answered – *'What sketch?'*

## Deb's Deli
4 Gardner Street (01273) 604925
Open Mon-Sat 9am-5pm

Although most of the tins and food in the window look as if they may well have seen their heyday, don't be taken in by this first impression. The selection here is amazing, ranging from potato lutkas to tinned snails, mushroom ketchup and a wide choice of deli fillings to go on normal bread, rye or bagels. And the cheapest smoked salmon and cream cheese bagel in town.

*Who will buy my lovely bread ?*

## Italian Shop
91/94 Dyke Road (01273) 326147
Open Mon-Sat 6am-7pm

Mediterranean heaven in the heart of the busy Seven Dials, with one the friendliest shop owners in Brighton. If he starts singing 'O Sole Mio' for you in front of the other people in the shop, just smile politely and say 'Lei ha delle gambe bellissime', which means 'you have a great voice'. The food is fabulous and if you're planning a picnic, the bread is made in heaven.

## The Pasta Shop
12b Meeting House Lane
(01273) 723522
Open Mon-Sat 10am-6pm Sun 12noon-5pm

Proper homemade pasta and a wonderful selection of fresh sauces which they can heat up for you to take away. Go and eat it on the beach and look down upon all those miserable suckers who bought a dehydrated burger from the pier.

## Spaghetti Junction
60 Preston Street
(01273) 737082
Open Mon-Thurs 10am-6pm,
10am-10pm Fri-Sat

First class fresh pasta (spinach and ricotta ravioli, fettuccine, etc), homemade sauces and ready-made meals to take home. Speciality melts are their forte. Ciabatta or foccaccia rolls start at £1.50 and fresh pasta is £1.90 per lb. Look out for their new range of desserts in the future. Also available for outside catering.

## Ryelight Chinese Supermarket
48 Preston Street
(01273) 734954
Open Mon-Sat 11am-6pm
Sun 11am-5pm

Smaller than Yum-Yums but with everything a good Chinese supermarket should stock.

## Taj Mahal Stores, Delicatessen and Food Stores
21a/b Bedford Place
(01273) 325027
Open Mon-Sun 9am-8pm

Specialist food retailers of Indian, Middle Eastern, Greek, Chinese and Malaysian grains and spices.

## HEALTH FOOD SHOPS

### Infinity Foods Coop Ltd.
25 North Road (01273) 603563
Open Mon-Sat 9.30am-5.30pm
Fri 9.30am-6pm

Brighton's much-loved health food shop stocks everything for your heart's desire. Yogi teas, organic turnips and tofu burgers all under one roof and bread baked on the premises. Whether you're a veggie, vegan, or allergic to yak hair, you'll find something delicious here. Useful too for its notice board (now in the window) where you can find accommodation, therapists and car-shares to Belgium.

### Organic Matters
1 New England Street
(01273) 689725
Open Mon-Sat 9am-6pm

Looking like a disused pub with two gold Taj Mahal domes on top, this place stocks everything from organic veg and herbs, to logs, furniture and hammocks. Round the back they sell direct off-cuts from oak, elm, beech and cherry which you can buy to make unique things for the home. At Christmas this is also the place for trees.

## SANDWICH BARS

### Veggie/Vegan Sandwich Shop
92a Trafalgar Street
(01273) 623332 Open Mon-Fri 8am-3pm,
Sat 11am-3pm

Tucked away at the bottom of Trafalgar Street and offering a tantalising range of meat-free sandwiches that aren't cheese and tomato. They also do a range of pizzas and hot and cold snacks.

### Lanes Patisserie
30 Ship Street (01273) 202106
Open Mon-Fri 9.30am-5pm,
Sat 9.30am-6pm

Good place to grab a quick snack if walking round the Old Lanes, as their sandwiches are possibly the cheapest in town.

If your feet need a rest there's a proper café upstairs. Locally known as 'The Pink Shop'. You'll know why when you get there.

### Pat's Place
128 Queen's Road (01273) 325278
Open Mon-Fri 8.30am-4pm
Sat 11am-5pm

Big portions and good quality are the order of the day in this tiny shop. The place is carnivore friendly and if it flies, jumps, ruminates or swims you'll find it here in some form or other. Try their lovely curried panda baguette.

## CAFÉS AND CAFE-BARS

*Places marked with an 'L' are licenced.*

### Alf Resco
On the seafront, between the two piers

The wafting odour of freshly baked lemon cake will lead you to this irrepressibly cheerful beach café which sensibly sticks to good coffee, slabs of cinnamon toast, freshly squeezed OJ, cracking cakes and excellent home-made Reggae compilations.

Stop here for breakfast on the way to work when the sun's shining and you'll lose all sense of time. And like the shop in North St, everything's one pound.

They open from Thursday to Sunday, close up to eat lunch when they feel like it, and take the winter off. I did say they were sensible.

And yes, the name comes from the old exchange:
*"Shall we eat Alf Resco?"*
*"Didn't we eat him yesterday?"*

### Billies
34 Hampton Place (01273) 774386
Open Mon-Sun 8am-5pm

Just up from Waitrose, at the very top of Hampton Place. Billies has developed a cult following amongst locals, largely thanks to its hash browns, at which it excels. One word of warning however, it's a small café with a TV that seems to be on most of the time, *'more for the benefit of the staff than the customer'* I was informed when I asked if I could turn it off. So bear in mind you might have MTV blaring in your ear while tucking into bread and dripping.

### The Dorset Street Bar (L)
28 North Road (01273) 605423
Mon-Sun 10am-11pm (food 'til 10pm except Sun till 8pm)

A visit to Brighton really is not complete without Eggs Benedict, a coffee and a pose outside the Dorset. As well as an ideal breakfast café, the Dorset also manages to be an excellent snack bar at lunchtime and sociable restaurant and drinking den at night. Offering a range of good beers, warm drinks and food ranging from mussels and fries to some fabulous hot meat baguettes, the Dorset has an enviable location on the corner of North Road and Gardner Street, where you can sit outside on warm summer afternoons and marvel at the misfits and style gurus parading through the North Laine. Or, if you're local, it's unlikely you'll pass an afternoon without spotting a host of familiar faces passing by to have a natter with (unless you've got no mates, that is). Finally, be on your guard for the manager Mark, (recognisable for his spikey black hair). He adds a certain madcap feel to the place and, if he likes the look of you, will belt out a few old 50s numbers while you're slurping on your drinks.

## Dumb Waiter
28 Sydney Street (01273) 270895
Open Mon-Sat 9am-5pm
Sun 10am-3.30pm

Fairly cheap café in the North Laine, with a pleasant atmosphere and a few seats outside. Reputedly one of the best veggie breakfasts in town, since the eggs they use come from stray hens they've rescued. Check the backyard if you don't believe me.

## Food for Friends
(see vegetarian restaurant section)

## GoodBean Coffee
39-40 Bond Street (01273) 723912
Mon-Sat 7.15am-6pm, Sun 9.30am-6pm
41 Trafalgar street (01273) 674608
Mon-Fri 7am-7pm, Sat 10am-4pm
16 Prince Albert street (01273) 727726
Sun-Thurs 8am-8pm, Fri-Sat 8am-10pm

If you're a coffee connoisseur you'll realise that this locally-based chain simply do the best cup of coffee in town. Drinks are prepared professionally by their baristas, who are the coffee equivalent of Tom Cruise in the film 'Cocktail' (but without having to juggle to impress you). The atmosphere is always friendly and lively, but that could be put down to all the staff and customers being high as kites on caffeine. While not offering full meals, there are snacks available, and their sandwiches are made by their own Brighton chefs with RSPCA approved meat. (By that I don't mean they make unwanted pets into sandwiches). They are currently growing at an impressive rate in Brighton and look set to take over the UK in the next few years.

## Infinity Café
50 Gardner Street
Open Mon-Sat 9.30am-5pm
(01273) 670743

Stylish veggie/vegan café, borne out of Infinity Foods' incredible success and with the food to match. Expect queuing at lunchtime, though you should always be able to find a seat upstairs.

## Kensingtons Café
1 Kensington Gardens
(01273) 570963
Open 9.30am- 5.30pm Mon-Sun

Tucked away upstairs at the corner of Kensington Gardens, this is the first Brighton café I ever visited when I moved here and I still have fond memories of the place.

It hasn't really changed much in 10 years, it still serves everything you can think of on toast, salads, jacket potatoes, a great breakfast, and more recently has started serving Mexican snacks like nachos. The food is reasonably priced and hits the spot if you're after a decent café snack. Inside there's plenty of seating, including these Happy Days style booths at the bottom. The décor is stylish but simple, but for reasons known only to themselves, a golf club and hockey stick appear to have been super-glued to the wall. On warm summer days, however, you'll probably want to plonk yourself on the balcony, read the paper, and drop coffee froth on the heads of passers-by.

A heated debate in Nia Café

## Lunar Bar and Coffee House
5a Castle Square, Brighton
(01273) 220014
Open 11am-11pm

Late-night café-bar located on the site of the now defunct Disco Biscuit.

With table service, a sci-fi theme and stylish décor, you can see a lot of effort has gone into the place, but as with so many of the Zel places in Brighton, it's another case of all style and no content. Still, service is friendly, the food is excellent (especially the Thai Chicken salad) and you can usually get a seat at weekends.

## The Meeting Place
Hove Sea Wall Kingsway
(01273) 738391 Open all year round subject to the weather

All-year-round, open-air café opposite Brunswick Square. On a warm summer morning it's a perfect spot to have your breakfast and read the paper in your pants, whilst getting a suntan. In the winter when it's snowing outside and the sea is crashing over the promenade it never seems quite as busy. Ranks highly if you want the traditional Brighton experience rather than the designer one.

## Moons (L)
42 Meeting House Lane
(01273) 323824
Open Sun-Wed 9.30am-5pm, Thurs-Fri 9.30am-5pm, Sat 8am-10pm

Traditional English style café-cum-licensed brasserie with good service. Extra brownie points for serving Horlicks, my favourite drink, as well as a wide choice of flavoured frothy milky drinks, both hot and cold. Not your typical Brighton café.

## Mock Turtle
4 Pool Valley (01273) 327380

Famous for its cakes. It may look like an old grannies' tearoom with lace table cloths but don't let that put you off. If you're a cake fan, you'll think you're in heaven. They also do take-away cakes. Bring a wheelie bin.

## Nia Café
87/88 Trafalgar Street
(01273) 671371
Open 9am-7pm every day

Fast becoming one of my favourite cafés in the North Laine, owner Sally has obviously been getting intimate with Jamie Oliver.

With simple décor, a commanding view of Trafalgar Street, laid-back music from the likes of Jeff Buckley, and inexpensive but delicious grub, I can even forgive Sally for pouring gravy over my friend, the last time I visited. Attention to detail is excellent here, order a mint tea and it arrives, in a pot, made from fresh leaves. It's these little touches that separate Nia Café from the glut of cheap and cheerful trendy cafés of the North Laine.

The food is Modern Continental (chicken breast in ciabatta, goat's cheese tart etc) but also on offer are more traditional meals like bangers and mash, while the breakfast choice even includes crumpets with honey and pancakes with maple syrup (for those, like me with a sweet tooth in the morning).

Take your slippers, park yourself here for the afternoon with a paper or a friend and you'll realise why nobody gets anything done in this town.

## Pickwicks Café
2 St. James's Street (01273) 686273
Open Mon-Sat 8.30am-6pm

Pancakes and sundaes are the two items shining through the good but basic menu. The café is named after the owner; a Mediterranean Dickensian character, whose baritone voice goes to prove that smoking makes you sound like Barry White. Don't do it kids.

## Pure (L)
George Street
(01273) 692457
Mon-Sat 11am-7pm
Sun 12noon-6pm

Licensed, stylish café with a continental menu ranging from mussels to Danish rissoles. Looks like an arty drinking den. Why not come here and do your postcards, as they have lots of free ones to give away?

Ahhh... friends again

## Rikki Tik (L)

18a Bond Street (01273) 683844
Open Mon-Sat 10.30am-11pm (food from 12pm-10pm) Sun 12pm-11pm

Painfully fashionable café-bar in the North Laine. The choice of grub is excellent, most of it seems organic and their range of juices and smoothies are fantastic (if a little over-priced at £3). Try the apple, ginger and celery drink for example. The food is surprisingly straightforward with a range of burgers, stews and soups, all pretty good value for under a fiver.

In the evening the atmosphere is that of a trendy London bar, with hoards of waif-like students itching to finish their media studies degrees and get jobs with the Big Breakfast. Like most of these trendy chains, it lacks a little soul but compensates with good food and all-evening happy hour on Mondays and Tuesdays. Front part is rumoured to be turning into a cocktail bar soon.

Over 40s must be accompanied by a teenager to get in.

## The Sanctuary (L)

51-55 Brunswick Street East
(01273) 770002
Open Mon 12noon-11.30pm, Tues-Sun 10am-11.30pm

Well-known and relaxed vegetarian café, with plenty of salads, soups and hot dishes of the day to choose from. Prices are not for the faint-hearted, in fact £2.50 for a slice of cake is a downright rip-off. The upstairs area, once home to idle layabouts playing chess has, over the years, transformed into somewhere people bring lap-tops and mobiles and small local businesses have their board meetings here. I spent three hours in there the other day on my mobile shouting 'buy, sell, buy' but nobody found it very funny, and I gradually got sucked into a conversation with someone about their tax-returns instead. There's also a space downstairs that's host to many evenings of poetry, music and Junk TV's infamous nights, although plans are afoot to turn it into a photocopying room.

## Tiger Bar and Canteen (L)

96 Trafalgar Street (01273) 693377
Open Mon-Sat 11am-11pm, Sun 11am-10.30pm (food stops at 9pm)

While perhaps the more discerning palate would be advised to eat elsewhere, this place serves as a good student hang-out on the edge of the North Laine and is popular for cocktails and drinks.

You can get snacks, such as melts, for under a fiver, but beware when busy as service may be friendly but it can be very slow. Someone really should tell them that vegetables are much nicer when warm and moist and that when you order Chicken Kiev you don't expect it to be from Tesco's.

## The Tin Drum (L)
95-97 Dyke Road (01273) 777575
43 St James's Street, Kemptown
(01273) 624777
Open Mon-Sun 12noon-11pm

Popular café-bar in the heart of the Seven Dials, that arose from the ruins of Brighton's dingiest and smelliest convenience store.

The house special Zakushki, is a selection of mouth-watering hors d'oeuvres, ranging from smoked salmon to pork, all served with rye bread, blinis and smetalia. There's a veggie one too and a wide range of flavoured vodkas to see you through the evening. They have a good selection of books and up-to-date mags at the back, which makes for a pleasant Sunday breakfast. And ladies, sit-com heart-throb Joe McGann is known to drop by occasionally for a glass of warm milk.

(The newly opened clone in Kemptown is almost identical but there are plans to also have launches for local artists on a monthly basis).

## Wai Kika Moo Kau
11a Kensington Gardens
(01273) 671117
Open Tues-Sun 10am-6pm

Veggie café in the heart of the North Laine with a New Age slant. Inside is one big splash of colour, from the artwork on the walls to the owner's shirts. The food is interesting and varied, ranging from deep fried Camembert with cranberry sauce and salad, to Mexican veggie grill. The tempura vegetables are particularly ageeable. For a North Laine café they've got the right balance of style and atmosphere, with genuinely friendly staff who, after a couple of beers, will dance on request to old Motown classics.

For trivia lovers, the name is pronounced 'why kick a moo cow' and takes its name from a Welsh village.

## IN THE MIDDLE OF NOWHERE

### Becky's Café
Top of Elm Grove
(01273) 628184
Open Mon-Sun 7am-3pm

A bit out of the way from town, and at the top of a bloody big hill. So why come here? The food is traditional British caff menu but the décor and layout provide some eccentric charm.

Originally a public loo, now adorned with red walls, large plastic gnomes and odd paintings that give the place a seedy, unintentionally surreal atmosphere.

Seek it out if you're in the area, or if you need some inspiration for your writing. The perfect setting for a sit-com.

**FOOD**

## Breakfasts in Brighton

*Forever plotting different ways to encourage you to buy each edition of this book, we are proud to launch this new feature which, each year, will provide the recipe for a unique breakfast dreamed up by some deranged local. Keep this safe as there are 25 to collect.*

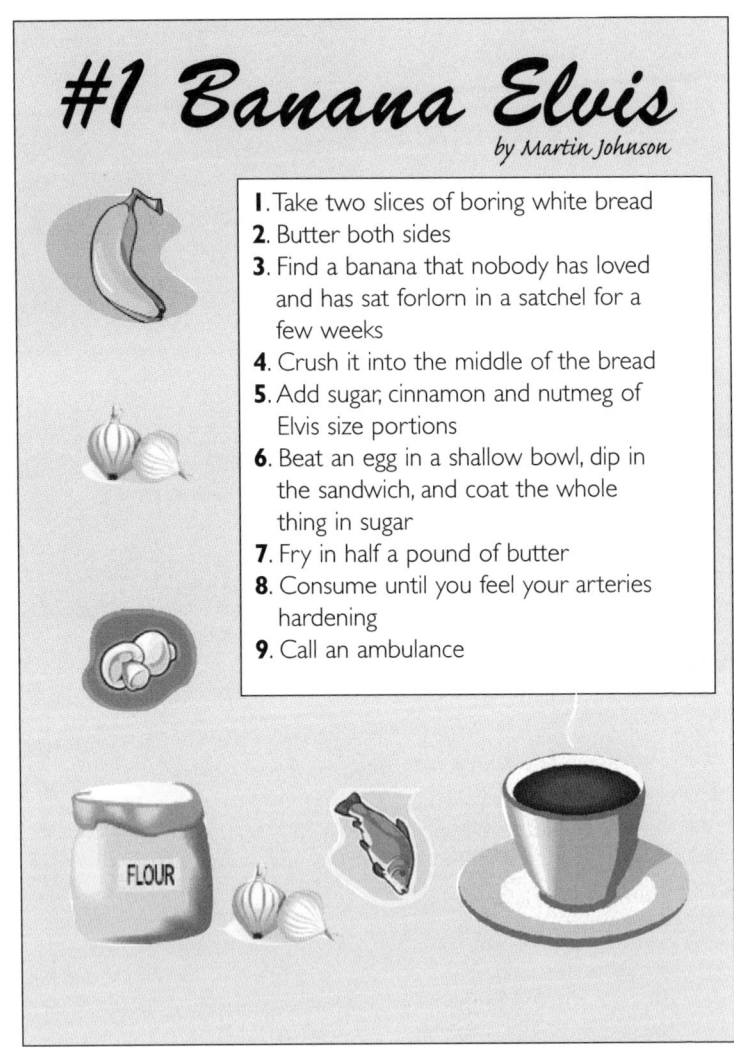

### #1 Banana Elvis
*by Martin Johnson*

1. Take two slices of boring white bread
2. Butter both sides
3. Find a banana that nobody has loved and has sat forlorn in a satchel for a few weeks
4. Crush it into the middle of the bread
5. Add sugar, cinnamon and nutmeg of Elvis size portions
6. Beat an egg in a shallow bowl, dip in the sandwich, and coat the whole thing in sugar
7. Fry in half a pound of butter
8. Consume until you feel your arteries hardening
9. Call an ambulance

*Thanks to Martin for this year's recipe, we mourn his imminent passing away. Look out next year for our celebrity recipe from Tim Booth, a breakfast bonanza based entirely on seaweed and local flora scraped off old fishing boats.*

# A Heart-Felt Defence for Greasy Spoons
*(by lard-lover Brian Mitchell)*

*There is more to life than longevity, as the patron of the greasy spoon will surely agree. Brighton, once boasting an embarrassment of such cafés, now seems simply embarrassed by them. In my 12 years here I have seen their number sadly dwindle, and with it the very café society that Costa and Zel are so eager to colonise. Below is a (wholly subjective) list of Brighton's top ten greasy spoons. Lend them your support, and your custom, before this remorseless gentrification leads to their extinction, and we end our days forking out £5 for a cup of latte.*

### Divall's Café
Terminus Road, opposite the station (01273) 328861

This would occupy first place, solely for being the only café I know that still regularly serves mashed potato; but there are many reasons for this accolade: the choice of vegetables is unparalleled; the value exceptional, the staff warm and friendly and the cryptic back-room, oddly congenial. When it closed down early in 1999, my life simply fell apart; its re-opening in time for the Millennium was a portent more propitious than any recorded in the 'Acts of the Apostles.'

### The Clock Tower Café
Dyke Road (a stone's throw from Waterstones)

Few can doubt that this café offers the best value anywhere in Britain. The proprietors' unstinting labour has kept the prices absurdly low. In ten years I have known them increase only once. The food is excellent; their chips particularly fine. Maybe the ambience is not always as welcoming as it might be, but at such low prices, it would be churlish to complain.

### Marion's
Beaconsfield Villas

Once Pam's Diner, these charming airy premises were acquired by the couple who had previously run the Top Ten in Kemptown. A very high standard is maintained throughout the menu. Worthy of special mention are the roast dinners, and the jam roly-poly, possibly the finest in town. Staff are also surprisingly amiable.

### Joe's Café
24 Upper Hamilton Road (01273) 553575 Open 8am-2pm

A trenchman's Valhalla, Joe's is required visiting for those who go to lunch as a warrior unto battle. The 'Gut-Buster' is not for the faint hearted – neither figuratively nor literally. Very much a worker's 'Caff', last orders are taken at 1.40pm, which is, alas, of little use to the severely hung-over. Also it would appear to have much in common with its spiritual cousin, The Athenaeum, as women are not allowed.

## Dave's Café
Lewes Road

One of the best breakfasts in town is available at this pleasant spacious café. The incongruity of mock-Tudor and prints of old street scenes together with a picture window and polystyrene ceiling only adds to the charm. The steak and chips are a snip at £3.95.

## Pete's Café
Ship Street Gardens

In the heart of the Old Lanes, tucked behind the heart-stoppingly over-priced 'Coach-House', sits one of Brighton's best-kept secrets. The chief incentive for visiting this cosy little victualler's is Pete himself, an unflappable Mediterranean giant of a man who would make even the most alienated hero of a Schubert song cycle feel at home. Go there and have your troubled soul soothed.

## Mrs Hudson's
12 Sydney Street (01273) 671266

Teetering on the brink of teashop respectability, Hudson's presents a slightly up-market alternative for pie and mash vulgarians. Presumably taking its name from Sherlock Holmes' landlady (who always made them a slap-up breakfast before a days' sleuthing) Mrs Hudson's is wonderfully antiquated compared to the rest of Sydney Street's more bohemian food outlets and boutiques. The upstairs room provides a welcome air of gentility, and the reasonable prices, the amiable (and in one case, impossibly beautiful) staff, and the much-feted home-made apple pie would ensure its inclusion in the most objective of top-tens. If you fancy a bath after breakfast, they're the only café I know in Brighton to supply one.

## The Diner
8 Montpelier Road

Good value, good food, pleasant surroundings, courteous staff, and an extensive menu commend this café for your attention. Perhaps, all in all, not one of the greats, but certainly no slouch.

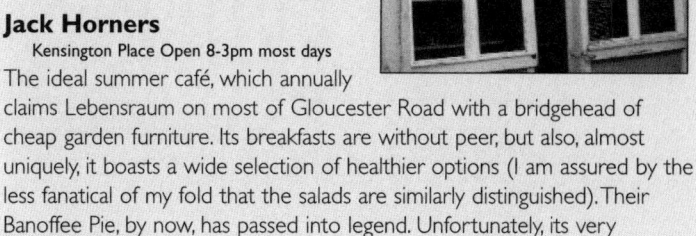

## Jack Horners
Kensington Place Open 8-3pm most days

The ideal summer café, which annually claims Lebensraum on most of Gloucester Road with a bridgehead of cheap garden furniture. Its breakfasts are without peer, but also, almost uniquely, it boasts a wide selection of healthier options (I am assured by the less fanatical of my fold that the salads are similarly distinguished). Their Banoffee Pie, by now, has passed into legend. Unfortunately, its very popularity can prove its undoing as it is often difficult to finds a table.

## The Kitchen Café
Trafalgar Street

The food here is invariably well prepared, and of an unarguably high quality. The roast dinners are satisfying and affordable. Two things conspire against a higher rating: firstly, the seating capacity which is minimal; and secondly, a lack of proper provision for smokers – no smoking tables in a greasy spoon are like atheist pews in a church.

*NB The Market Diner is not included in this list, because being an all-night café, it properly deserves its own category. Nonetheless, drunkards everywhere give thanks to the god of greasy spoons for creating it.*

## In Memoriam-
Egromont's
The Dials Café
The Village Café-
Foray's Friar Tucks
Gillfillian's
The Dallas Café
The Lorelei
The Phoenix Brewery
The Plaice to Meat
The Trafalgar Café
Mr Bradshaws

# RESTAURANTS

## CAJUN & AMERICAN
### Blind Lemon Alley
41 Middle Street
(01273) 205151
Open Mon-Sun 12pm-11pm
www.bluescompany.co.uk

Immensely popular restaurant offering cool blues and tasty southern food. Their speciality is homemade char-grilled burgers, which come as meat or veggie.

The tucked away entrance makes this restaurant a bit of a find, which is good news if you like to avoid over-touristy places. Sundays are your best time to come, as local legend Phil Mills has been doing a live Blues set in the tiny upstairs room here for years, and if you don't like it, you can throw your onion rings at him.

If you want to eat here at weekends, especially on Sunday nights, make sure you book ahead of time, since capacity is limited to 50.

I love this place and cannot praise it enough.

### Old Orleans
1-3 Prince Albert Street
(01273) 747000
Open Mon-Sat 12pm-11pm
Sun 12pm-10.30pm

Popular Cajun restaurant in the heart of the Old Lanes. Visually it's like some awful themed pub-grub chain, but for meat-lovers the food is tremendous and plentiful, which I guess with main courses between £10 and £15, is what you'd expect.

The Red Snapper here is delicious, or for the really adventurous why not wrestle with an alligator steak?

**DEAF LEEK TROUSERS**

In a cheap copycat style, ex-Radio 1 DJ 'The Hairy Cornflake' has opened up a similar restaurant 'Deaf Leek Trousers' just down the road. The food is Welsh cuisine featuring some guy in cowboy boots playing old Alarm songs on a banjo. No need to book, it's always quiet.

## CHINESE
### China Garden
88 Preston Street
(01273) 325124
Open every day 12pm-11pm

If you were to judge this place by its décor it'd probably not fare well. It may look flash but with the exception of the monographed carpet, a lot of effort seems to have gone into styling it on the interior of my grey 1980s Renault 5. This was probably the height of fashion 15 years ago but it wouldn't go amiss to remove some of the Athena pictures and have them humanely put down. Fortunately however, the food here is of such high quality and the service so impeccable and perfectly timed, that to avoid this place for the sake of a few tacky features would be a real shame.

Having eaten here several times with large groups I can vouch that everyone has savoured every morsel, from their hors d'oeuvres platter right through to the toffee banana at the end, and the food has received nothing but glowing praise from all concerned. Everything is fresh, full-flavoured and far removed from the typical stodgy Chinese take-aways we've become accustomed to. If you're a veggie you'll need to ask for the special vegetarian option as it's not on the menu, but is possibly the best I've ever tasted.

**A final tip**: Watch out for the pianist at weekends. He's lovely to listen to when you're sitting in the waiting area, but don't get a seat near him when you're eating, as he tends to get over-excited when playing 'Windmills of my mind' and it might interfere with your digestion. Try instead to get yourself a sea view if you can, as the restaurant has a great location overlooking the battered remains of the West Pier. Highly recommended.

## Cheung's Restaurant
6B Queen's Road
(01273) 327643
Open Mon-Sat 2pm-3pm, 5.30pm-12am
Sun 1pm-12am

Authentically located on the first floor, this dark, seedy place always makes me think of the movie Chinatown. The food is excellent and the gyrating tables are fun, but to anyone who's not in full possession of their faculties it can be a little daunting. Don't get stoned before you go or you'll end up eating nothing at all.

## Yum-Yum Noodle Bar
22-23 Sydney Street
(01273) 683323

Refreshingly untrendy noodle bar. For the price you get a good selection of Chinese and Indonesian, and entertainment comes free courtesy of the window seat. The food is good, and with starter, main course and tea for two for under £10, is definitely good value for money. Worth visiting when shopping in the busy North Laine.

## ENGLISH
### Harry's
41 Church Road
(01273) 727410
Open Mon-Sun 9am-10.30pm

Remember how in The Beano every week one of the characters would foil a couple of burglars (dressed in black striped shirts and carrying a bag of swag), and they'd be rewarded with a slap up meal of bangers and mash at the local nosh-up? This is a very, very posh version of that restaurant.

## FISH AND SEAFOOD
### Regency
131 Kings Road (01273) 325014
Open Mon-Sat 11am-10pm

This distinctive seafront fish restaurant wouldn't look out of place in a 70s Carry-On movie. Everything on the menu is of outstanding quality, although I'd particularly recommend their seafood platters, they're excellent value, and the calamari can be chewed without having to take out a dental policy. From £4 for the basic haddock and chips, to £12 for the Dover sole. If you're after an inexpensive sit-down fish and chip dinner with plenty of choice, forget Harry Ramsden's and come here instead.

### English's Oyster Bar
29-31 East Street
(01273) 327980
Open Mon-Sat 12noon-10pm
Sun 12.30pm-9.15pm (ish)

High-class restaurant with a reputation for having the best seafood in Brighton. A cold seafood platter for two goes for around £40.

## FRENCH
### Cripes Creperie
7 Victoria Road (01273) 327878
Open Mon-Sat 11am-11pm,
Sun 11am-10pm

Done out in the style of a cosy French bistro, this is a perfect spot for a romantic meal. The crepes are delicious, portions are huge and the menu is so appetising it takes a good half-hour of drooling to decide. Just add a bottle or two of Cidre Breton and the scene is set.

Having recently changed hands, the new owner has confirmed that Cripes will remain essentially the same, but promises *'more traditional choices on the menu, better wines, more sweets and a killer cheese platter.'*

At £12/14 for a main meal, this food is very reasonably priced, which means if you're planning on going down on one knee after two bottles of cider, you won't have to skimp on the diamond.

## Crepe Dentelle
65 Preston Street
(01273) 323224
Open Mon-Sun 7pm-11pm,
Fri-Sun 12noon-3pm

You can't get any more French than Chef Philippe, whose family have been tossing crepes since the 40s. His attention to detail has turned this restaurant into a little French gem, with checkered tablecloths, candle light and Edith Piaf in the background (her music, not the corpse).

The food selection here is truly impressive, ranging from savoury pancakes to sweet, with lots of veggie options.

The pancakes have all been given French men's names like 'Crepe Jean-Paul', of which the chef is proud. Would it work in English I wonder? *'A Charlie pancake for me and my wife would like Roger without onions please.'* Perhaps not. French cider is served in the traditional bolée, for that earthy, country flavour. And to round it all off, Philippe and his wife like to warm up your bellies before you go home with a free French liquor at the end of each meal.

## La Fourchette
101 Western Road
(01273) 722556
Open 12pm-2.30pm and 7pm-10.30pm,
closed Sun and Mon lunch

Decorated in a cheesy French farmhouse sort of way (framed bunches of hay on the wall and stray chickens in the room) this small restaurant on the high street offers classic French dishes done in a sophisticated way.

The menu has some excellent choices (for carnivores) such as skate with veal juice, scallops with leek and saffron sauce and escalope de fois gras with caramelised turnips, all of which were mouthwatering and tender. I happened to visit with two French ladies whose critical palates were delighted with the food, while I was simply delighted with the two French ladies. Be careful however when tucking into your meal; the food presentation comes from the Le Corbusier school of piling everything up in one enormous tower. Stick your fork in at the wrong place and, like in Kerplunk, everything rolls off onto the table.

The restaurant's only drawback is its size; the larger food connoisseur might find it a squeeze in here, while monstrously large menus and small tables meant that all three of us managed to knock cutlery on the floor whilst there.

All things considered, it may be on the small side but this is a place of exceptional quality food. You won't find better French cuisine anywhere else in Brighton.

**The Gingerman**
21a Norfolk Square (01273) 326688
Open Tues-Sat lunch and dinner

Local chef Ben McKellar has turned this unremarkable building in a quiet side street into a celebration of modern French cuisine. A small room, simply decorated, belies a purist approach beautifully executed.

From the fresh-baked rolls served with olive oil and balsamic vinegar on arrival, to hand-made petit-fours, the attention to detail throughout the meal is consistently designed for inconspicuous pleasure.

Meat features heavily in the main courses, with creations such as pork fillet with figs and squab pigeon (not the Churchill Square variety, we presume) on celeriac puree, but rather than going overboard on eclecticism, Ben's real strength is in the intelligent perfection of his sauces. He has a rare ability to make cod or spinach taste divine.

Three courses here will set you back about £22 and the wine list is well-balanced if restrictive in its inclusion of only French wines. A big favourite with local Labour apparatchiks.

# INDIAN/JAZZ-FUNK-FUSION
**Black Chapati**
12 Circus Parade Tel: 699011
Open Wed-Sat 7pm onwards

It's ten years since Steve Funnell burst onto the Preston Circus scene with this incongruously located temple to bold fusion cuisine. In the early days it was brutally minimalist, and some will remember him lecturing to the entire restaurant on exactly what they were eating. Any diners spotted talking amongst themselves during these sermons would be asked to share the joke with the rest of the class.

Today the approach has softened: mellow yellow décor, chairs that it's possible to stay on for more than half an hour and only an occasional sight of the red face through the kitchen hatch. But there's still a stern feel about the place – the first line on the menu is an admonition to smokers.

It's all about the food, really. Steve's approach to the blending of Asian and European cuisine is unique and a consistent gusto runs through the menu which, in pleasant contrast to modern vogue, is framed in understated language. The spices sear lightly across the roof of your mouth and the range of ciders is as good an accompaniment as the small, well-chosen list of wines.

The message would seem to be 'serious diners only', but there is enjoyment to be had from the sense of occasion, the delicately handled service and the sheer uniqueness of the place.

**Bombay Aloo**
(see vegetarian restaurants)

# ITALIAN
## Alforno
36 East Street(01273) 324905
Open Mon-Sat 12noon-11pm

Immensely popular in summer as this tiny restaurant spreads outside into East Street. Sit out, watch the world go by and enjoy the free street entertainment during the day. The best pizza in Brighton according to my Italian girlfriend.

## Alfresco
The Mikmaid Pavilion,
Kings Road(01273) 206523
Open Mon-Sun 10am-12midnight

Looking like it's out of some 60s Italian movies, Alfresco is an enormous glass-panelled building with a commanding view of the beach and a spacious round balcony on the first floor, which means you don't have to fight for a precious sunny spot during those two minutes of heat in the summer.

While the food is your standard Brighton idea of what Italian grub should taste like, this is balanced by its idyllic surroundings. Pizzas start at £5 for a Margherita.

## Donatello
3 Brighton Place
(01273) 775477
11.30am-11.30pm Every day

Many years ago I was having breakfast at a Little Chef in Bedfordshire when I swear I heard a chef shout, *"Don't forget to order another box of omelettes"*.

It struck me that 'A Box of Omelettes' could well be the title of a treatise on the slow decline of processed food during the Eighties.

For those who missed that unforgettable period, it is encouraging to know that there is still a restaurant where you can relive the experience.

## JAPANESE
### Sapporo
38 Preston St (01273) 777880
Open every day, lunch and dinner

Stylish and expensive teppanyaki bar in a street of many restaurants. Teppanyaki was apparently conceived during the American occupation of Japan after observing the GI barbecues. They went one better and developed a delicious and theatrical version where the customers sit around a huge hotplate while the chef juggles pepperpots over a sizzling selection of meat and fish.

The set menus are on the last pages, and for £29 the Sapporo Feast consists of sashimi, tempura and miso soup, followed by a blur of beef fillet, salmon, squid, whole prawns (the tails are exquisite) and buckets of fried rice. Wash it all down with warm sake and congratulate yourself heartily.

The chefs are mostly Filipino and are natural entertainers. Diners are flanked by obscenely agreeable clusters of Asian waitresses who light your cigarettes and perform the Singapore Airlines smile at every opportunity.

### Moshi Moshi
Bartholomew Square
(01273) 719195
Open daily 12pm-11pm

After establishing themselves with three successful sushi bars in the Big Smoke, Moshi Moshi has demonstrated a new level of ambition by taking on the 'Curse of Bartholomew Square'. Ignoring the obscurity that has swiftly followed any attempt in living memory to set up a working eatery in this windswept graveyard of civic space beside the Town Hall, they demolished the old rotunda and started anew.

The result is a sort of sub-007 screened cube, the entrance an opening fully fifteen feet wide, with temperature cunningly controlled through a system of underfloor heating.

First impressions are stunning; between wooden slatted floor and textured red ceiling a great conveyor belt snakes around light rattan benches and a long bar.

As you sit, you are faced with an endlessly renewed, slow-moving display of small plates containing colourful samples of sushi, sashimi, tempura and other delicacies. The simple beauty is that when something tasty-looking passes by, you pick it up. It may turn out to be pickled octopus with horseradish, but you can always hide it in your pocket if you don't like it.

You can also order off the menu. Sushi sets on stylized chopping-boards, bento boxes (a double decker starter and main course) seaweed-wrapped tamaki rolls and teriyaki combinations. Each table holds a jug of soy sauce, red-hot horseradish and plenty of lovely gari (sliced pickled ginger) to cleanse the palate.

Though wine is available, you can indulge yourself in a choice of hot and chilled sake, sake sours or Asahi beer. Service is focused on guiding you through the unfamiliar experience, and is thoroughly professional. You are never committed here; you can as easily leave after a nibble as submerge yourself in a three-hour blowout.

This may not be Japanese cuisine at its zenith but the food is surprisingly good value, and the belt makes for top entertainment. Simply spike the drink of the person next to you, stick a cuddly toy and a set of steak knives on the belt, and you should be able to convince them that they're on the Generation Game.

## JAMAICAN
### Tamarind Tree
48 Queens Road (01273) 298816

Caribbean restaurant with an authentic and chilled out feel to it. You should plan to make an evening of it here as the relaxed pace means that your food may take some time to arrive. Bring your own drinks or try some of their exotic juices or hot chocolate.

The Jerk Chicken and Callaloo Soup are particularly good and don't be put off by some of the more obscure ingredients. They've written a section at the beginning of the menu which has these fantastic dictionary definitions like something out of 'Call My Bluff'. Well recommended.

## LEBANESE
### Kambi's
107 Western Road
(01273) 327934

This place is a real favourite of mine. The mood always seems very lively in here and conducive to good conversation. Food-wise the meat grills are fabulous and I particularly like the batata harra (sautéed potatoes with coriander, garlic and lemon).

I came here one night when a group of us shared a seemingly endless platter of different Lebanese dishes and I cannot describe how delicious every single one was. If that's not enough, at the end of the night you get to smoke the Shiha (pronounced sheesha) which if you're not familiar with, is like the thing the caterpillar smokes in 'Alice in Wonderland'. The tobacco is flavoured with strawberries and just one puff and I'm craving Marlboro Lights again. It's bring your own booze here as well and if you can't stay, every single dish that you can eat in, you can take away. The Falafels are particularly well-loved.

If you're in at the right time, you might be lucky enough to catch a travelling band of musicians who occasionally drop in and play Eastern European folk music. They do requests and so my girlfriend once paid good money for them to come and serenade me while I ate. Instead, bizarrely, they played happy birthday to her, so we all joined in with the words. She now has two birthdays a year, like the Queen.

## MEXICAN
### L Mexicano Ltd
7 New Road (01273) 727766
12pm-12am Mon-Sun

I've only ever visited here late in the evenings, after being thrown out of the Colonnade pub next door, so I have a warped view of it being a late-night stumbling-into-the-curry-house kind of place.

Designed as a brightly coloured cave, this is a genuine Mexican-run restaurant where they like it hot and they like it full of beans. TexMex it is not, the food is of good standard, plentiful and varied.

Late night visitors don't seem to be a problem, I've stayed here with friends until 1.30am without feeling like we'd overstayed our welcome.

If you like Mexican food, you'll enjoy it here, or if you want a decent meal after the pubs have closed and can't face another kebab, you won't regret it either. Just be ready for a spot of windypops the next day.

## MODERN CONTINENTAL
### Havana
32 Duke Street (01273) 773388

Not for the penny-conscious, Havana is an elegantly decorated and spacious restaurant, giving the impression that 'riff-raff' would not be welcome. The food matches the surroundings, as does the price, and a main course without veg starts at around 15 pounds. The food is stylish European cuisine, cooked to perfection, and the meat dishes I have tried here (liver, kidney, duck and veal) are succulent and tender.

Service, however, does not really match up to the surroundings. I twice had to chase after my half-finished drinks after the waitress whisked them away, and with such rip-off prices (£6.95 for a Martini) you might be tempted to smuggle in your own bottle. A little bit too Nouveau Riche for my liking, but if you want to impress a first date, or mum and dad are paying, you won't regret it.

## New Whytes Restaurant
### 33 Western Street (01273) 776618

*'This is the kind of place to take a first date if you want to impress them, but feel uneasy with vertically cooked food. The service is so good that if you forget to complement your date on their dress, the waiter would have remembered for you.'*

Alex Berardi, author of
'The Scantily-Clad Chef'

Tucked away down one of Hove's many side-streets, this small scantily decorated restaurant offers modern, but unpretentious cuisine, with a heavy slant towards a lot of English meat dishes (including pigeon). The menu changes every two months, and at £14 for a main course, is excellent value. It is, however, the personal touch that really makes this place special, and the service here is the best I've ever experienced in Brighton. Where else would the waiter nip out to the local pub to bring you back your favourite tipple?

It's probably worth taking up smoking for the night here though, as the downstairs smokers room is far more inviting than the austere formality of the upstairs area, but while the décor isn't exactly lavish, the attention to detail and value-for-money far outweigh the likes of Havana.

Look out for their lobster nights, (offering a five-course meal and a whole lobster), and other events such as their Celebrity Charity Launch drawing inspiration from popular Regency Dishes.

## THAI
### Aum Thong
60 Western Road (01273) 773922
Open 12pm-2.30pm and 6pm-11pm,
Sun 6pm-10pm

You know you're in an authentic Thai restaurant when the menu says things like 'Thai food is always cooked with real hrebs.', and my favourite, 'if you fell you don't like Thai food...' which perhaps is some kind of ancient proverb.

The menu here is immense, and particularly rich on seafood dishes, with all main courses around £5-8. While the mood can seem a little lacklustre during the day, in the evening it's perfect, with subtle lighting, a warm atmosphere and genial staff. Much of the food is of an excellent standard; the Tom Kha Hed soup is dynamite, as are many of the curries, meat and seafood dishes. The duck, which is always a tricky one to get right, might be a bit foamy and fatty for the more delicate palate. Not fancy but certainly authentic.

### Sada Thai Cuisine
4 Lewes Road
(01273) 677608

This place comes highly recommended by a couple of close friends who eat here regularly. If, however, it doesn't reach the standards you've come to love and respect from this book, we'll hunt them down like pigs and get your money back.

### The King and I
2 Ship Street, Brighton
(01273) 773390

Located at the bottom of Ship Street right by the sea, The King and I is another good quality Thai restaurant. While some of the food has been adjusted for western palates, if you want the more traditional dishes, simply ask. The front door is always locked, so make sure to press the buzzer. When they answer, say *"Sawadi Kah"*.

George Bernard Shaw explains to friends how being vegetarian can bring you back from the dead

# VEGETARIAN

## Bombay Aloo
39 Ship Street (01273) 776038
Open Mon-Thurs 12noon-11pm Fri-Sun 12noon-12am

All-you-can-eat vegetarian Indian buffet for £4.50. Bajis, salads, dips and main curries with rice. Starve yourself for three days and clear them out.

## Food For Friends
18 Prince Albert Street (01273) 202310
Open 8am-10pm, Sun 8.30am-10pm

This stylish vegetarian café-restaurant in the Old Lanes has been around for years and made a name for itself with its excellent choice of veggie food, cakes and genial atmosphere. There are always 3 or 4 specials every day, as well as a selection of salads and cakes, all homemade. The stir-fry with quiche is usually a pretty good option followed by the yoghurt with fresh fruit. Having eaten here regularly over the last 6 years, I do feel that with ever-predictable menus, smaller portions and poor mid-mornings choice it is, however, time for a bit of a re-think. The worst time to visit seems to be around 11am when they tend to run out of breakfast and there's nothing to eat until noon. Best to visit for lunch or dinner, when they have a BYO booze policy, the candles come out, and it all gets very relaxed and laid back.

## Terre À Terre
71 East Street (01273) 729051
Open Tue-Sun 12noon-10.30pm
Mon 6pm-10.30pm

Beautifully presented Nouvelle Cuisine. From its very beginning round the corner in Pool Valley, this stylish restaurant set the scene for vegetarianism with a difference. It proved that a meal can be delicious, sophisticated and look appetising, even without meat.

This is not a restaurant for those who want to binge, but for those who like attention to detail and care put into the dishes. Expensive and pretentious, or stylish, well-priced food? The debate continues among friends, but it's busy every night of the week. Booking is a must.

## Trogs Organic Vegetarian Restaurant and Café Bar
124 King's Road (01273) 204655

I still haven't had the chance to try out the food at this much-loved seafront restaurant, but it comes strongly recommended, and is a definite favourite with local veggies and friends.

Worth a visit alone if Neel is working behind the bar*, for it seems that eccentricity is warmly welcomed here and legend has it that barstaff are employed on the strength of how imaginatively they answer a series of bizarre questions put to them by owner Alison. Apparently Neel got the job for his reply to, *'What kind of clothes look best on your pet?'*

*see eccentrics guide

# FOR A SPECIAL EVENING

## Bali Brasserie
Kingsway Court,
First Avenue, Hove
(01273) 323810
Open 6pm-10.30pm Sun-Fri,
Sat until 11pm

Found at the far end of Hove and done out in wicker, bamboo and plastic plants, this place is straight out of 'Love Boat' and 'Fantasy Island.' If Barry Manilow lived in Hove, he would eat here.

The setting is made complete at weekends by live music in the bar from Lola, who sits on a stool singing stuff like Nancy Sinatra and Lee Hazelwood to backing tapes, and says things like – *'If anyone has a birthday out there, come on up and we'll sort you out with something reeeaal special.'*

A word of warning though, kitsch fans. Even at the weekends, it can be pretty dead in the bar, so I recommend it only as a place for big groups. It'll help if you get dressed up, come en masse and create the atmosphere yourself. Incidentally the food is Indonesian and Malaysian. It's good, but a bit pricey.

*'Look boss, it's de plane, de plane'.*

## The Hungry Monk
Jevington near Eastbourne (01273) 482178

This one's for the devilishly romantic among you, and famous for being the birthplace of Banoffee Pie. The food isn't cheap but the whole set up here is utterly charming, even if it is a bit of a bugger to find.

On arrival they escort you to a small lounge to sample aperitifs and bite-sized appetisers, and make you feel like lord and lady of the manor. After a couple of sherries you are invited to dine in the main room, which, with its low ceiling, open fireplace and dim light, contribute to the perfect intimate romantic meal.

The portions are huge, the food is delicious, and if you go for the Banoffee Pie at the end (which you must) be prepared to leave three times fatter than you were before you went in. Men, it's probably best to propose to your partner before the pie, as she may not want to marry someone with a tyre round their waist.

# THE BEST FISH AND CHIPS

(according to Dave 'more scraps please' Mountfield)

*Brighton has many advantages as a town, but really good fish and chip shops is not one of them. Perhaps it's the embarrassment of other, more exotic cuisines in the town that has served to marginalise our humble national dish; perhaps it's the bank holiday crowds that allow poor-quality outlets to flourish, but one golden rule must be adhered to when seeking greasy Nirvana in Brighton: go inland, young man.*

## Bardsley's
Baker Street (off London Road)

I come from the Midlands, where no self respecting chippy owner would feel his job was done if he or she didn't send you away with an enormous cholesterol bomb of well-cooked (maybe even double fried) chips, and a fishy, battered golden crispy behemoth. Sadly, the only chippy I've found that equals this demanding criterion in Brighton is Bardsley's, where quality, quantity and value are up to even the most match-fit Midlands chippy. They even serve Pukka pies; the only legitimate chip-shop pie, which also hails from the Midlands.

The key to any chippy is obvious. To paraphrase Bill Clinton *'it's the chips, stupid'*. And this is where they really deliver. Large portions of well-cooked, tasty golden fingers and a superior batter mix for the fish.

Of course, everybody has their own opinion on these things, and places such as Sing Li on Guilford Road comes close on a good day, but for me this is still the best in town.

***Cheeky also recommend...***

## Bankers
116A Western Road
(01273) 328267
Open Mon-Sun 11.30am-10pm

An excellent take away and sit-down chippy on the high street, whose classic 60s décor makes you feel like you're starring in some kitchen sink drama. The fish and chips are near-perfect and can also be cooked in Matzo meal (a Jewish alternative to batter which is definitely worth trying). If you're still feeling peckish afterwards, you are a glutton, but I can recommend the cheesecake. Don't miss the indoor guttering effect above the counter. What's that all about?

## FOOD

### TAKE AWAY

#### Famous Moe's
Brighton (01273) 676867
Hove (01273) 779779

Well-loved take-away in Hanover. The pizzas are good value and come with a better than average variety of toppings, together with some of the creamiest coleslaw I've ever had. Go for one of their cheap deals for two people and you've got the perfect excuse to be a greedy pig and have banoffee pie after eating a whopping great pizza.

#### Kambi's
107 Western Road
(01273) 327934
See restaurant section.

#### New Hong Kong Chinese Take-Away
49 Preston Street
(01273) 327788

Quality food and good prices.

#### Nishat Tandoori
58 Preston Street
(01273) 321701
Open Mon-Sun 5.30pm-12am

Best Indian/Goan take-away, and the atmosphere in this place almost beats going out for the evening. Be ready to trade a few jokes with the staff, but in particular look out for its two celebrity chefs.

One is a punk who wears a little woolly hat everywhere (including the bath apparently) and the other, David, is known locally as Woody.

At one time he looked remarkably similar to the famous comedian Woody Allen, but over the years some bizarre transformation process, that we don't properly understand yet, has turned him into the spitting image of Peter Sellers in 'The Party'.

# SUSSEX RETAILER OF THE YEAR !

## FAMOUS MOE'S PIZZA ™

**Delicious pizza's delivered to your door**

ORDER ONLINE
*www.famous-moes-pizza.co.uk*

| BRIGHTON | HOVE |
|---|---|
| **01273 67 68 67** | **01273 779 779** |
| 20 SOUTHOVER ST | 57 HOLLAND RD |

Free drink with your order on presentation of this book

---

Student discounts with card, cocktails and shooters,

party bookings welcome, outside seating up & down, unique lighting atmosphere,

comfortable sofa seating, cool bar, coolest place.

## The Fringe Bar

We have DJs and music most nights of the week and serve a fabulous range of Italian and English classics all day including Breakfast, Lunch and Dinner.

'The Fringe Bar' & 'The Bamboo Bar'
10 Kensington Gardens, North Laines,
Brighton BN1 4AL
TEL: 01273 684426

OPEN 9am-11pm     7 Days a Week

**FOOD**

### Piccolo
56 Ship Street
(01273) 203701
Open Mon-Sun 11.30am-11.30pm

Pizzas here are good and cheap (£4-£5) however, the hectic atmosphere and rushed service might not be to everyone's liking. I've forgotten the number of times I've used their fantastic take-away option, but really should try something other than their Hawaiian.

## WHERE TO BUY BOOZE AFTER 10.30PM

### Southover Wine Shop
80/81 Southover Street (01273) 600402

This is one of only a few off-licenses in Brighton that stays open until 11pm. Don't ask me how they wangle it, but you might just find this information a godsend one day.

If that's not enough, they stock over 40 Belgian beers, have a great selection of spirits, sell fireworks all year round and even sell bread and milk as part of a special Sunday service.

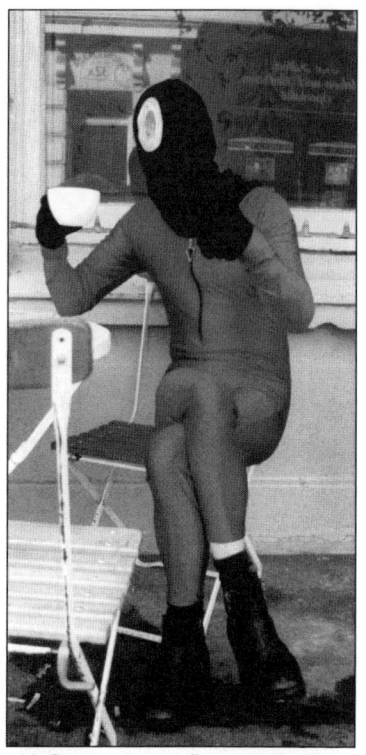

Mr Cyclops enjoys a coffee outside the Dorset

**BRIGHTON BUDDIES**
**LATE NIGHT EATS**
THE COOL PLACE TO MEET
20% STUDENT DISCOUNT
MON-THURS

**THE NIGHT PEOPLE'S CAFE**
THE ONLY 24-HOUR CAFE/BAR IN SUSSEX
46-48 KINGS RD, BRIGHTON
TEL: 01273 323600

# Watering Holes...

*Chances are that during your visit to Brighton you might be tempted to pop for a swift half somewhere, so you'll be pleased to know that we have bars to satisfy every member of society, no matter how depraved.*

*Saying that, Rabbie's bar, Brighton's only Scottish pub (complete with tartan carpets) has finally closed down. I guess there are limits to people's depravity.*

## FASHIONABLE DRINKING DENS

### Alicats
80 East Street/ Brills Lane (on the seafront, opposite the Green Bagel and beside the Prodigal)
(01273) 220902

This is one of the coolest, most secretive bars in Brighton, and surprisingly unique. The sprawling sofas, dingy red lighting and décor makes me think of some of the coffee-houses in Amsterdam. The atmosphere is definitely chilled-out and laid back, though the music can sometimes be a bit loud for talking over.

Busy at weekends, with a young discerning crowd, but not always the best place if you get claustrophobic. During the week it's much mellower. As my friend Tim said, *'If the Fun Lovin' Criminals drank in Brighton, they'd drink here'.*

And may I add that in some other universe the Velvet Underground would have had the odd Babycham here, too. Bars do not get much seedier than this.

### Coopers Cask
3 Farm Road, Hove
(01273) 737026

Chocolate and love-hearts at the bar, free tampons in the ladies', excellent food, table service, music mags to look at and sweets at the end of the night. Seems like someone's been doing their homework as to how to create a good atmosphere.

This charming gay-friendly bar may be quite a way into Hove, but don't be put off, it's easily one of the best places in town for pub grub, and a recent re-furbishment has meant that finally those revolting ornamental eggs have gone forever.

**WATERING HOLES**

## The Fortune of War
157 Kings Road Arches (01273) 205065

Long-established seafront pub, which gets ridiculously busy at the weekends in summer. If you want to hang out with the crowds on the beach it's a good starting point, but it'll take you a couple of days getting to the bar. Why not bring your own beer and hang out nearby anyway?

The much-coveted window seat with sea view will not be yours unless you start queuing in February, but you could be lucky during the day when it's quieter.

## The Hop Poles
13 Middle Street (01273) 326503

Another gem from the same guys who run the Coopers Cask. Jars of sweets behind the bar, table service, gay-friendly…it's basically the Coopers with more seating, which must be a good thing. The beer garden can be a welcome retreat if the music is a bit loud, and being throwing distance from the Cinematheque, the Hop Poles makes a good spot for post-movie discussion over a pint and a bag of bon-bons. One of the best pubs in the Old Lanes.

## The Office
8 Sydney Street (01273) 609134

Once the site of a gruesome murder when the pub was the notorious Green Dragon. Now it's a characterless place with a terrible name, where men and women dressed in Gap and Jigsaw clothes stop off to chat to their partners on their mobiles. Surely Sydney Street deserves a less banal pub than this?

## The Open House
146 Springfield Road
(01273) 880102

Proving that with a little imagination Zel still have a few surprises up their sleeves, the Open House is a beautiful and stylish new pub, situated next to the London Road Station. Expansive and decorated with colourful art, it has three main areas, one resembling a front room with sprawling sofas and art-work on the walls, whilst the main bit by the bar has big wooden tables and occasionally plays host to live music..

The mini games room at the back has Table Football and Air Hockey, which is a nice touch, but having enthusiastically taken the plunge on

Wait a minute, isn't that John Peel ?

my first visit I discovered the Air Hockey game does make an awful racket and won't make you popular with people nearby trying to chat. Outside, the garden has a sort of roof terrace feel, and is again decorated with art (an amphibian theme) and a water sculpture. If you don't live nearby, I recommend making the trip up the hill if you're in the vicinity of Preston Circus, or try it as a pre-movie bar if visiting the Duke of Yorks.

## Palmers Bar
Queen Square
(01273) 325812

Another secretive little basement bar hidden away near the ice rink. Once a brothel, now a rather special pre-club den with DJs, tapas, cocktails and fresh fruit smoothies between 5 and 7pm.

The layout is intimate and chilled out, but there are only a few tables so get there early for a seat, as it can be a bit of a squeeze at weekends. I once saw a 50s documentary at the Cinematheque about teenagers, which had been filmed down here. Everyone had fuzzy beards and they danced like on Happy Days. The beards may have gone but otherwise things don't change much in this town.

## St James
16 Madeira Place
(01273) 626696

In the heart of Kemptown, another modernised trendy pub it may be, but not in the ever-predictable style. Smart move.

The food is the same as that served at the Great Eastern, which means that it is a priority spot for Sunday lunch. The staff are young and friendly and promote the place as a hang-out for students and the young-at-heart.

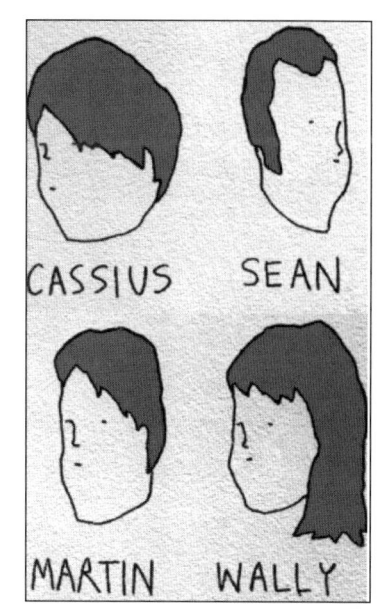

Last time I was in, a girl tried to pinch the book I was reading. What is the world coming to when even your trusty paperback is no longer safe from the hands of leggy young blondes?

## St Peter's Bar
London Road, near Grubbs

An odd little chill-out bar that looks strangely out of place down on the London Road, but I can never put my finger on why.

Pokey but charming with the odd DJ to set the mood, it's the sort of place you'd come to plan a heist (and I know a man who would). The faces painted in the back are worth a look too.

## WATERING HOLES

### The Shakespeare's head
 1 Chatham Place on the corner of
 New England Road
 (01273) 329444

One of the better Zel pubs, and thankfully not working on the ethos that the louder the music is, the happier the punters will be. There's a good ambience to the place, with lots of room for sitting, good beers, and a huge fat Henry the Eighth in the corner. He used to be chained to the ceiling of the Walmer Castle for years, until someone took him down to dust him one day and he ran off in search of a pub that would treat him with more dignity.

### The Sidewinder
 St. James's Street

A pot-pourri of postmodern design in the far-flung reaches of Kemptown, this Zel pub has Buddhas, tribal masks and bird cages sitting amongst its chic colonial-style décor and leather sofas, and is occupied almost entirely by fresh faced young slackers lolling around, smoking Marlboro Lights, and swapping Glastonbury anecdotes. Being the exception to the rule in this neck of the woods however, the style works perfectly and as well as the laid-back atmosphere, the pub provides good food, hip music, and a beer-garden with a couple of seats straight out of the Flintstones.

### The Walmer Castle
 95 Queen's Park Road
 (01273) 682466

Once home to cheesy poetry nights, acoustic evenings and an enormous Henry the 8th, the Walmer had a Zel-style makeover a couple of years back and is now a bright, trendy hang-out in the far-flung reaches of Hanover. The décor won't be to everyone's taste; the bright orange walls, TFI Friday-style writing on the outside, and the South American symbols on the walls are, for me, already a bit naff, but the pub has a genuine warmth to it and the staff are very chatty. Its plus points are the range of beers on offer, a good selection of food, and two beautiful fish tanks in the back room.

Considering some of the grizzly pubs on offer down Queen's Park Road, if you live locally, you'll be clamouring to return.

## The Western Front
11 Cranbourne Street
(01273) 725656

Found just next to Borders by the Churchill Square Shopping Centre, this place has recently been refurbished and looks all the better for it. Its location means that it inevitably attracts the out-of-town crowds and hoards of foreign students who congregate outside Borders, waiting for the Pan pipe band to turn up. But during the day and mid-week it makes an excellent town centre hang-out and serves consistently good food.

Last time we were in, six phones went off in the space of 5 minutes. Ah, the sweet sounds of the upwardly mobile. Lemon with your Hoegaarden, Sir?

## Zel Pubs

These are a chain of monstrously trendy pubs found in most corners of the town. Usually done out in bright colours and decorated with an array of ethnic artefacts, fish-tanks and lava lamps, they were once unique but are now expanding at an alarming rate. Doesn't anyone want to sit on rickety chairs in quiet bars anymore?

Attracting more of a young, fashion conscious, student crowd, they can be ideal as pre-club bars to get you in the mood, but be ready for a spot of over-crowding and loud music, especially at weekends in places like the Mash Tun and Fish Bowl in the town centre. On quieter evenings The Open House, The Sidewinder and the Shakespeare's Head are much more agreeable.

Having over 20 pubs in Brighton, Zel, while putting new life into some of the grotty old pubs, have had the good sense to leave other places alone (such as the Marlborough and Victory) for which we thank them.

Combining modern food and 'stylish' surroundings with over-priced beer is their winning formula, leaving me wonder what the future holds for the good old British pub in Brighton. Having taken over my old local the Tap and Spile, renamed it the Game of Life and painted a wall mural outside that looks like a Marillion album cover, I do worry sometimes...

**WATERING HOLES**

## WHERE TO SAMPLE A BIT OF LOCAL COLOUR

### The Bugle
24 St. Martins Street (01273) 607753

Original Irish pub down the Lewes Road with long-established folk sessions Wednesdays and Sundays and an Irish landlord with a red nose to prove it.

### The Colonnade
10 New Road (01273) 328728

This is the bar for the Theatre Royal next door. It's a wonderfully oddball place at the best of times and the atmosphere can range from that of a morgue to being at a Simon Callow party with everyone throwing their arms around each other, shouting – 'Darling I thought you were simply wonderful'. Look at the signed photos on the wall ranging from Nora Batty to Jeffery Archer if you don't believe me.

The last time I was in here the barmaid (a Bett Lynch lookalike) was playing War of the Worlds and the guy next to me was reading a Frank Muir book. This place is super-cool, it's just that no one in Brighton knows it, yet. Don't be surprised to see Rod Serling sitting in the shadows.

### The Evening Star
55/56 Surrey Street
(01273) 328931

The good news is that this pub is an independent brewery that has some really outstanding beers with a new one on tap nearly every day.

The bad news is that, yes, it does have its fair share of middle-aged blokes with big bellies who always win at pub quizzes and have things nesting in their beards.

At the weekend, however, the crowd is more varied and the barstaff are friendly and welcoming. Worth a visit for the beer alone.

## The Greys
105 Southover Street
(01273) 680743
www.greyspub.com

This tiny but celebrated pub has been an institution in Brighton for as long as I can remember. Renowned for its Belgian chef, who can rustle up Lobster Bisque, Roast Guinea fowl and even more exotic dishes like 'Joie de Jacques Cousteau' with the twinkling of his magic wooden spoon, it's unsurprising that the food here is legendary. Combined with some excellent music evenings from Blues and Folk heroes and you have a pub that really has no need of lava lamps and designer furniture to create its personality. Inhabited by roguish landlord Mike and a motley collection of dysfunctional middle-aged drinkers, it does lean towards being a *locals' local*, but new faces are made welcome, and the stuffing and mounting of American visitors is now kept to a minimum. With new beers on tap every two months or so, combined with a menu of Belgian beers, they should keep even the beardiest of real ale drinkers happy. If heaven had pubs, this would make a fine local.

## The Hand In Hand
33 Upper St. James's Street
(01273) 602521

Another independent pub in the heart of Kemptown with the beer brewed locally on the premises. The Olde Trout (named after the landlady) comes recommended and they also do a nice line in German beer, chocolate and hard-boiled eggs.

Look out for the naked Victorian ladies on the ceiling and the sad collection of mouldy ties.

It's a very small place so don't always expect a seat, especially at weekends when their masses of regulars (middle-aged men with beer bellies who always win at pub quizzes...) are there.

Get the manager talking about his time in Bavaria and before you know it, the Lederhosen are out and the oompah music is on.

### You might like to know that:
- They do a late breakfast which is a real gem at £3.25.
- You can take home 8 pints half an hour before closing.
- It's a handy drinking hole for after a service at the Spiritualist Church.
- This is strictly a non-pulling pub!

## The Heart and Hand
75 North Road (01273) 624799

This pub's obvious great selling point is its famous jukebox, which features the likes of Love, The Electric Prunes and Scott Walker. Beyond that it's just a small old-fashioned bar in the North Laine. The staff can be pleasant but the pub does tend to sometimes attract an odd mix of old-school Brightonians and cliquey musicians, who aren't very friendly, unless you're famous or you know someone who is. Have a drink, spin some tunes but don't expect to make many friends. If they all ignore you, put on the Tim Buckley track 'Once I Was' twenty times and leave. Why that track? Stick it on and you'll find out.

## The Iron Duke
Bottom of Waterloo Street

One for the ghostbusters. This typical small locals' pub in Hove is only worth a visit because it is reputedly haunted by several ghosts. The bar-staff will tell you stories about strange smells and things moving around, but most of them are pretty nonchalant about it all. The first time I ever went in, one of the optics came crashing down off the wall. The landlady just shrugged her shoulders and said, *'ghosts as usual.'* Strictly for the Shaggys and Scoobys.

## The London Unity
Islingword Road
www.welcome.to/thelondonunity

While the front bar has an old jukebox and more seating, it's the back room in the London Unity that I've always had a particular fondness for; it seems to have a magic all of its own. Like a cross between the Onedin Line and some museum of strange curiosities, the room is done out in dark wood panelling and has an odd collection of artefacts, ranging from old model ships to weird paintings of shoes and tribal masks. Look out also for the African statue wearing a crash helmet. These idiosyncrasies, combined with the subdued lighting give the place an intimacy lacking in many Brighton pubs. This is a place to come to tell dirty jokes, share conspiracy theories or have wild affairs with strangers.

The landlord here is also part of the pub's heritage. He's just like a regular punter, in that he seems to be here purely to have a natter and get pissed. Last time I was in he was chatting up a couple of young girls at the counter, oblivious of the fact that two customers were throwing ice-cubes at him. Everyone around the bar had to keep ducking as ice smashed all around the room but still his conversation went on unabated. This is a pub full of real characters. Top marks all round.

## The Regency Tavern
32 Russell Square (01273) 325652

One of Brighton's best-loved pubs where gay couples, locals and grannies sit side by side. Done out in exotic gold leaf palm trees, plastic flowers and adorned with gold cherubs, it could easily be a set out of 'The Avengers'. Even the gents' is decorated with a glitterball and mirrored tiles. In spite of all that, there's still something peculiarly Victorian about the place, which adds to its charm.

At weekends look out for one of the barmen, probably the most outrageously dressed man in Brighton and looking like an extra from an 80s pop video. If that's not enough, it's reputed to do some of the best pub lunches in Brighton and is also haunted by several ghosts.

Be Seduced... Be Intrigued... Be Refreshed...
BY THE LUNAR WOMAN
STARRING:
GORGEOUS COCKTAILS
PREMIUM SPIRITS & LAGERS
LASER SHARP DJS
SUMPTUOUS WINES &
FINGER-LICKING GOOD FOOD.
NOW SHOWING AT:
5 CASTLE SQUARE,
AT THE BOTTOM OF
NORTH STREET,
BRIGHTON.
TELEPHONE: 01273 220014
lunar

## WATERING HOLES

### WHERE TO GO FOR A GOOD NATTER

**Basketmakers**
12 Gloucester Road
(01273) 689006
Food served 12pm-2.30pm and 5.30pm-8.30pm weekdays, 12pm-3.30pm Sat, 12-4pm Sun

It took me a good while to find this place when I first moved to Brighton, it's very discreetly tucked away in the North Laine area and this is surely one of the reasons it seems to be so well loved by Brightonians. One of the last great unspoiled local pubs, with no frills, no pumping music, no trendy lagers, no vile colours on the wall and excellent pub grub. What is unusual about the place however is that you can leave messages inside the tins on the wall, and at the same time look for any that have been left. I hid one for you lot in the Huntley and Palmers Dundee Cake tin, though I can't guarantee it'll still be there now. The one I replaced said:

'Ruth Hutt licked my face.' Make of that what you will.

### The Battle Of Trafalgar
34 Guildford Road (01273) 882276

A fight in this pub is as likely as Elton John's hair growing back of its own accord. Instead, it's a relaxed local with plenty of seats, a bar billiards table and a small beer garden, which isn't the usual empty concrete patio and a dead cat.

The crowd here are really friendly and there's no reason why you shouldn't end up feeling like a regular after your first visit.

Look out for the landlord, he's the spitting image of Mr. Fisher, the old head-teacher out of 'Home and Away', who is, according to one e-mail we received last year, *'a nice bloke, but steer clear from the subject of cricket, or you'll never get away'*.

### The Cricketer's
15 Black Lion Street
(01273) 329472

Done out in red Victorian-style furnishings with wallpaper to make your granny blush. Deserves a mention because it's one of the oldest pubs in Brighton* and gets a mention in 'Brighton Rock'. A mixed crowd of young business types, clubbers and locals make sure it's always busy, uncomfortably so at weekends. Come when it's quieter and you can see how gaudy the furnishings really are.

### The Geese
### (have flown over the water)
16 Southover Street (01273) 607755

A perfect excuse for taking a well-earned break half way up Brighton's mountainous Southover Street. The Geese is a peaceful Irish pub that, with its inviting fireplace, big windows and absence of beer garden, somehow seems better suited to cold winter evenings, when you can sit by the fire with a Guinness, read the paper and keep Jack Frost at bay.

*the Black Lion next door is said to be the oldest

The pub is decked out in wood panels, little green velvet curtains, a fireplace, the obligatory collection of artefacts (in their case clocks) and two friendly resident dogs. CC is the shaggy black one while the other is Murphy, a teenage dog who '*needs to be fixed*' according to the barmaid.

One-time winner of Brighton's best pub award and host to a regular Traditional Music Night on Tuesdays, you get an idea why Hanover is so cherished for its good pubs.

On a more irrelevant note, I once hid my ex-girlfriend's shoe in the Christmas tree here one year, and she never found it until the next day. Our relationship was based on seeing who could be the more annoying, and seeing as though she left me and went to live in Thailand, I think I was the winner.

## The Great Eastern
103 Trafalgar Street (01273) 685681

Unspoiled with any clutter, except for the shelves of books at the back, this is another perfect place to come with mates for a chat.

You need to get here early though because the tables near the bar will be too cramped if there's more than four of you and there's only a few at either end of the pub. The place is run by particularly friendly bar staff, often made up of customers who liked the pub so much they decided they might as well get paid for being there. Also renowned for its pub grub from Annie's Kitchen, which does everything from classic to exotic food.

Drunken buffoons in the Quadrant

# WATERING HOLES

## The Quadrant
12-13 North Street (01273) 326432

After several threats to knock it down and build a much-needed drive-through burger joint, this peculiar little bar seems to be staying put for now. In an area where crappy theme pubs are the norm, it's refreshing to find a place that hasn't had the predictable facelift, yet doesn't feel like an old man's pub.

Two winding staircases connect top and bottom, and the journey from the top bar to the gents in the basement will keep you fit if you've got a weak bladder. Looks like it should be haunted.

## The Rock
7 Rock Street (01273) 697054

Once renowned for its cabaret and music nights (David Devant and his Spirit Wife started out here) but these days the upstairs room is home to pool tables and a rather nifty table football game instead. The owner has a thousand and one stories to make your hair stand on end and will insult you if he likes you. It's quite a way out in Kemptown, but on a cold winter's night when you need that ideal pub to settle by the fire, have a game of chess and talk about the good old days, this is the place to come. Being a stone's throw from the very fashionable Sussex Square, don't be surprised to see the likes of Gaz and Kevin Rowland drinking in here from time to time. Watch out for a bloke called Carl forever trying to sell tickets to people to see his flat round the corner, where Ozzy Ozbourne wrote the seminal rock song 'Paranoid'.

## UNABLE TO FIND A CATEGORY

### Nan Tuck's Tavern
63 Western Road Hove 901273) 736436

Bizarrely located close to Palmeira Square, this place is part of a chain of themed pubs, whose subject is all things ghoulish and supernatural. Inside you'll find skeletons, old horror films on the telly, strange chemistry sets bubbling away and a life-sized nude model of Jeremy Paxman. It's definitely worth one visit (just to experience the scary toilets if nothing else) and once your curiosity is satisfied you'll never, ever, ever, ever, want to come again. What puzzles me is: who would actively choose it as a local, apart from Brighton's frazzled Goth community? I could see it working in West Street with all the other lousy pubs, but out in deepest, darkest Hove it seems an odd choice of location. Saying that, the Hove lot are a creepy bunch.

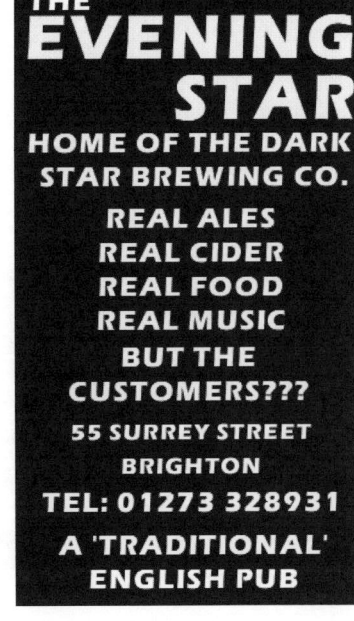

---

**THE EVENING STAR**

**HOME OF THE DARK STAR BREWING CO.**

REAL ALES
REAL CIDER
REAL FOOD
REAL MUSIC
BUT THE
CUSTOMERS???

55 SURREY STREET
BRIGHTON
TEL: 01273 328931

A 'TRADITIONAL' ENGLISH PUB

## COCKTAIL BARS

### The Blue Parrot
New Road (01273) 889675
Closed Sun-Mon

Tucked away close to the Colonnade pub, this small upstairs bar specialises in exotic and classic cocktails. Get a balcony seat over-looking the Pavilion and it's a perfect way to start or finish an evening in style. They do a terrific Piña Colada, or for the less adventurous, half a shandy with a cherry. All cocktails cost £4.

## AFTER-HOURS DRINKING

### Sumo
9-12 Middle Street (01273) 823344
Open 8pm-1am, free before 10pm

Mixing 60s futuristic and 90s minimalism and somehow resembling the drinking den from 'A Clockwork Orange', this unique and stylish bar is worth seeking out. As a general policy they won't let in big groups of men, preferring instead to cater for the stylish twenties to thirties crowd who want somewhere sophisticated to meet and chat.

You can tell that a lot of thought has gone into the place, with the emphasis on subdued music, table service, and cocktails, as well as a wide choice of beers. Soon to be reverted back to an Internet café-bar. See section on internet cafés for more details.

### The Star Of Brunswick and Vats Bar
32 Brunswick Street East
(01273) 771355
Open Monday until 1am
Tues-Thurs until 12.30am

While The Star of Brunswick is your average local Hove pub, downstairs Vat's Bar is a little-known but wonderful after-hours drinking hole. There's usually a small fee to get in (a quid or two) but you can carry on boozing until late, without the hassle of standing around in a crap club with nowhere to sit and having to listen to Steps. It can get a bit hot and claustrophobic down there if really busy, but otherwise it has a pleasant seediness to it.

**WATERING HOLES**

Tuesday nights at Vats are host to the fabulous and outrageous Dave Lynn cabaret, attracting a gay/straight crowd, whilst Thursday is DJ night.

Food is served right up until 12.45am (a full menu to boot) and mid-week it's free to get in if you go through the bar before 11pm. (£2 otherwise). Weekends entrance £2/3.

### The Grosvenor Casino
Queens Road (01273) 326514

Free to get in (provided you've had the foresight to get a free membership card, which permits 6 guests) and open until 2am. If cheap beer, gambling and breakfasts don't interest you, it's still worth a visit just to experience their carpet.

(See gambling section for more details)

> **EVERY DRINKER'S UTOPIA:**
> **A Guaranteed Lock-in on a Saturday Night**
>
> There is a pub in town that guarantees a lock-in every weekend, and usually stays open until the small hours of the morning. Last time I was there some smart Alec borrowed some lipstick from a female friend and, before we knew it, everyone in the pub looked like Robert Smith for the night. If you get in touch and convince us you're not a copper, we might be kind enough to let you in on our secret drinking den.

# the george

vegan & vegetarian food

get an
## appetite
for life

food served:
mon-thurs: 12-9.30pm
fri-sun: 12-8pm

brighton's first vegan & vegetarian pub, offering quality food at reasonable prices in a friendly atmosphere...

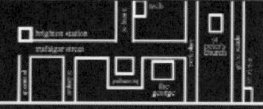

the george, 5 trafalgar street, brighton. 01273 681 055

# the prodigal

*dedicated to...*

*food served 11.45-7pm*

*life, liberty,*

*beer-food-wine*

*food and drink*
*...and other less serious matters*

80 east st, brighton, east sussex, bn1 1ju
**tel:01273 748103**

**WATERING HOLES**

# A Pub Crawl in Hanover*

*A host of fabulous pubs await you in this area of Brighton, and if you're in town for more than a couple of days I thoroughly recommend coming here for a boozy night out. Your starting point is Southover Street, past St. Peter's Church, opposite the Level. Yes, I know it's steep but no whinging. Walk up a short way, wait for the smokers to catch up, then start by visiting The Geese (Have Flown Over The Water).*

*It used to be just called The Geese, until the guy who re-painted the sign admitted that he couldn't paint geese and that he had just painted a stretch of water instead. Hence the name acquired the extra bit in parenthesis. But I digress; it used to be my local and is a small friendly Irish pub. Opposite is The Greys, another tiny pub, famous for its superb Belgian chef and music nights. The owner has a black sense of humour and the pub's advertising slogan is pretty amusing too. Make sure you eat here some time during your stay, although you'll need to book well in advance.*

*Up the hill from here you'll find The Napier. For some reason it seems to be a popular haunt for disgruntled teachers, but leave them to their disgruntling because there's a great beer garden outside. Watch out though for the cat from the house next door leaping in your pint. Even further up the hill your trail takes you to the trendy Pub with No Name, a favourite with the Skint crew. Stick on a woolly hat and anorak, give yourself a cool name like 'Loinclothsally' and enjoy the vibe. If you have drunk enough, the idea of 'doing aeroplanes' back down Southover Street should start to be appealing by now. Keep going until you reach Hanover Terrace. Circle for a while then parachute out.*

*Walk down this street and look out for house number 88. A student transformed it into a big smiley face a few years ago as an art project and it's stayed like that ever since. At the end you'll find the equally hospitable London Unity, and further up, the new improved Constant Service. Steve Coogan likes the odd pint in this area, so if you see him, award yourself 20 points and remember to ask him to autograph your buttocks. You will be so drunk by now, that this idea will form naturally in your head anyway.*

*When it's throwing-out time you must have a pizza at Famous Moe's, then crawl back home. And if it's Saturday, remember you promised to get up for 7am sharp to check out the Sunday market...*

*see other pub sections for further reviews

# HAN(G)OVER

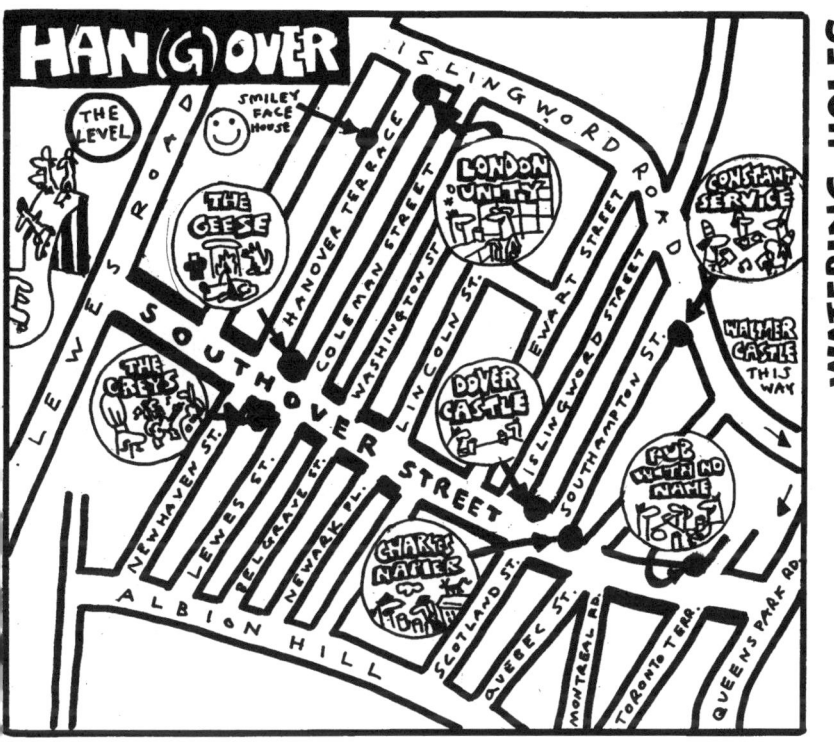

**WATERING HOLES**

# Discotheques

Home to the famous Zap Club, Skint Records and The Big Beat Boutique, Brighton's club scene boasts everything from cool underground Jazz and Retro, to House and Garage nights, as well as being home to the biggest gay club on the South Coast. Combine this with regular visits from big-name DJs, plus our own Norman Cook and Phats & Small, and it's not surprising that Brighton's clubs are packed every night of the week. What other town can boast over 30 clubs, all within walking distance of each other, and most a stone's throw from the beach?

One of the very special things about Brighton is that unlike so many other towns and cities, the clubs here do not merely represent that weekend escapism from drudgery and boredom. The club scene here does not wait for the weekend, if anything some of the best nights are mid-week and even Sundays are starting to become fashionable. Clubbing in Brighton seems nothing less than a shameless celebration of living in a party town, which is probably why carnival-type music, like Big Beat, Latin Jazz and 70s disco, is particularly popular here. And with special club nights, like Vavavavoom! and Wild Fruit, the scene has a dimension of glitz and glamour that Manchester, even in its heyday, could never have provided.

Please check local press for club-night details, as they can change on a monthly basis.

## The Beach
Kings Road Arches (01273) 722272

Found between the two piers on the seafront, this spacious club, with a stylish Mediterranean flavour to its design, is one of the more popular of the many seafront nightclubs. Inside, the room has been divided into different sections, including a restaurant area off to one side. The bar is huge and looks like it should have featured in James Bond's 'Goldfinger'.

Once the home to the 'Big Beat Boutique' but the Skint team upped and left when the Concorde 2 opened last year, so it's now back to banging House, 70s disco and old Funk tunes at the weekends, and the Beach seems ever popular for it.

The only thing a bit disconcerting here is trying to find exactly where the dance floor is, as it's a bit ill defined, but it's a big club so don't worry, you won't have to Breakdance with someone's armpit in your face. Attracting a friendly, unpretentious crowd, The Beach is a popular pick-up place. Get here early if you want to guarantee entry though, especially at weekends. It can be a lonnnnngggggg wait in that queue sometimes, especially if you end up sandwiched between cackling hen parties.

## BN1 Club
Inside the West Beach Hotel, 135 Kings Road (01273) 323161

Small basement club, which favours Drum 'n' Bass and cutting-edge House. It's all UV and white walls down there, which is not really my thing, but they do have these interesting little booths you can go sit in, and claim as your thrones for the night, but get there early because there's only a few.

## Casablanca
Middle Street (01273) 321817

Specialists in Latin-Jazz and Jazz-Funk, and particularly refreshing in that they have live bands at weekends, and not just DJs. With such a strong DJ culture here, you forget sometimes what a pleasure it is to dance to live music, especially when the bands really know how to let rip.

**DISCOTHEQUES**

The club has two floors, and although it's a bit annoying that you can't take your drinks between the two, the top half is basically just a bar (with a naff car theme) so I'd recommend sticking to the downstairs bit. Shame that the dance area is between the bar and the exit, but if the funky music and those horns don't move you to dance, you're in the wrong club.

### The Catfish Club
19-23 Marine Parade (01273) 698331

Underneath the Madeira Hotel, this oversized school hall has been home for many years to an evening of Northern Soul and Motown.
This is generally a place for an older crowd, with regulars in their thirties (and even forties) coming to indulge their passion for this music. The venue is awful, but it seems to be the only place in town where absolutely anything goes on the dance floor. So if you're tired of practicing those high-kicks at home, you now know where to go.

### Concorde 2
Madeira Drive (opposite the Peter Pan amusement shed) (01273) 571154

Built out of the ashes of the Water Rats (a one-time greasy bikers hang-out) the Concorde 2 took over from where the original Concorde left off, by putting on excellent club nights and live bands. Home once again to the legendary Big Beat Boutique (every other Friday) you'll need to get here early, as the Skint crew (including Norman Cook, Lo-Fidelity All Stars and such like) still attract very big crowds.

Other days of the week expect legendary Hip-Hop nights, local bands, touring bands, Drum 'n' Bass, and of course Vavavavoom!
And for goodness' sake, try and wear something that doesn't clash with the paint job in there.

Key players in the pasty-faced Indie community

## The Core Club
12-15a Kings Road
(01273) 326848

Tiny basement club next to Dr Brighton's on the seafront, with a heavy slant towards Garage, Electronic, Underground Pop and other weird stuff.

Attracting Brighton's oddball community of non-club clubbers, this small venue manages to somehow squeeze in plenty of small-label bands, which usually push down the capacity to about 12.

At time of going to print, however, the Core Club was having a major refurbishment, which, when complete, should mean plenty more space to swing those sequined Adidas bags.

## The Cuba
159-161 Kings Road Arches
(01273) 770505

Sandwiched between three successful clubs down on the seafront, this place suffers a bit from an identity crisis, which is a shame because the layout is, in some ways, far better than many of its neighbours.

Like the Zap, the club's design is split level with arched brick ceilings, and set out with wooden floors and plenty of cool seating areas. It should be a great club, so why the queues for the other clubs on the seafront stretch into eternity, while this place is half-full for most of the week is a mystery. At weekends it does get pretty packed for popular Hard-House and Garage nights, but the best night to visit is still Viva Las Vegas on Thursdays.

Knobbly Knees competition at the Joint

## Enigma
10 Ship Street
(01273) 328439

The Enigma is somewhere you used to go if you couldn't get into The Zap, but nowadays it has a groovy crowd all of its own, most notably on Saturdays for 'Phonic Hoop', run by the legendary Rob Luis. On the night this long, low and very dark room plays host to an eclectic style of hip-hop-tech-funk-etc, and draws an even more eclectic crowd, from boozy students and Rastas to gurning men with their shirts off.

For blokes who have given up trying to pull, there are two large TVs with lo-fi computer games, however these are situated next to the girls' toilets, so the night is always young at Enigma.

Dress code: A hooded top

**DISCOTHEQUES**

## DISCOTHEQUES

### The Escape
Marine Parade (01273) 606906

This cool Art Déco building, done out in mauve and sky-blue, and overlooking the seafront, is still one of the most successful clubs in Brighton. With winning formulas for music and promotions, it attracts a young, to very young, horny crowd, who love getting tarted up and partying.

Despite countless refits and changes of promoters over the years, The Escape is still somewhere you can count on if you like your music hard and loud and your fellow clubbers dressed up and 'with it'. The longest running night is 'Thank Funk' on a Friday when the club splits into two. This night has been running upstairs in the bar for seven years and is still going strong. Its popular mix of funk and disco has now pervaded most clubs in Brighton, but this is where the eclectic music mix that you associate with Brighton started.

On Saturday nights both floors of the club are opened for the successful 'Dolly Mixers', produced exclusively by women, who really make an effort to decorate the club (and their clubbers) in accordance with the monthly themes.

The bouncers on the door have been here for years, (although they have been known to pop home from time to time). The most recognisable is Pete (aka. Attila the Hun) who puts the fear of god in every punter who tries to get past him, but he's really an old softy at heart and if you tickle him behind the ears he'll invariably start to hum 'Everlasting Love'.

Dress code: backless dress for the ladies, crotchless panties for the boys.

### A Cheeky Tale

If you look above The Escape you'll see a flat, which has a commanding view of the beach and, in particular, the phone box in front of the club.

These two guys I know, Mark and Bruce, used to live up there, and some nights after the club had almost cleared out, they'd ring up the phone box, wait for some pissed-up clubber to answer, take a note of how he was dressed, and then play these weird 50s adverts down the line to him. It would start with some cheesy music and then go:

*'Hi, and welcome to the world of Lux soap, a new powder that'll get your clothes whiter than white.'* – and then a different voice would say:

*'You are wearing a blue hat.'*
*\*Click\**

## The Event 2
West Street (01273) 732627

The largest club in Brighton, specialising in chart, disco and dance, and popular with students and weekend revellers. Don't take the place too seriously and you'll have a good time.

At weekends the dance floor is a sea of Top Man and Top Shop fashion, and the place certainly has its fair share of virgin clubbers. It is of course a blatant meat-market, but the nights are generally cheap, unpretentious and unashamedly glitzy.

Also host to occasional big-name gigs and special London club nights.

## The Gloucester
27 Gloucester Place (01273) 688011

It's been around since 1692 and still going strong. Expect cheap and cheerful nights with every taste catered for, from House and Indie, to 70s and 80s revival nights.

Hardly at the cutting edge of fashion, but there's plenty of space inside and a dance floor straight out of Saturday Night Fever. The crowd seems unpredictable at the best of times, especially during the week. Sometimes it's full to capacity, other nights there's just a few Goths sat in the corner eating jelly.

## The Honeyclub
214 Kings Road Arches
(01273) 202807

This seafront club is a well-loved students' haunt during the week, and packed at weekends for its House nights. It's also popular with the gay scene, and is one of the few clubs in Brighton to open every day of the week. The party here never seems

Lady Laverne at the Honeyclub

to stop, and with such full-on hard-edged Dance music playing every evening, it's only a matter of time before the poor building has a nervous breakdown. Attracting big name DJs now, The Honeyclub is moving slightly away from being just 'cheap and cheerful'; though it still manages to over-do it with the smoke machine. With a new chill-out area, there are more places to sit down and relax now, and watch the fashion gurus parading around in the latest cheesy high-street garb.

Saturdays here are a must, if only to witness Drag Queen Lady Laverne turning away punters at the door for being too ugly.

## DISCOTHEQUES

### The Jazz Place
10 Ship Street (01273) 328439

Noted for its fabulous Salsa and Jazz music spun by resident DJ Russ Dewbury, this popular but tiny basement club is a real gem.

It is small (think of your bedroom with a bar), and you can't exactly slip off into the corner with someone, but tangoing cheek-to-cheek is the next best thing.

Intimate, relaxed and with a genuinely friendly crowd, you should have an excellent time here. If you love the music, listen to Surf FM on a Sunday night for more of the same.

### The Joint
West Street (01273) 321629

Done out in quite a kitsch style, with heavy red lighting and leopard fur seating, it's not surprising that classic nights such as Dynamite Boogaloo still run here.

This small basement club is usually a drum-machine free zone and plays everything from 60s Soul and R 'n' B to Indie, Soundtracks and Easy Listening. There are plenty of seats and a good L shaped bar where you get served fairly quickly. Expect a mixed crowd ranging from Small Faces lookalikes and Mod chicks, to weekend revellers. Sharp outfits are de rigueur at weekends if you don't want to be stared at contemptuously. Dynamite Boogaloo is still a tremendously entertaining night, expect to see Boogaloo Stu, dressed like some enormous toffee, crooning his way through a few familiar favourites. Other weeks you might get treated to some insane telly, or if you're very lucky you'll get to see a performance by the much, much larger than life 'Dolly Rocket'.

### The Ocean Rooms
Morley Street (01273) 699069

Probably the strangest club in Brighton. Its three floors include a cocktail bar upstairs, a large restaurant area on the ground floor and a dance floor downstairs.

The cocktail bar is very decadent, with poufs, soft red lighting and the biggest red-velvet settee I've ever sunk into. Both the cocktail bar and the restaurant (with its huge tables and plenty of seats) are ideal chill-out areas and, for Brighton clubs, unusually conducive for a good natter. It's only the dance-floor downstairs that lets them down, as it's still stuck in the 80s.

Mid-week the club attracts students and a young crowd, while at weekends it's an older, dressier crowd that descend, but I can't help get the feeling the place is still searching for a real identity.

If you want a club where you can relax and chat, without worrying about over-bearing noise and elbows in your beer, it's worth a visit, but don't expect it to always be busy. This could easily be one of the best clubs in Brighton. With a recent change in management and new club nights, keep your fingers crossed for the future.

## The Paradox
West Street
(01273) 321628

Taking itself slightly more seriously than The Event, this place tends to attract a slightly older and more image-conscious crowd. The interior is done out with mirrors and carpets and has a pretty big dance-floor, for lots of arm-waving.

Full of clubbers in their late teens, the music ranges from Chart and Disco to Hi-Energy and 70s-80s themes. Queuing at the bars at weekends can be a nightmare though; I've waited up to half an hour to be served before.

Next door is their other club, the Barcelona, which opened to their older crowd who got fed up with sharing a dance-floor with young kids. For most nights it's for the 25 or over crowd, so please bring an Ikea catalogue as proof of age.

The Paradox is also home to Wild Fruit, when it's hi-energy and House Anthems, drag heaven, and an excuse to dress up in your girlfriend's (or boyfriend's) sexiest clothes. (See special club night reviews)

## Pressure Point
Richmond Place (01273) 235082

Upstairs above the pub, this small venue has a good PA (which is woefully underused) and puts on a handful of different club nights each week. Don't expect much in the way of character, it's little more than a small hall with a bar, stage and nowhere to sit. The best night is still 'Bust the Box', a debauched monthly party session.

## Tavern Club
Castle Square (01273) 827641

This place has been a popular spot for Indie music, ever since Brighton's legendary Basement Club committed suicide after one of the DJs left a Shed 7 record playing all night by mistake.

The Pav Tav (as it's sometimes known) is basically a function room above a pub, but has enough character to suit the style of the club nights here. Subdued lighting, a wide bar and a few sofas make it intimate and friendly, and the Indie nights are always heaving. Every Thursday, Brighton's Indie contingency drag their skinny bodies down here for 'Mad For It', to demonstrate that no matter how hard you try, you can't dance to Oasis. Friday nights have, for a while now, been home to 'Fresh', a Lesbian night which is gaining ever-increasing popularity. Come Saturday, it's back to the Doors, Beatles and 200 nicotine-stained, pasty-faced kids in need of a good square meal.

Dress code on the door is pretty strict: dyed black hair and trainers are compulsory. If you're ginger, don't even try.

## Volks Tavern
Madeira Drive (01273) 682828

Despite a recent major refit, which added a small downstairs bar to the venue, The Volks still has a down-to-earth vibe, and as it is slightly off the beaten clubbing track, pulls in a crowd who are there for the music and not the pose.

Friday nights are host to Lunarcy, an excellent and extremely popular TechTrance fest hosted by Chris Natural (and his mum who bounces the door for him!)

Saturdays is home to Danger Diabolique, which replaces the long-running Bubblegum Factory, but is in effect the same night, with its Psychedelic music and freaky punters. This is the place where you can spot all the Retro haircuts you have seen sported around the North Laine during the week.

The Volks makes for a sweaty night out, and well worth it when they open the doors at the end of the night, let the cool sea breeze in and everybody stumbles out onto the pavement in a messy, but satisfied state.

Dress code: Paisley shirt, Beatles wig and corduroy.

## The Zap
189-192 Kings Road Arches
(01273) 202407

Under the arches, right down onto the beach, this is probably Brighton's most famous club. It is home to some of the UK's top club nights, which have featured the latest and the greatest on the decks, from Carl Cox to Boy George. Although no longer top dog, and despite its ever-growing grottiness, The Zap is still enormously popular with the more serious clubbing crowd, and the weekend (and weekday) queues

Say Cheeeeese...

## SPECIAL CLUB NIGHTS

### Vavavavoom!
*Alternate months Last spotted at the Concorde 2, but check press for current venue*

Set up over 4 years ago by local diva Stella Starr, Vavavavoom! has grown to become something of a phenomenon.

Based on the 50s Burlesque tradition, the club night features saucy cabaret acts, strippers, go-go dancers, a live band, guest singers and many other surprises. Each event is themed and with a strict dress code; it is the punters who make the effort with their costumes that really keep 'Vavavavoom!' unique. Previous themes have included Voodoo Horror, Circus Freaks, Elvis and Underwater. This is a very flirty, sexy club where inhibitions are cast to the wind, and its gay, straight and fetish crowd demonstrate that the emphasis is on fun, not sleaze.

Past highlights have included the three-breasted lady, live mixed-sex wrestling and Stella stripping whilst sprawled on a gigantic gorilla's hand.

The best club night in Brighton without a doubt.

prove it. The Pussycat Club on a Friday is now in its fifth year of mixing pumping House with a bit of glamour, and is still going strong.

As you enter this cavernous space there's a big dance floor area and stage to your left, surrounded by plenty of balcony space, and a chill-out room upstairs, with separate bar and a few chairs and tables.

Currently favouring House, Garage and 70s music, The Zap pulls a crowd of glammed-up young starlets that have made it past the tough entry examination at the door. Watch out for the floor in there; accidentally drop your tank top, and it will forever smell like a beer-towel and ashtray.

**COMING SOON TO A VAVAVAVOOM NIGHT NEAR YOU**

**REVENGE OF THE FURRY NIPPLE II**

**WITH STELLA STARR AS THE NIPPLE TASSEL SWINGING HOT MAMA**

## DISCOTHEQUES

### Wild Fruit
*First Monday of every month at the Paradox*

Well-established and glamorous night for extroverts and anyone who fancies sticking on a frock, false eyelashes or anything that glitters. This club night was originally targeted exclusively at the gay scene but word somehow got around, and pretty soon everyone wanted to come. Still predominantly attracting a gay crowd, this is an evening of serious flirting, high camp, dressing up, and uplifting House and Garage music. If you've just moved from Skegness, prepare to be shocked.

### Pussycat Club
*Every Friday at the Zap*

In its fifth year now and seeming more popular than ever, this colourful night attracts a mixed gay/straight dressed-up crowd, determined to prove that this is the best Friday-night club in Brighton. The music is hard uplifting House, and Glam attire or fancy dressed is strongly recommended.

## AT A GLANCE...
**Big Beat:** Concorde 2
**Chart/Disco/High-Energy:** The Paradox or The Event? You decide.
**Drum 'n' Bass:** BN1 Club
**Easy Listening/Soundtrack/ Retro:** The Joint/ Volks Tavern
**Goth/Industrial:** The Gloucester
**Hip-Hop & Breakbeat:** Pressure Point and sometimes The Jazz Place
**House and Garage:** The Zap, The Escape, The Cuba, Honeyclub
**Indie:** The Pavilion Tavern/ Gloucester/ Escape
**Jazz/Funk/Salsa:** The Jazz Place or The Casablanca (if you want it live)
**Northern Soul/Motown:** Catfish (or The Joint at the weekends)
**Reggae:** Volks, Roots Garden at the Jazz place or Concorde 2
**70s/80s:** Popular mid-week alternative at many clubs, try The Zap, The Gloucester or The Beach
**Weird Electronica/ Underground Pop & Kraut Rock:** The Core Club/ 'Clang!' at the Volks Tavern

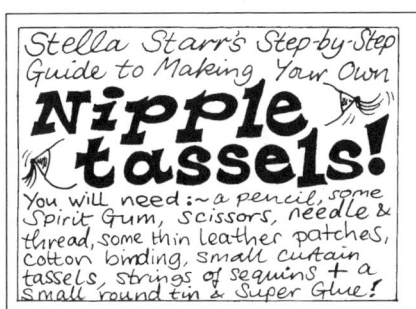

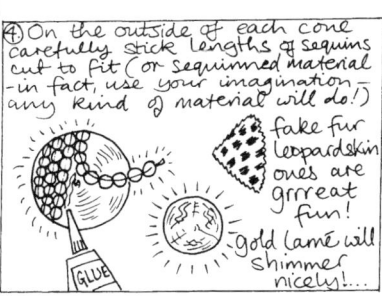

## Stella Starr's Step-by-Step Guide to Making Your Own Nipple Tassels!

You will need:— a pencil, some Spirit Gum, scissors, needle & thread, some thin leather patches, cotton binding, small curtain tassels, strings of sequins + a small round tin & Super Glue!

① Take a small round tin (or any round object roughly the same diameter as your nipples) & draw round & cut out the circles of leather.

② Cut into the middle of each circle & form cones:
overlap
Glue this together with Super Glue... carefully!

③ Cut off the right amount of cotton binding to cover inside of each cone. Glue. The binding helps the cone stick to your nipple!
Cut small pieces of this cotton binding
N.B. The 'cone' is known as a "pastie".

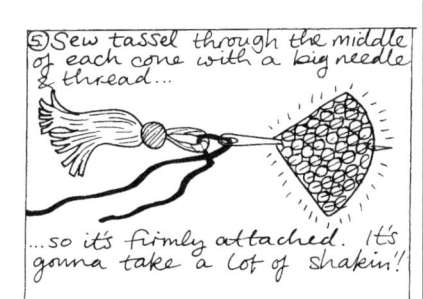

④ On the outside of each cone carefully stick lengths of sequins cut to fit (or sequinned material — in fact, use your imagination — any kind of material will do!)
fake fur leopardskin ones are grrreat fun!
gold lamé will shimmer nicely!...

⑤ Sew tassel through the middle of each cone with a big needle & thread...
...so it's firmly attached. It's gonna take a lot of shakin'!

⑥ Now take the Spirit Gum & carefully brush on to both your nipples & the tassels, then wait a few minutes for both surfaces to get "tacky" & stick, pressing very ~~firmly~~ to your breasts!
SPIRIT GUM — v. important stuff!!
Paint gum inside the cone!

⑦ Now — Shake it, Baby, Shake it!
You can make any shape nipple tassels — hearts, stars etc.
Peel them off carefully (like removing a plaster!) & clean your nipples with SURGICAL SPIRIT & COTTON WOOL. Use them again & again! S☆

## CINEMAS

*See the latest Hollywood movie Friday night, a David Lynch season on the Saturday, then a documentary about SM on the Sunday. Here's how.*

## WHERE TO SEE THE LATEST BLOCKBUSTER
### The Odeon
West Street (0870) 5050007

The biggest cinema in the town centre, and with the Event nightclub next-door, handy if you're taken with the urge to snog a few strangers after the film.

### UGC Cinema
The Marina 0541 555145

Eight screens with all the latest movies from Tinseltown. You won't find anything adventurous in their billings, and it is located below the multi-story carpark in the Marina, but if you like modern swanky cinemas, you won't be disappointed. Besides, if the film's crap you can always take a walk on the Marina breakwater and pretend you're in 'The French Lieutenant's Woman'.

## INDEPENDENT CINEMAS
### Cinematheque
9-12 Middle Street (01273) 384300

Upstairs at the media centre, this sixty-odd-seater cinema has established itself as the place for cutting edge, rare and experimental films in Brighton.

Run by Ben, Michael and Adrian of the Richard O'Brien appreciation society, it is a melting pot of documentaries, cult movies, rare screenings and shaved heads. This is fringe cinema at its best, covering everything from UK horror seasons and occult documentaries, to US underground and rare oldies.

Comedy fans should keep an eye out for rare Buster Keaton films and the much-loved annual Laurel and Hardy Christmas special, complete with mulled wine and home-made biscuits (provided Marty doesn't scoff them all).

## Duke Of York's
Preston Circus (01273) 602503
www.picturehouse-cinemas.co.uk

Found at the end of London Road, the building is bright yellow and has a large pair of stripy legs sticking out from over the balcony. It's easy to miss however, as all the houses on the street have copied the idea, and now there are hands, elbows and feet sticking out all over the place, as far as the eye can see.

Having celebrated its 90th birthday in September 2000, the Duke's can claim to be the oldest independent cinema outside London, showing a fairly wide selection of cult, art house and world films. They have a nice bar upstairs, and rather than the usual cinema junk food, do a selection of cakes and a nifty hot chocolate. The auditorium itself looks magical with coloured lights around the screen, and the red velvet seats are the most comfortable in Brighton. In fact the only thing I'd change about the place would be to crank up the heating a bit in winter.

Thoroughly recommended for all movie enthusiasts and if you fancy seeing one of their late-night screenings at the weekend, buy your tickets in advance as they often sell out. Cheap days are Mondays and Thursdays before 6pm.

### DUKE OF YORK'S TRIVIA

Built for theatrical impresarios Violette Melnotte and Frank Wyatt, Violette was the iron fist in the velvet glove, always known to staff as Madame, and when one of the actors at the theatre gassed himself, she instructed her solicitor to reclaim the cost of the gas from his estate.

The legs once belonged to a cinema in Oxford known as 'Not the Moulin Rouge' (which originally stood opposite the house with the shark in the roof*), and every Sunday at 3pm, they do the Can-Can.

*see the Cheeky Guide to Oxford for the full story.

## ENTERTAINMENT

**CINEMATHEQUE**

THE INNER WORLD OF THE ENGLISH
1939-1979: UK HORROR SEASON
PLUS FRINGE FESTIVAL + CIRCUIT
BREAKER + VERHÄNGNIS + MORE

## THEATRES

### Brighton's Little Theatre Company
Clarence Gardens (01273) 205000

Founded in the late seventies by Sid Little (of 'Little and Large' fame), this converted chapel, tucked behind the Pull and Pump, has been home for many years now to the cosy amateur company who do everything from Ayckbourn to Shakey. Avoid the back seats if you go, there are low slung beams that can obscure the view and spoil it, but keep a look out for Sid, he still pops up occasionally to see the odd farce, but he's porked out a bit now and looks more like Eddie.

### Gardner Arts Centre
Sussex University Campus, Falmer (01273) 685861

This late 1960s purpose-built arts venue looks like it's straight out of a TV comedy drama starring Peter Davidson as a bumbling lecturer who inspires his rebellious rabble of students by accidentally turning up drunk and naked to one of his seminars. That aside, the Gardner Arts Centre is a large venue, with gallery space and a café-bar, which has really pulled out all the stops over the last couple of years with its meaty choice of events. Their programme now features everything from alternative comedians, theatre and cult films to art exhibitions, dance groups and workshops, while their music events range from the likes of Yo La Tengo to traditional music from Azerbaijan.

The venue is seating only, perfect for dance and theatre, but it can feel a little bit formal at times for stand-up comedy and cutting-edge music events. All things considered, it's well worth the hike out of town and afterwards you can sneak into the student bar opposite for cheap beer.

### The Komedia
Gardner Street (01273) 647100
www.komedia.dircon.co.uk

Impossible to miss, owing to the fact that its outrageous red lighting turns Gardner Street into an enormous brothel every evening. That aside, it's a blessing to have a theatre in town that doesn't churn out the usual old cobblers, year in, year out. Instead this is a place to see new comedy, cutting edge theatre, world music and just about any other modern performance art you can think of. Prices can be a bit intimidating at times, but its usually worth the gamble, the quality of what's on here is normally very good. They also offer an excellent restaurant (The Curve Bar) plus Internet access upstairs, and frequent late bars at many of the shows in the downstairs cabaret space. Monthly highlights include the 'News Revue' and 'The Comedy Dairy', both of which are un-missable.

## New Venture Theatre
Bedford Place (01273) 746118

This converted school does about nine productions a year, usually covering more difficult and unusual plays. For fans of amateur theatre, done with luvvie gusto.

## The Sallis Benney
Theatre University of Brighton, Grand Parade (01273) 643010

This place is as dead as a dodo for six months, but out of the blue it will have live music, plays and dance, and then suddenly go back into hibernation again. It's like some drunk relative who's been woken up at a party and dances their way across the living room only to collapse unconscious in the kitchen moments later. Definitely worth keeping an eye on during the summer term, as all the performance-art students put on free events here for a couple of weeks as the final part of their degrees, before settling down to a life of unemployment.

## Theatre Royal
New Road (01273) 328488

For the more conservative theatre-goer. It's the usual souped-up collection of farces, thrillers, Shakespeare and musicals, but for that authentic old-style theatre experience you can't beat it. The auditorium is fabulous; plush red seats, 20p binoculars and viewing boxes. I once saw Barbara Windsor in the nude here but that's another story.

Dress code – loafers, slacks and a cardie. Monocle optional.

## Akademia
14-17 Manchester Street (01273) 622633

Student hangout which doubles up as a theatre and café. The food is good and, to fit with student lifestyle, cheap and plentiful. As well as the odd bit of theatre, expect to find comedy nights here too. And it's not just exclusive to students, so you don't need to sneak in disguised as Rick from 'The Young Ones'.

## CULT & DIY TV
### Junk Television
(01273) 882313
buckinfudgy.com/junktv

I've seen episodes of 'Monkey' and 'Fantasy Island', madcap home-made films, animation, adverts with funny overdubs, silly competitions and loads more at these nights. Held downstairs in the Sanctuary Café (see Food Section) a few times a year, be ready to expect an evening of bizarre goggle-box programmes.

Things are quiet in summer as they usually take their show on the road, so September to May are the best times to catch them here. If you've made the odd film in the past, bring it down or send it to them and get it viewed. Brighton's answer to Exploding Cinema.

> **Past Highlights**
> **Blue Movie** – 'A porn film shot from the distance of 1 inch.'
> **Bring Along Your Worst Vinyl** – 'An evening of musical horror'
> **It's A Jazz Thing** – 'Free Jazz meets quantum physics and someone gets stuck inside his charity shop coat.'

Scene from local cult classic 'Mr Cyclops and the Ginger Moustache Mystery'

## ENTERTAINMENT

### COMEDY

**The Krater Comedy Club**
Weekly at the Komedia (01273) 647100

Usually running Saturday and Sunday nights, the Krater Comedy closely follows that tried and tested Jongleurs formula, found nationwide. Regularly compered by Stephen Grant, known for his speedy delivery, the Krater is unquestionably popular, but does, however, demonstrate the frightening lack of original material of most of the comedians currently trawling round the national circuit. Attracting stag and hen parties in their droves (a growing Brighton epidemic) this is hardly a discerning audience but at least they don't seem to mind listening to men and women in their mid-thirties drone on about their pathetic sex lives. With moronic heckling and mobile phones going off every 10 minutes, this is my idea of comedy hell, but maybe I'm just a miserable bastard.

**NewsRevue-Brighton**
Monthly at the Komedia
(01273) 647100

Based on the successfulNewsRevue-London, now over 20 years old, NRB managed to establish itself as a top Brighton comedy night after only the first show. Packed with songs, sketches and digs at the usual suspects (the police, politicians, crap TV and the Spice Girls) the performances are fast-moving, well-executed and slick.

Far from being groundbreaking satire from the likes of 'The Day Today', NRB follows the well-worn paths laid down by shows like 'Beyond the Fringe', and 'That Was the Week That Was'. The evening is perfectly split into two forty-minute performances, and although there'll be times when you can see the punch-line coming from a mile away, the pace of the comedy leaves you little time to dwell on this before being bombarded by another great one-liner. Look out for their end of year shows around Christmas time.

## ENTERTAINMENT

**STOP!**
NO, IT'S OK, I'VE FORGOTTEN...
WAIT, IT WAS SOMETHING ABOUT COMEDY,
ERRRR....CHEAP BEER! THAT WAS IT! THEY'VE GOT THESE ACTS...
COMEDY AND STUFF, AND SOMETHING....
SOMETHING ABOUT SOMETHING......IT'LL COME TO ME NOW,
WHAT WAS THE PLACE CALLED? **AH-HA!**

THE SEMI-SKIMMED
**COMEDY DAIRY**

STUPID NAME IF YOU ASK ME, BUT I'M TOLD ITS **THE PLACE TO BE**
OR WAS IT THE CLOCK TOWER CAFE? CAN'T REMEMBER.

Tuesday November 9th
doors 7.30pm  £4/£2 conc.    **THE KOMEDIA** BOX OFFICE: 01273 647100

### The Semi-Skimmed Comedy Dairy
One Tuesday a month at the Komedia (01273) 647100

Having grown out of a Brighton sketch group 'The Ornate Johnsons' and the Zincbar (Brighton's long-running and successful equivalent to the Gong Show) the Dairy is, without doubt, one of the most original, perverse, and bizarre comedy nights that ever existed. Spawning a whole host of near-genius yet dysfunctional care-in-the-community comedians, the acts here are a far cry from the shirts-out-lets-talk-about-masturbation brigade that you typically find on the circuit.

Its compere is Dave Mountfield, a rosy-cheeked garden gnome with a bawdy sense of humour, whose years of working with Jerry Sadowitz have toughened him up to deal with the rowdiest of audiences. His technique of lunging at hecklers with scissors and giving them novelty haircuts has certainly kept crowd abuse down to a bare minimum.

In actuality, the audience is another winning quality of the Dairy, for while the night still attracts certain performers who churn out jaded stuff about drugs, signing on and being single, it is the bizarre comic characters and strange and disturbing monologists that really win the audiences' respect. Expect to see the likes of Joanna Neary and Glen Richardson performing as Rubik's Snake (a terrible 80s synth-duo from the West country), Adam (who looks like Otto from the Simpsons) performing his bizarre fables, or Dave Suit doing his novelty reverse stripping routine.

Reminiscent of the originality and freshness of 'Vic Reeves Big Night Out', the Comedy Dairy is already a legendary night.

**TUESDAY 8TH AUGUST**
STAND-UP, CHARACTERS, SKETCHES, COMPETITIONS

WITH A **GLASS AND A HALF** OF
MUSIC, LATE BAR AND **THE SLIGHTLY ODD**...

the SEMI-SKIMMED
**COMEDY DAIRY**

'I CANNOT EXPRESS THE EXTENT OF MY DISAPPROVAL'
LORD CADBURY

**IT'S BETTER THAN CHOCOLATE**
DOORS 7.30    **THE KOMEDIA**    £4.00
SHOW 8.30 PROMPT   BOX OFFICE: 01273 647100   CONCS £3.00

# Comedy Dairy Profile #1 Gerard

Tall, lanky, and usually pissed, Gerard is, for my money, one of the most original comedians I have ever seen. Panting his way through his set, hunched over the microphone, his comedy is a dark and psychotic stream of consciousness, surrealism, and media angst. Inspired by "paranoia", Gerard's targets seems to swing wildly from Wittgenstein to crap pop acts, ("Alanis Morissette unplugged? Wouldn't you like to see that? I mean, why keep her alive?"), while at other times his fears get the better of him setting off a series of disturbing one-liners, worrying for example about his girlfriend...

*'I found a photo of Peter Sutcliffe in her drawer....and it was signed.'*

I once heard a story about Gerard, from my next door neighbour, that one particular night, after dropping acid on the nudist beach, Gerard rolled into work at the Quadrant Pub sporting a cork moustache and tripping badly. Finding himself sacked on the spot for being 'too dangerous', he headed for home but decided to cheer himself up by putting his elbow through Hannington's window, to retrieve a handbag that his girlfriend had taken a shine to. In a moment of rare lucidity he realised that perhaps this wasn't the best thing he could have done, hung the handbag on a lampost, ran home and hid in a cupboard above the kitchen door.

A few minutes later the police arrived, after a tip-off. Let in by Gerard's girlfriend, they searched the house to no avail, but just as they were about to leave, they heard a noise from the cupboard. One policeman asked if anyone was in there. Professional to the end, Gerard cried out *'No!'* and soon found himself being escorted down to the copshop.

After several hours of questioning, the police decided to let him off with a caution, putting the incident down to 'high jinx', combined with the pity they felt after Gerard's heart-wrenching and shamefaced confession that he was a closet transvestite.

## LOCAL WEBSITES AND WORKSHOPS IN COMEDY
**brighton-hove.org**

This spoof website (a take on the council site brighton-hove.gov.uk) has a Mark Thomas style approach to many local issues and debates. Includes such gems as the 'No place to Pee' campaign (lamenting the decline of public loos and their inevitable transformation into cafés). At last, a Brighton website worth visiting.

### Comedy Workshops with Gerry Maguire Thompson
11 Jew St BN1 1UT, tel or fax (01273) 206000 gerry@pavilion.co.uk.

Local comic author and columnist Gerry Thompson has been running 'Hands On Comedy' workshops for some time now for beginners, professionals and corporate organisations at the Komedia theatre and other venues. Gerry is the author of several books, including the best-selling 'Cats are from Venus, Dogs are from Mars'.

## GAMBLING

### The Grosvenor Casino
Queens Road (01273) 326514
Open until 4am

Step into this 80s movie set, situated just across from Brighton station. Their carpets, array of vile merchandise and the rather surreal alchemical paintings on the wall alone merit a visit, but there's much more besides. Membership and entrance are both free, (although it takes 24 hours for them to validate your ID) and once in, along with the roulette wheels and pontoon tables, you can enjoy cheap drinking until 2am, and have the best value breakfast in town. Six of us had breakfast in here one night with a couple of drinks and it only came to £13, but as my friend Pete astutely pointed out at the time, *'it's subsidised by losers'*.

The roulette tables start at 25p a bet, and the Pontoon and Poker start at £1 but there are other tables with higher stakes if you're feeling brave, or you can just watch the professionals in action. And did I really hear the girl say – *'Good Evening Mr. Paradise'* – to one of the regulars as we were leaving?

### International Casino Club
6-8 Preston Street (01273) 725101
Free membership and admission

Taking itself perhaps more seriously than The Grosvenor, as you step in and hear the lilting tones of Phil Collins and Philip Bailey singing Easy Lover you'll realise these guys mean business. The downstairs bar is usually quiet and has a big telly that drains away the conversation as soon as you arrive, and find yourself drawn into a documentary about Doug McLure. Like the Grosvenor, the décor reeks of the 80s, with mirrored walls, fake wood panelling and a clientele to match.

### The Greyhound Track
Nevill Road, Hove (01273) 204601

With all the Parklife nonsense good and buried, now you can go to the dogs and have a laugh without feeling that you have to be ironic about it. It's a few quid to get in, and the minimum bets are a pound. Forget trying to figure out how the betting works, just pick the dog with the silliest name, use the touts outside for better odds, and watch out for the lasagne.

## ADAPTATRAP PERCUSSION

LARGE SELECTION OF WORLD
PERCUSSION INSTRUMENTS:
CONGAS, BONGOS, DJEMBES
TABLAS, SANZAS, BELLS, REQQ
DIGERIDOOS, SHAMEN-BOWLS
GONGS, BODHRANS, BENDIRS
RATTLES, KORAS, GUIROS, TIME
TAPES, BOOKS, REPAIRS, ADVICE
MAINTENANCE, WORKSHOPS
HUMANS, FALOOKAS

**26 TRAFALGAR STREET
BRIGHTON BN1 4ED
TEL 01273 672722**

---

## GARDNER ARTS CENTRE BRIGHTON

www.gardnerarts.co.uk

**BOX OFFICE : 01273 685861**
e-mail : gardner-arts@pavilion.co.uk    www.gardnerarts.co.uk
Gardner Arts Centre University of Sussex, Brighton, BN1 9RA
**RING US FOR YOUR FREE DIARY OF EVENTS**

---

## DUKE OF YORK'S Premier Picture house

www.picturehousecinemas.co.uk

24 hr info 01273 626 261
Box-Office 01273 602 503

- BRIGHTON'S LEADING ARTHOUSE CINEMA
- THE BEST IN NEW INDEPENDENT AND FOREIGN LANGUAGE RELEASES
- CULT AND CLASSIC REPERTORY SHOWS
- DISCOUNTS FOR STUDENTS MON-THU
- REDUCED PRICE MATINEES MON - THU
- £3 LATE SHOWS EVERY FRI & SAT
- OPTIONAL MEMBERSHIP
  INCLUDES 2 FREE TICKETS.
  REDUCTIONS OF UP TO £1.50 ON ALL SHOWS.
  PROGRAMME MAILING. 2 FREE PREVIEWS.
  DISCOUNTS AT KOMEDIA & BORDERS BOOKSHOP.
- FREE EMAILING VIA OUR WEBSITE

www.picturehouse-cinemas.co.uk

---

## WHAT ARE YOU DOING TONIGHT?

theatre   music
   comedy   live literature
cabaret      children's theatre

**The choice is yours...**

**BRIGHTON'S MOST VIBRANT & WELCOMING VENUE**

KOMEDIA

**Box Office 01273 647100**
GARDNER STREET • NORTH LAINE • BRIGHTON
www.komedia.co.uk

# Music

*Let's begin with a joke...*

A bass player's girlfriend comes home to find him giving a particularly painful Chinese burn to their ten-year-old son. She begs him to stop and asks why he's inflicting pain on their loved one.

*'Because he's de-tuned one of my bass strings,'* he says angrily.

*'But that's no reason to treat him like **that!**'* She exclaims.

*' Yes but the little bugger won't tell me which one it is.'*

## LIVE MUSIC VENUES

### The Brighton Centre and East Wing
Kingsway Brighton Seafront
(01273) 290131

Fancy seeing Simply Red for £30 or would you rather have dysentery? Whatever your tastes, when the big guys are in town this is where they play. It's one of those classic 50s buildings you find in every large town or city, that somehow seem to have been fashioned on Gatwick Airport. Still if you've come to throw your knickers at Tom Jones, you're not going to care too much about the décor are you?

In a sort of strange Russian doll kind of way, the East Wing is a slightly smaller but equally featureless room for all those acts that couldn't fill the Centre. The analogy applies all the way down to the loos where Leo Sayer played a comeback gig last year.

### Concorde 2
(see club section)

### The Free Butt
Pheonix Place (01273) 603974

Not a sexual favour, instead this small venue has been home for many years to countless local band nights of every description, from Ska to Indie to Hardcore. You can see a band or three here just about every night of the week, and it's easily spotted for its revolting colour. If you're in a band and looking for somewhere to play, this will probably be your first port of call.

### Gardner Arts Centre
(See theatre section)

### The Lift
Queen's Road
(01273) 779411

This tiny but magical venue is tucked away up Queen's Road, above the Pig in Paradise.

Countless evenings have been spent here, some awful, some astonishing. I have seen some brilliant gigs, spoken word events, god-awful cabaret and the odd fire. Brighton's most eclectic venue is even regular host to different jazz bands, which to my shame I've yet to experience. Check the board outside for what's on that day, phone or sneak a look in the local press.

## Pavilion Theatre and Corn Exchange
New Road
(01273) 709709

300-odd capacity venue in the centre of town which, after a refurbishment, is back in use for larger gigs, theatre productions, comedy and contemporary dance. It is also home to the legendary Brighton Jazz Bop, now in its 13th year. Look for their brochure round town.

## Ray Tindle Centre
41/ 42 Upper Gardner Street
Alan Sherman
(01273) 819184

Having been in hibernation for a year or two it's good to see this place being used at last. This community-run venue is exactly what you'd expect; hot and smoky with crap school carpets, but that's what rock and roll's all about. With a capacity of about 200, expect to see local band nights and other events.

Having come to a dead end trying to discover the true identity of Ray Tindle, I can only conclude he was a minor Brighton celebrity, who, on his death bed, left all his money to build a community venue, having had the foresight that there would be a lack of venues for middle-sized Post-Rock acts of the new millenium.

**THESE GUYS PUT ON GOOD GIGS**

## Melting Vinyl
Contact Anna & Steve (01273) 325955
Info@meltingvinyl.co.uk
www.meltingvinyl.co.uk

Looking like they've been pulled out of the Yellow Submarine cartoon, the duo of Anna and Steve are responsible for undoubtedly some of the best gigs in town, as everything from Garage-Pop to weird Electronica comes under their wings. Their Friday night slot at the Core Club was, for some time, a runaway success, but with the Core Club being refurbished at time of going to print, we're still not sure whether they'll return there. As well as this they do a lot of gigs up at The Lift and are now starting to put on bigger events at the Pavilion Theatre, Concorde 2 and occasionally the Old Market in Hove. Expect way-out sounds, Electronic pioneers, Lo-Fi, Garage Pop and some of the coolest bands on the planet. Go to their gigs and support these fine people, it would be awfully quiet here without them.

MUSIC

**MUSIC**

*melting vinyl presents some swoonsome pop from Belle & Sebastian labelmates*

**salako + Mint**
*jeepster*

**FRIDAY 14 APRIL
THE RAY TINDLE CENTRE
UPPER GARDNER STREET
(NEXT TO HEART & HAND)
8—11PM •£3.50/3 CONCS**

### Disastronaut
The Lift Club (01273) 779411
www.disastronaut.co.uk

American Jeff puts on a ton of gigs at The Lift (where he lives with his monkey) ranging from the shambolic to the sublime. Mellow-Country and Critical Beat acts seem to be particular favourites, but be ready for anything on a Jeff night. For a real taste of Brighton you should go to one of his gigs at the Lift at least once in your life but don't be surprised if he DJs and sings for half the night, he's just a little egocentric. The Lift is currently host to his well-publicised Slack Sabbath nights, which attract DJs from the outer limits and underground Electronica scene.

(For more stories on Jeff, see Eccentrics Guide)

### Timebomb Jukebox
Alan (01273) 298095

Responsible primarily for good local band nights at The Free Butt and the Ray Tindle Centre, and probably a good promoter to start with if you're a local band after your first gig.

### Raw Pony
(01273) 777346

This collective of good eggs from Lura Luxx and Bemsha Swing put on a host of gigs at The Lift and The Free Butt under the mantle of Post-Rock and Post-Hardcore. Previous acts have included American Jazzcore act The Sorts and Black Heart Procession.

### Sir Ian Helliwell
Geiger HQ (01273) 731743

Tipped to be the next Dr Who, recently knighted Sir Ian Helliwell puts on regular film and music events in Brighton. Responsible for the fabulous Pioneers of Electronic Music Festival in 1998, he has since hosted many evenings of experimental super 8 films at the Cinematheque with electronic soundtracks from the likes of Fridge to the theremin tweakers Louis et Bébé Baron.

## HOW TO FIND OUT WHO'S PLAYING

*All the local magazines will give you a run-down on who's playing, and where. Some of the best places to pick up information are the record shops themselves, which might have posters for last minute and low-key gigs. Edgeworld Records is particularly good for finding out titbits of information on all things underground.*

## WHERE TO GET TICKETS

### Edgeworld
Kensington Gardens in the North Laine
For Electronica/lo-fi affairs.

### Rounder Records
In the Old Lanes (01273) 325440
For bigger gigs and special club nights.

### HMV
61-62 Western Road (01273) 747221

### Dance 2 Records
129 Western Road
(01273) 220023 /329459

## LOCAL RADIO

### Southern FM
Did someone mention Alan Partidge?

### Surf FM 107.2
(01273) 386107

During the day the music is the usual chart fodder, but it's worth tuning in to the morning slot just for John Chittenden, as, chances are, he'll be making a novelty milkshake out of the previous night's curry or doing a saucy feature on celebrities who shave their private parts. In the evenings, things toughen up and Surf play some way out cool dance tunes and keep you in touch with what clubs and gigs to go to. My favourite show for years now on Surf has been 'Totally Wired'. This is on 11pm-1am every day of the week and plays underground Electronica, Post-Rock and old classics from the likes of Captain Beefheart.

Of course by the time this goes to print it might all have changed, been bought up by Chris Evans and confined to playing Ocean Colour Scene 24 hours a day. Remember how Nazi Germany started.

**MUSIC**

# THE POP CELEBRITY HALL OF FAME

It is a well-established fact, that apart from Nick Berry, everyone in Brighton is a musician of some sort. Below is a helpful guide to the pop-stars of past and present who at some time have graced our streets. I must admit though, some of it could be based on hearsay and an over-active imagination.

## FAMOUS FOR 15 MINUTES
**These Animal Men** – (NME darlings who lived entirely off speed and hair dye)
**Tampasm** – (noisy all-girl band who appeared on the Girlie Show before splitting up and heading off to Secretarial School)
**Frazier Chorus** – (Kitchen Dreamers)
**Peter and the Test Tube Babies**
**The Piranhas**
**Sharkboy**

## FAMOUS NAMES WHO HAVE GRACED OUR TOWN
**Kirk Brandon** – (Spear Of Destiny)
**Genesis P. Orridge** – (Psychic TV)
**Kevin Rowland** – (Dexy's Midnight Runners)
**Foz** – (The Monochrome Set)

## STILL THROWING TELLIES OUT OF WINDOWS
**Gaz** – (Supergrass)
**David Thomas** – (Pere Ubu)
**Tim Booth** – (James)
**Martin Rossiter** – (Gene)
**Jeff Noon** – (I know he'd want to be here)
**Annie** – (Elastica)
**David Van Day** – (Dollar)
**The Levellers**
**Fatboyslim**

Simon Johns of Stereolab, about to give birth to a Mini-Moog

### CLEARLAKE
This year's 'band most likely' award goes to Hove 4-piece, Clearlake, previously known as

Blur your eyes, and the second guy along in Clearlake looks like he's got huge hands

'Not Bit of Wood'. Mixing the music hall charm of 'David Devant and his Spirit Wife' with the song-writing capabilities of Syd Barrett and The Kinks, Clearlake's first single 'Winterlight' made Mark and Lard's record of the week, and judging from the quality of their other songs (including the very wonderful 'Jumblesailing') and live performance. I hope to be seeing them on Jools Holland before too long.

# An Insider's Guide to the Local Band Scene

by Steve from 'Melting Vinyl'

It may be the salt in the air from the sea that can rot guitar strings, or just that woozy air of apathy that gently seeps into every Brightonian's pore, but for a town of its size, and with a healthy number of live music event attendees, notable home-grown acts are a little sparse. What follows are the acts that this writer has blessed with his seal of approval; take it as twisted as his bitter little prejudices allow...

Brighton, being the home of all things 'Mod', has an alarming number of dull blokes with hair combed down in front of their ears, merrily twanging away in praise of the man Weller. Avoid these groups.

If you're visiting, you'll no doubt be aware that your own fair town probably has its own versions, and holidays are about getting away from the mundane and everyday. So if you require glamour, excitement and an all-girl band playing Kraut-rock, Electrelane fit the bill perfectly; all serious faces, metronomic drums, a Farfisa organ, and no Weller tributes. After an initial single on 'Skint', they are now off to pastures new, and as we go to print, they are merrily designing fold-out covers for their quadruple magnum opus 'We are the Lane'.

With a town jam-packed full of ex-students, serious instrumental guitar bands come with the street furniture. There's a constant Post-Rock nucleus centred around the axis of long-running guitar abusers 'I'm Being Good'. It almost seems that anyone who has ever seen the band play live has gone off to form strange Jazz-time guitar acts with the obligatory 'weird' instrument. And they all seem to live in The Lift, on Queen's Road, Brighton's centre for the weird and wonderful.

Away from planks of wood with strings on, bedroom boffins are dotted amongst the hills of Brighton, carefully sampling the traffic and their flatmates' cornflake munching, creating perfect sound collages to lay over some phat beats, and then never play them to anyone. A notable exception is the man they call 'Pilote', whose beat-trickery can regularly be witnessed around the town, and on record too (check out his album 'Antenna').

The music scene down here can be staid and dull, but occasionally it can get your fillings a-rattling. Just avoid bands with 'The' as a prefix, and you should be safe. Oh, but then there's 'Anal Beard'...

# MUSIC

# WHERE TO START LOOKING IF YOU WANT TO JOIN A BAND

## The Friday Ad
(free from any newsagent)

In the music section you'll find about 5 to 10 adverts for musicians wanted. It's usually stuff like REM tribute bands and pub blues bands but you do get the occasional curiosity that might prick your enthusiasm enough to pick up the phone.

## Edgeworld Records
Hive, Kensington Gardens

Scan the walls carefully and you'll find a handful of intriguing ads for Lo-fi, Mellow Country, Electronica and the odd Hardcore band. Probably your best port of call unless your idea of style is cowboy boots and long permed hair.

## The Guitar and Amp Shop
79-80 North Rd

A large selection of adverts, but what a depressingly dull bunch most musicians are.

*'Influences include Ocean Colour Scene, Cast.......zzzzzzzz'.*

Get the picture? But still probably the most popular place for ads, so don't avoid it simply because of my prejudices.

If you are a bass player or drummer the world is your oyster and bands will kneel down and beg you to join, even if you do only like playing slap-bass or keep time like Moe Tucker.

If you are a songwriter looking for a band however, your ad will join another seven thousand hopefuls and probably read something like this:

> JUST DRUMS, KEYBOARDS, FLUTE, HORNS, BACKING VOCALS, RHYTHM and LEAD GUITAR NEEDED TO COMPLETE THE LINE-UP FOR A NEW AND EXCITING BAND WITH RECORD COMPANY INTEREST.
> INFLUENCES INCLUDE TRAVIS AND OASIS.
> NO TIME-WASTERS, ANYONE OVER 25, WELSH MIDGETS OR HIPPIES.
> TEL 56472 ASK FOR SPIKE

# GETTING A GIG

## OPEN MIC
There are plenty of open mike spots in countless pubs around Brighton that will welcome you with open arms, provided you're not planning on playing 'Stairway to Heaven' on bagpipes. (Actually that appeals in a rather perverse way). Some will be awful and others will be worse but you might just meet some kindred spirits or at least get some free beer for the evening. To find out where they are, grab a few of the listings guides in the cafés and newsagents and just go along.

## BUT WHAT ABOUT *MY* BAND?
If you want your band to play here, your best bet will be to try the small venues like The Free Butt and The Lift, and any other places you see advertising local bands. Send them a demo, get someone to recommend you or sleep with the promoter.

## PROMOTING YOUR GIG
Don't expect to pull a crowd. It is notoriously difficult getting people to come and see you in Brighton when there are so many other potentially better things they could be doing. Stick up a few posters around town but expect to discover the next day that all 500 of them have mysteriously disappeared. Try and bring a few friends instead, using bribery or blackmail. Failing that, get on your knees and weep until at least one of them promises to come. Failing that, ask your parents.

## THE SOUNDCHECK
You will be told to arrive at the venue strictly for 6pm, no later. This you do, even though the sound-guy does not show up before 7, and he's had a few already. After the headline band have sound-checked for around 2 hours, you will be given 5 minutes for your sound-check owing to the fact that the doors are about to open. During your sound-check you will notice that the other band will probably giggle at you for a couple of minutes then walk off and ignore you for the rest of the night. Do not be alarmed, this is nothing out of the ordinary. It just means they think you are talentless geeks who are destined to go nowhere fast, unlike them.

Meanwhile on stage you can't hear your vocals at all. When you tell the guy on the mixing desk he will say 'that's as high as I can get'. He is however referring to the cocktail of drugs he took earlier. Beyond this point, he will only hear your voice backwards in his head. As the hallucinations and paranoia kick in, he will stagger out of the venue and never be seen again until the following evening. Your sound-check is now over.

## MUSIC

### THE PERFORMANCE

You are set to go on stage at 8.40pm but hang on until ten past nine in the hope that there will be more people in the room than the barstaff. The bass player's dad walks in, so on you go. On stage you can hear nothing but feedback and look around for the mixing guy. After 5 minutes he appears momentarily in the room, gives you the thumbs up and disappears again. You frantically wave at him but he's gone. You soldier on.

### AFTER THE GIG

The bass player's dad says 'well done lads'. He tells you that it was a shame the vocals couldn't be heard and asks you nicely what the high pitched whine was throughout the set. Meanwhile the promoter who promised you £20 has gone home and someone's nicked your guitar tuner. The diminutive singer from the other band with eye make-up and a glittery shirt is really pissed now and he comes over to tell you that you were crap before swaggering back to snog his 13-year-old girlfriend.

Well done, you have survived your first gig. Don't be too disheartened though, your ego will be a little bruised but that's all. You have learned a lot and after a bit of a practice you'll soon be ready for your next one.*

Where did it all go wrong?

*I think it only fair to say that despite all my cathartic ramblings, I had a hell of a lot of fun playing in bands over the years.

# A Short Essay on Busking

If you're thinking of earning some extra cash, this can be a fun way of doing it. Don't expect too much enthusiasm from the locals however, there are a lot of regular buskers to compete with. The foreign language students will not be your best market either. Generally they will stand around for ten minutes, have their picture taken with you and then bugger off to McDonalds without paying anything. All things considered, I recommend that you sell your soul and aim straight for the tourists.

Your best bet is to go for the novelty approach and make yourself stand out for the day-trippers who will see you as a 'unique experience', even if you have been standing outside the Palace Pier for the past ten years hammering nails up your nose. Look for a good spot where a lot of people are passing by you, ideally somewhere where they might stop and watch (ie not a busy high street). Why not look around for some empty shops to stand in front of? If you stand in a doorway quietly strumming your guitar and singing Nick Drake songs to your feet then you will join another twenty hopefuls around the Lanes. And don't be afraid to make a fool of yourself, people will pay good cash for this. Be bold in asking for money but don't be pushy. If you have an act with another person, have one of you going into the audience now and again with a hat. Some punters are put off paying by the sheer exposure of leaving the crowd to drop those precious coins in your box.

Why not try the odd bit of audience participation? It will draw interest from the crowd, as they thank the lord that they weren't picked. I was unlucky enough to have been selected as straight man last year for an escapologist outside the pier whose entire act seemed to have been based on watching Bottom a couple of times. He humiliated me with awful jokes and spent twenty minutes just putting on a straightjacket and then taking it off again. But by his shouting and confidence he pulled a big crowd and made a lot of money in a very short time, so good luck to him. Saying that, if I ever see him again I will kill him.

One final tip. If you have a pet, bring it. Buskers with animals make loads of money. Bring along your stick insect collection and your woolly mammoth. The more unusual the better. Look out for the guy with the grey rabbit in the Old Lanes, I don't know how he keeps it from running away, it must be nailed to something. But he knows he's on to a good thing.

# MUSIC

## BUSKING DONT'S
### Didgeridoo
No longer a novelty.

### Drums
These have a habit of irritating anyone with a shop or office within a one mile zone of you and will make you extremely unpopular.

### The Penny Whistle
All love of this instrument has been beaten out of me over the years by countless buskers who think that I will be fooled by them simply blowing and randomly moving their fingers up and down.

### Mime
It didn't work for Howard Jones and David Bowie and it won't work for you.

## WHERE TO BUSK IN SUMMER
### Brighton Place
Opposite Donatello's in the heart of the Old Lanes

Probably the most coveted spot in Brighton. Every summer there's a full-on pan-pipe band who haven't seen the 'Fast Show' yet. Get there early, and expect a bloodbath.

### Where Kensington Gardens meets Sydney Street
The guy who plays Blues guitar at Blind Lemon Alley restaurant used to busk here, but you don't see him around anymore so make the best of it. This spot has a big turnover of pedestrians but there are also a lot of retailers around so don't make it too noisy. And don't expect the punters to stick around, there are too many alluring shops around you. It's a good spot if you have a short novelty act like setting fire to yourself.

### Gardner Street
It's a car-free road on a Saturday and quite conducive to the odd spot of busking. Don't play Oasis on your acoustic guitar here though, it's very predictable and you will have a fairly discerning audience. Be different, play Fatboyslim on a Bontempi organ. Try and make the buggers smile.

**Down On The Seafront**
The closer to the Palace Pier you get, the more punters you will get. But it can get noisy down there too, especially by the roundabout. I'd find a compromising spot between the two piers and be prepared to deal with a few lager louts. Many, many years ago, a group of us used to busk right down on the seafront, opposite the beach. That was a great spot but we did suffer from getting a crowd up on the promenade, which stood, looked down, clapped, and then left without paying. Saying that, if anyone had thrown money down, I'd probably still be recovering from the bruises.

## WHERE TO BUSK IN WINTER
You can't busk inside Churchill Square as the Gestapo will throw you out but you can go to the Imperial Arcade where at least you're out of the rain and cold. Plus the acoustics are great there. Don't expect a huge turnover of pedestrians and don't spend all your earnings on novelty items from the Condom Store.

You could also try Market Street, beside Hannington's, which is also sheltered and gets very busy, especially at the weekend.

# MUSIC

# The Wheel of Life of a Brighton Musician

**1.** You answer an ad in the Guitar and Amp Shop and spend the evening with an unhinged alcoholic in his bedsit, listening to demo tapes of his old group.

**2.** After another year of this you decide to form your own band and bring some purity back to pop music.

**3.** You audition hundreds of guitarists until you find someone who owns an original 70s Telecaster. Even though he can't play it, you know a cool guitar when you see one and this is way more important.

**4.** You wait another 3 years for a bassist and drummer to come along. The bassist is a frustrated guitarist, while the drummer is merely a psychopath who doesn't particularly like music but enjoys hitting things. They'll do for now.

**5.** At your first gig at the Free Butt the drummer hits the singer in the other band, your guitarist fails to notice that he is playing the wrong set and then gets in a strop about it, and you have a sneaking feeling that the bassist played slap bass on one of the tracks. Your friends tell you that you sound a bit like the Stereophonics, which is ironic because you hate them.

**6.** You record a demo, have 40,000 made, spend a week arguing over the track listing, send one copy to John Peel and put the rest under your bed where they remain still.

**7.** After 6 months the bassist announces that although still committed to the band he has formed his own band called 'Latafunkapanda' playing Jazz-Funk covers, and you are alarmed to notice that he is starting to wear corduroy and grow a goatee.

**8.** Your demo returns from John Peel with the message- *'sounds too much like Stereophonics.'*

**9.** The drummer by now has taken a preference to hitting the bass player rather than his drums and the only way to calm him down seems to be regular heavy doses of ketamine.

**10.** You discover the existence of a Swedish synth-pop band with the same name as you.

**MUSIC**

**11.** The bassist announces that he is leaving to concentrate on his Jazz-Funk career so you hide the drummer's stash of ketamine and unchain him.

**12.** You read in the paper that the Brighton band you really hate have just done a Peel session.

**13.** The drummer phones from prison to say that he can't make the next 400 rehearsals.

**14.** The guitarist comes round to your house, you smoke a joint together, reminisce about the good old days and moan about all the bands you know who have sold out. You jam through a couple of Oasis numbers, and then he goes home.

**15.** A month later you turn on the telly and see the guitarist on 'Stars in Their Eyes'. The words *'tonight Matthew I'm going to be JK from Jamiroquai'* are like daggers through your heart.

**16.** You move into a bedsit, start drinking heavily and put an advert in the Guitar and Amp shop.

*The cycle is now complete.*

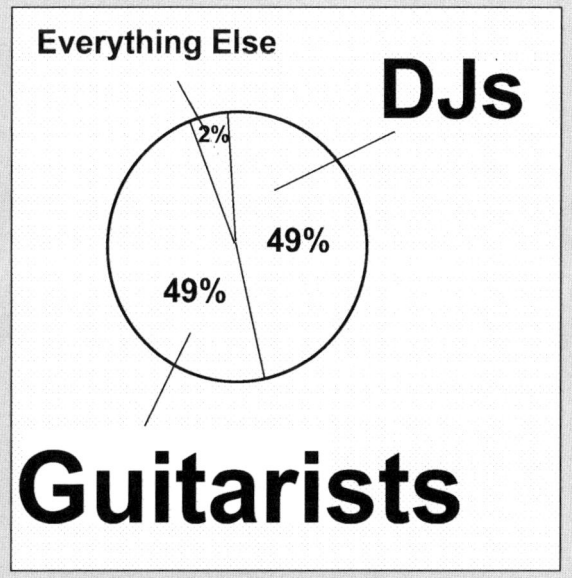

Everything Else 2%
DJs 49%
Guitarists 49%

**Brighton Musicians Pie Chart**

## LOCAL HEROES

# Local
# Heroes

*This chapter is a homage to some of the local people I admire, who have all bravely dragged themselves out of the gutter to become entrepreneurial champions of the unique, beautiful and bizarre.*

### Peter Pavement and Slab-O-Concrete Publications
www.slaboconcrete.com

One-time grave-digger with a passion for underground comics, Peter turned his back on busty heroines and men in tights having a mid-life crisis, when he set up Slab-O-Concrete 8 years ago, focussing instead on cutting-edge comic art and underground pop-culture. Now one of the UK's most dynamic underground publishers, Slab release over 20 books a year from such cult artists as Billy Childish, Jad Fair, and Jeff Noon, with themes ranging from surreal stories and political satire, right through to a collection of pornographic comic strips.

No longer craving solace with the dead, Peter now shares his office with Brighton's other DIY duo, Anna and Steve of Melting Vinyl, although he does occasionally bury the neighbours' dead pets, *'just for old times' sake'*.

Championing the underdog, Peter still encourages new comic artists to send their work for potential publication, providing it's quirky enough and original.

*For more information try the website above.*

The Hand of Glory

## Hexagon Archive
www.hexagonarchive.com

The Hexagon Archive is an independent resource that collects rare and unusual material related to the occult. It has an extensive photographic library featuring relics such as ritual swords, magic wands, genuine witches' curses and Shamanic rites. Run by a trio of mad geniuses, they are one of the few groups of people allowed access to Stonehenge for historical and research purposes. The archive houses a vast array of CD Roms, documents, books and research, all connected to the art magical. These include one of the only medieval recipes for the ghoulish Hand of Glory (a candle formed from the hand of a hanged man) while some of the most interesting texts are the secret rites used by the infamous sex magician, Aleister Crowley.

Located in the heart of Brighton, the archive will be organising an annual festival in June: Occulture, an esoteric event that has in the past featured pagan exorcists, cult busting mystics, the Church of Satan and some of Britain's most powerful occultists.

Hexagon welcome submissions of all esoteric material bar UFO's, declaring, *"We'll talk to anyone except crazies!"*

## www.acmeartshop.com

This is the website for local artist Chris Macdonald, and it displays his beautiful and strange sculptures made from found metal objects and carved wood. Ranging in price from a few pounds to several hundred, this is surely the work of a man who fell down Alice's rabbit hole and never returned.

*'My brain often works like that of the 19th century French philosopher who suggested that the wind is caused by trees waving their branches'.*

Chris MacDonald

**LOCAL HEROES**

### gallery-daville.co.uk
Beautiful and surreal, the images and words of local artist Greg Daville have always touched something deep in the unconscious, where the monsters under the bed still lurk. His website covers a whole host of art, past and present, although, for me, it is the 'Fourth Door Images' that are the most stunning. In Greg's art, strange creatures inhabit centre stage in dream-like landscapes, with images ranging from mythical towers to fetish models.

If you like unusual, yet striking images, pay this site a visit.

All artwork is modestly priced and can be mail-ordered from the site.

### www.hedweb.com/brighton
50 bizarre Brighton deaths catalogued by local munchkin Dick Witts, ranging from poisoned chocolates to the trunk murders and the tale behind the death in the Green Dragon. Dully presented and associated with a website of self-indulgent tosh, the tales themselves, however, merit a read for those in need of further local stories, and anyone with a love of the macabre.

# Local Legends & Eccentrics

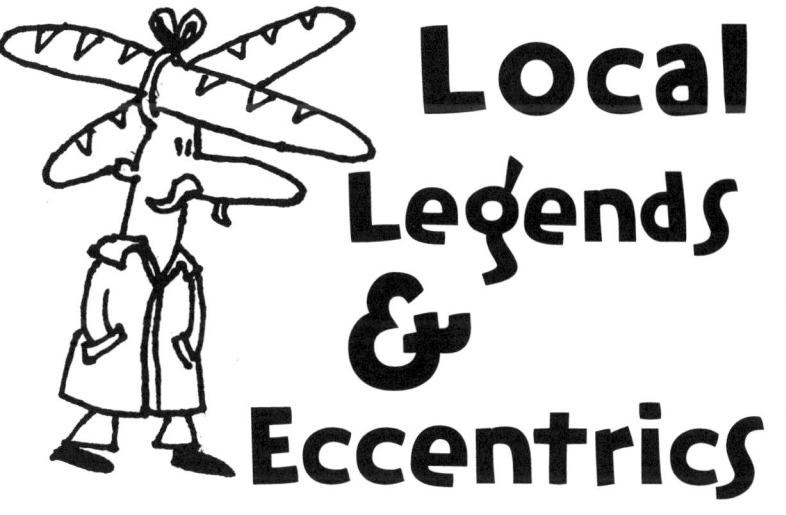

*Brighton has always had more than its fair share of outlandish individuals and below is a guide to some of the town's fruitiest and most loveable characters. But does anyone remember the bread man, who used to wander the streets of the North Laine between 6 and 7 in the morning with two French loaves strapped to his head like helicopter blades? Now he **was** a loony...*

## Mad Jack

This loveable toothless old-timer frequents several cafés around the North Laine such as Zerbs and The Dorset, where he is an affirmed regular, usually charming a cup of tea and a cake out of the owners on a daily basis. Full of life, but two buttons short of a cardigan, Jack will generally declare it to be his birthday most days of the week, claim to be building a brick and will usually call you Martin. My favourite story about Jack is when he was spotted in Zerbs one day unscrewing the lid off the charity box by the till. Carefully he took all of the coins out the box, counting them as he went along until they were all out on the counter. With equal gravity he started to replace them, again counting as they were returned. As the last coin went in he announced,

'It's one pound short!!' and began eyeing the other customers accusingly. After no-one owned up to the crime he turned back to face the person serving, and said quietly, *'cup of tea please'* and placed a pound coin on the counter.

**25 points**

## LOCAL LEGENDS & ECCENTRICS

## Drako Zarhazar

Possibly Brighton's greatest eccentric, Drako Zarhazar's life-story reads like some improbable work of fiction, having danced at the Moulin Rouge and London Palladium, modelled for Salvador Dalí's 'Crucifixion of Christ', starred in films by Andy Warhol and Derek Jarman and also having survived two serious road accidents and comas.

Decorated with exotic tattoos and piercings, Drako is someone you simply couldn't mistake, even in Brighton. His head sports a tattooed triangle, while his face is adorned with bright blue eyebrows, facial piercings and an impressive Daliesque wax moustache. Visit his flat and it is somewhat like stepping into the pages of a pornographic psychedelic cartoon, for all the walls are adorned with phallic images. From flaccid to fully erect, there are thousands of them everywhere, sometimes stuck casually onto a traditional painting, while others are accompanied by humorous comments.

Ask him about his films and Drako usually seems fairly nonchalant about them all, preferring instead to describe his favourite movie moment as *'one night in Rome when someone filmed me putting a candle up someone's arse, which I lit, and then with a big whip, whipped out the flame'*.

Nowadays Drako rarely ventures out and unless you happen to spot him shopping around Kemptown, the only place you might see him perform is at Vavavavoom!, the Burlesque-style club night where he occasionally stands naked on a plinth for the evening, encouraging the gaze of passers-by.
**50 points**

## Drako recalls meeting Dalí for the first time.

'I remember being invited one day to a house on the outskirts of Paris. I walked down the stairs to a pool in the basement, and swimming naked in the pool were two beautiful girls. I remember coming and sitting on a big couch next to Salvador Dalí. He didn't say anything to me but kept watching these two naked girls swimming, and I suddenly noticed Dalí's hand moving up and down next to me. He was looking at these beautiful girls... and he was wanking.

And I thought to myself 'here I am on the outskirts of Paris, sat next to the famous painter Salvador Dalí, with him wanking over these beautiful girls. Isn't life incredible?'

## Sir Ralph Harvey

A well dressed and genteel man sporting the fading moustache of a brigadier, Ralph travels the world battling the likes of Vikings and Saxons with military re-enactment societies, while his own outfit make regular appearances around the country dressed as Dad's Army (Ralph, of course, plays Manwaring).

Perhaps more surprisingly Ralph is one of the country's leading authorities on the Occult, heads his own local coven following the Wiccan religion, and is responsible for sorting out much of the poltergeist activity around the Shoreham area.

Having also regularly worked as an actor, at the height of his fame he played Hercule Poirot on Belgian TV where he became a household name, until the Agatha Christie estate stopped the TV company from using the famous detective's name. From then on, even though he dressed the same and played the same role, Ralph had to be known as 'Inspector Sprout', and somehow it was never the same.

Look for him as Captain Manwaring, parading down on the seafront during the May festival, or in town giving lectures on the Occult.

**40 points**

## LOCAL LEGENDS & ECCENTRICS

## American Jeff

With tattooed sideburns, shaved head and dressed in some outlandish fashion, American Jeff rolled into town 9 years ago claiming he had been chased out of Cincinnati for showing fist-fucking films. While his mannerisms, voice and image are frighteningly similar to Dick in the film Hi-Fidelity, Jeff's unique qualities come from his inexhaustible efforts at plotting his own world domination. Although he's still something of an enigma, virtually everyone in Brighton seems to know plenty of gossip about him, though mysteriously their stories never seem to tally. Over the years Jeff has been a filmmaker, writer, DJ, mime-artist and painter, and is currently trying his hand at music with his country band 'Welcome to Beaver Country'. Dressed in everything from bow tie, suit and woolly hat, to post-apocalyptic luminous overalls and wellies, Jeff can be found wandering the streets putting up posters or performing at the Lift. Love him or loathe him, Brighton would be a duller place without Jeff.

**20 points**

## Brian Mitchell

Brighton's answer to Tony Hancock, Brian can be spotted shuffling around the greasy spoon cafés of Brighton, fag in hand, and dressed in a three-button suit or corduroy (or both). Living in a 1950s bubble all of his own, Brian harps back to the days when everyone drank tea, ate bacon butties for breakfast, smoked filterless cigarettes, and only sailors had tattoos. Wonderfully at odds with the trendy side of Brighton, Brian has beavered away for years writing musicals, performing in comedy sketches and practicing turning alcoholism into an art form. With a laugh loud enough to stun a badger, he can easily be located in the dark at comedy events around town, although having been commissioned to script the new Basil Brush sitcom for the BBC (with his partner Joseph), he is solely to blame for bringing the catchphrase 'Boom, Boom' back into fashion. If approached, it's unwise to offer him a drink, but if you do, under no circumstances mention that you happen to like Laurel and Hardy, or you'll be cancelling all appointments for the next three days.

**30 points**

## Graham Duff

The ambling hulk of Graham Duff can often be seen in Brighton, ferreting around record shops in search of a vinyl fix and mumbling to himself as he experiments with his latest comic character. Sporting a beret, always at a daringly jaunty angle, he is one of Brighton's best-loved comedians and over the years has contributed extensively to radio, television and stage. He can even be heard DJing on Surf FMs Totally Wired show, and yet still finds time to run an orphanage.

Graham's previous exploits have included the 'A-Z of Drugs' (with James Poulter) which took a comedy slant on the pros and cons of narcotics. With two blokes travelling around the world with a suitcase full of herbal highs and a lot of time on their hands, however, the show became more and more about their own personal experiences. This followed with the 'A-Z of Taboo', covering all the ranges of sexual perversion. Again, with two blokes travelling around the world with a suitcase full of bondage gear and time to kill, you can probably guess the rest. Despite looking like a psychopath, Graham is really just a pussycat with a bald head.

**35 Points**

### Graham Duff tells the Carol Vorderman story

*'Well, this was years ago when I didn't know who she was, she was just on Countdown then, and I was in this comedy club in the North and I tried to chat her up. I liked the way she was dressed, you know, leather trousers and tight jumper…classic Vorderman.*

*I thought I'd pulled as we stood laughing at the final act together so I asked if she wanted to do half a tab of acid with me, and she didn't look too impressed. She ended up snogging the main act and going off with him instead.'*

When asked if it was offering her the acid that blew his chances, Graham cheekily replied,

*'Not necessarily…..I figured that maybe she was already sorted.'*

**LOCAL LEGENDS & ECCENTRICS**

## Neel

Found loitering around the photo booth in Brighton station late at night, invariably dressed as a Prozac tablet, Cluedo character or in his floral gimp outfit, Neel has devoted his life to pushing the boundaries of photo-booth possibilities.

Spending days on costumes, backdrops and make-up for each new project, Neel then saunters down to the station (sometimes with a bevy of monsters, film-stars and models) and gets to work.

One of his more 'unusual' photos has included him dressed as Trevor Jordash (the man buried under the patio in Brookside) the photo of which featured Neel with white make-up, zipped inside a body bag with a lump of fake concrete on his head. For another idea he redecorated the photo booth to look like the shower scene from 'Psycho' and had Gwen (from the shop Pussy) covered in water and blood peeping over a shower curtain playing a rather distressed Marion Crane. Naturally this attracted the attention of the police, who thought he was making a porn film.

Apart from getting a full-grown Dalmatian dog in the booth with him, Neel's most ambitious project to date came early in 2000 when he arranged his own funeral at Brighton Station. His reasoning being, *'I've always wanted a funeral party, and thought it a shame that I wouldn't be there to enjoy it with my friends.'*

The invite read: 'Everyone has to die one day...I'm just organised.' Having made himself a coffin, he then sent out invites to his 24 closest friends, asking each of them to come dressed as one of the many different characters required at a funeral. Vicars, undertakers, grieving widows, the Sally Army, a choir and even an Elvis impersonator all happily turned up, and after a bit of dutiful grieving and a speech by the deceased, one by one they all filed into the photo booth for their picture, ending with Neel, dressed as a corpse.

**35 points (60 if you end up in one of his photos)**

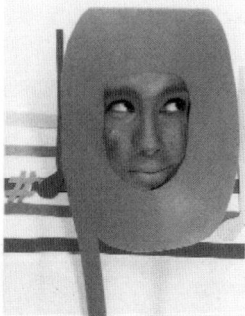

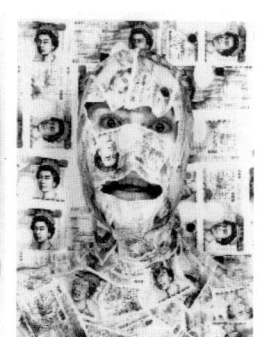

# LOCAL LEGENDS & ECCENTRICS

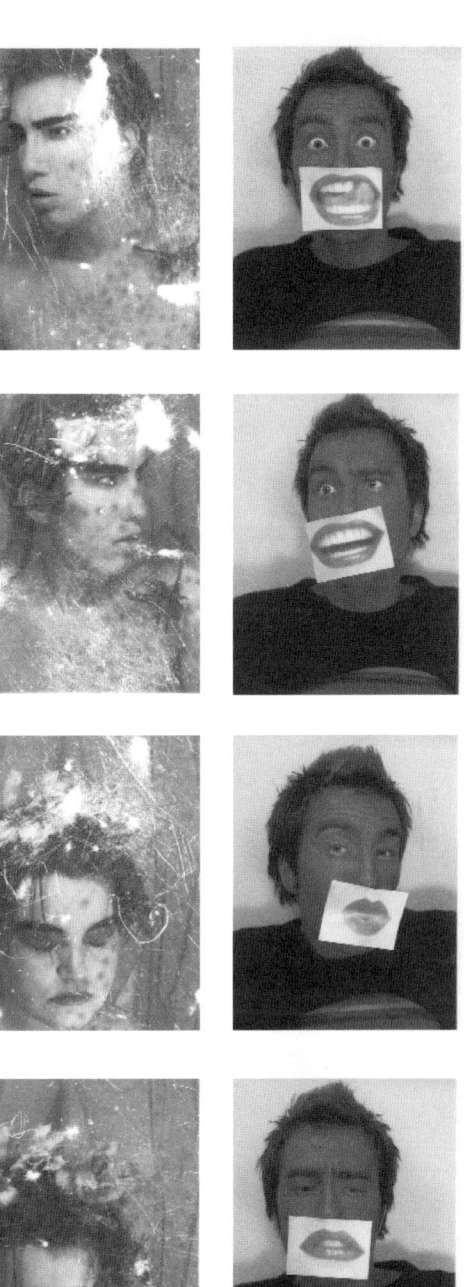

## Coopers For Haircuts

An appreciation by Dave Mountfield

Baker Street sweeps gracefully between the Art Déco majesty of London Road Co-op and that great stamping ground of the 8-Ace crowd, the Level. On this fine thoroughfare, opposite Bardsleys, the second best chip-shop in town*, can be found 'Coopers, Ladies' and Gentlemen's Hairdressers'.

To the casual passer by, there is little to give away the unusual nature of the establishment within, except the hand written sign saying 'haircut 120p', the fly-blown articles of a brave Desert Rat still cutting hair at 147, the bizarre, badly-toupeed voodoo dolls heads, the adverts for hair treatments preferred by Clark Gable, and the leering, swearing face of an ancient, tiny, goblin-like man staring at you.

But once you have entered the portal, an exciting new world of hairdressing possibilities awaits you.

To start with the décor: the stylish minimalism of Nicky Clarke has been banished in favour of a dark, dank, interior (linoleum themed) and with great attention to little details, such as the many years of dust and grime on every surface. Flies have been thoughtfully added to the terrifying open vat of pomade, last used when Dennis Compton was down playing Sussex in the County Championships of 1958. Lifestyle magazines have been replaced with informative right wing publications dealing with the Vietnam War, and the walls have been charmingly decorated with a seemingly random selection of items and cuttings.

In a style reminiscent of the Son of Sam, this image is re-enforced by the heady aroma of old man and cat piss, which pervades throughout.

The demographic make-up of Mr Cooper's clientele is predominantly the more mature gentleman, and thus cut styles run to a short-back-and-sides or the more raffish 'trim'.

**LOCAL LEGENDS & ECCENTRICS**

As I was, for many years, one of his younger customers, I was not always afforded the deference and politeness he extended to those some 50 years my senior. Mr Cooper would often point out quite brusquely that my hair was touching my collar and therefore 'long', and as such I was to be surcharged a further 20p. After demurely agreeing to this hike, he would point out how helpful it would be if "all these fucking hippy scroungers" could be rounded up and dealt with in various uncompromising ways. Egged on by his elderly colleagues, his diatribe would veer to the right of Mrs Thatcher, dealing succinctly and in pithy language with such issues as immigration, tax, the weather, gays, politicians, sporting figures and so on. I would lie back, as his trembling hands shaved my sideburns with a cut-throat razor, and listen to a golden stream of discourse and opinion. Of course, occasionally I would get a cut, more often than not a bald patch to boot, but it was worth it to hear this man talk! He will tell you he cut Field Marshall Montgomery's hair in World War Two, and even has cuttings from the Evening Argus (a publication of Papal infallibility) to prove it. If, however, you study photos of Rommel, the 'trim' looks eerily familiar.

These days I earn enough money to think nothing of spending up to £5 pounds or more on a haircut. But I still look back on those dole cut days with affection, and was saddened to see a closed sign for many months on Mr Cooper's door.

Imagine, then, my delight when recently I saw him back at his trade, cheerily swearing and dribbling on the top of another satisfied customer's head.

I unhesitatingly recommend a trip for an unusual but practical haircut, for as we are swept into the sea by a tide of homogenised Zel pubs and cleverly named eateries, this may be your last glimpse of a Brighton rapidly fading into legend.

*Let him who has wisdom know the best fish and chip shop in Brighton is on the Upper Lewes Road. See 'Best fish and chip shops' in the Food section

## LOCAL LEGENDS & ECCENTRICS

# Adventures with Brighton's most Eccentric Shopkeeper

These genuinely bizarre tales come from my own and others' experiences of Brighton's mysterious Mr. R, a sort of unhinged version of the shopkeeper from Mr. Ben. I heard recently of one customer, who, when discovered by Mr. R to only have 5p to his name, was offered a teaspoon of dried milk powder in exchange for his meagre bounty. Another acquaintance was refused entry to his shop on account that he was 'wearing the wrong buttons on his shirt', although Mr. R did kindly offer to sew on the correct ones, if he didn't mind waiting.

And finally, one customer was deeply perplexed when Mr. R started explaining to him how elephant skin waistcoats can be kept clean with white bread. Then mid-sentence he paused and said:

'But you know Sir, I just don't understand how elephants stay clean in Africa though, as there's no white bread out there.'

## FORNICATING BABOONS

*Hello, can I help you Sir?*
I'm just browsing thanks.
I start to weave my way around the bundles of suits hanging up in the shop. The shopkeeper follows close on my heels:
*Tell me Sir, why are the South Downs so cold?*
I beg your pardon?
*The South Downs Sir, why are they so cold?*
Er, well I don't know, I'm not a geography teacher.
*Aren't you Sir? May I ask what you are Sir?*
Well I…. I teach music sometimes.
*Do you Sir? Would you like to come upstairs and play my piano?*
Pardon?
*My piano Sir, it's upstairs. Would you care to play for me?*

I find myself saying 'yes, alright' and follow him upstairs into a room that is inconceivably packed with clothes and junk. In the corner there appears to be the remains of a piano, covered in dust and a whole array of paraphernalia. I take a heroic leap across the room and land near it. Getting the lid open is tricky owing to all the heavy objects on it. I get it half open and play a couple of notes. It is appallingly out of tune and I tell him. He does not appear to be listening, but instead is talking to a rack of ties in the corner of the room. He sees I have finished and says:

*Perhaps Sir would like to come back and give piano lessons here?*

I mutter something vaguely negative, but he continues unabated:

*My uncle Sir, was a famous violinist. Played to millions. Mantovani personally approved of him. Of course he's dead now. Buried underground. You could dig him up if you wanted to. But that wouldn't prove that he really played the violin though, would it?*

We move downstairs. At the bottom of the stairs he bends over to pick something up from behind a dense pile of suits. It's a book of English Politics from the 1960s. He opens it up and inside is his name and the year 1968:

*I'd like to go back to school Sir. I left when I was only 15, but I did win a prize once.*

I presume it's the book. It isn't. The reason for him bringing out the book in the first place is never made clear.

*We could have any book we wanted, so I asked for 'The Human Zoo' by Desmond Morris. Do you know him Sir?*

I nod.

*But the headmistress wouldn't allow it Sir, all those fornicating animals. Not Homo Sapiens, but animals Sir. We are Homo Sapiens aren't we Sir?*

What did that mean??
I nod.

*Of course I was nearly old enough to be a father Sir, but not old enough to look at pictures of fornicating baboons.* Pardon?
*Would you like to buy this book Sir?*

He motions to the book in his hand:

Isn't it special to you?
*No Sir, I've already read it. But I don't think that you could afford it Sir.*

A customer has been standing by the door now for five minutes.
I point this out to him. He doesn't look around but asks:

*What is your definition of a customer Sir?*

He moves away and faces the customer. It's an old guy with a jacket in his hand. He speaks slowly:

I bought this jacket from you and I'm happy with it but one of the buttons has come off.
*Well you can't be that happy with it can you Sir?* **He says nastily.**
I just want the button replaced. Have you got a button box?
*I'm sorry Sir, I don't understand.*
A button box.
*A button box Sir?*
Yes, a box with spare buttons in it.
*I'm sorry, I really don't understand. What is Sir's definition of a button?...*

## Some Velvet Morning

*Hello, can I help you Sir?*
Well I'm looking for a…
*Certainly Sir.*
And he leads me around the labyrinth, offering here a tweed overcoat, there cavalry pantaloons. Eventually I put my foot down and force the issue:
Actually I'm looking for a double-breasted velvet suit.
The world falls from around us and a heavy feeling hangs in the air.
*Velvet?*
Yes that's right, I say somewhat cautiously.
Black and double breasted.
*But……..velvet?*
Yes, but if you don't stock velvet I'll……
*Am I right in assuming Sir wants a suit?*
A man's suit? Made from...what was it......'velvet'?
Yes.

And suddenly noticing the very thing not a step away I pronounce - Like that one.
But it's too late.
*In all my years in the business, I've never heard of anything like it,* he says incredulously.
*A suit.*
*A man's suit!*
*MADE OF VELVET!!!*
I decide to cut my losses and ask for any suit, just to end the spiral of recriminations against velvet. The storm breaks.
*Of course Sir! I've just the thing.*
And with that he brandishes forth the crumbling apparel of Napoleon. The thing has epaulets, gold braid and jodhpurs!
As I'm hurriedly leaving I hear him say:
*Of course it is a little generous in the waist, but we could pad it out with citrus fruit no doubt......*

\*Thanks to Martin Johnson for supplying me with this tale

185

# Brighton in Books & Movies

## BRIGHTON IN THE MOVIES

### Brighton Rock
1947 Dir. John Boulting

Discover a Brighton of Bovril adverts and brylcreem. This classic Graham Greene story set in the 30s has plenty of scenes from the Old Lanes, Queens Road and the West Pier. Richard Attenborough plays Pinkie Brown, an evil small-time gangster who tries to cover up a murder by marrying a young girl who could give evidence against him. The ending is better in the book (aren't they always?) but it's a genuinely chilling account of the gangster scene that once flourished here. Doctor Who fans should look out for William Hartnell.

**Classic line from the film:**
*'People don't change, look at me. I'm like one of those sticks of rock. Bite all the way down and you still read Brighton.'*

### Quadrophenia
1979 Dir. Franc Roddam

Welcome to the Brighton of Triumph Heralds and Wimpy bars.
A troubled young Mod visits Brighton with his mates for a wild weekend but gets carried away. You know the story, I'm sure.

The fighting scenes take place on the beach and down East Street in front of the blue pub on the corner (the New Heart and Hand) that is now The Prodigal.

To find the famous alleyway where Jimmy and Steph had sex, go down East Street towards the sea, and near the end look for the shop LTS and a sign for an alleyway that reads 'to little East Street'. It's down there. This was once a graffitied Mod shrine, but all that seems to have gone now, and the next Mod revival is not due for another 10 years. Yes, the doorway is still there (now black) but it's locked, so no, you can't pop in and have a shag. Imagine how many people have tried though.

**Classic line from the film:**
*'I don't want to be like everyone else, that's why I'm a Mod see.'*

## Villain
1971 Dir. Michael Tuchner

This Richard Burton movie from the 70s is a tough bruising thriller with Burton playing a vicious gay criminal. Set in London, he does however find his way to Brighton to visit his dear old mother. But the game is eventually up when he gets nabbed by the fuzz on the West Pier.

## The Slade classic FLAME
1975 Dir. Richad Loncraine

Thanks to Ian for mentioning this particular gem to me. The plot charts the rise of Midland pub band Flame (played by the Brummie boys) who eventually become Glam superstars. Of course it all goes awry after one too many Babychams on tour, and ends with a brawl in the famous Grand Hotel. Look out for Tom Conte as the manager.

## Oh, What A Lovely War!
1969 Dir. Richard Attenborough

Attenborough's first movie is an over-ambitious and slightly pompous affair, telling the story of the First World War through allegory, mild satire and way too much singing. The West Pier is the platform for telling much of the story of the events leading up to the war, and the film also includes many fine shots of the seafront and the Downs.

Despite its many faults, it's an interesting piece of British movie history, with some occasionally stunning scenes. The scene in the trenches on Christmas day, when the Germans and English soldiers nervously meet in No Man's Land and share a drink, is a beautiful cinematic moment. The film also boasts an incredible cast, ranging from the thespian gods of Laurence Olivier and John Mills, right the way down to the Fairy Liquid Queen herself, Nanette Newman.

## The Fruit Machine
1988 Dir. Philip Saville

Gay drama set around the seedier tourist areas in Brighton. Shots of West Street, the amusement arcades and the Escape club.

---

### OTHERS TO LOOK OUT FOR
**Jigsaw**
1962 Dir. Val Guest
**Tommy**
1975 Dir. Ken Russell
**Mona Lisa**
1986 Dir. Neil Jordan
**Under Suspicion**
1992 Dir. Simon Moore

### AVOID LIKE THE PLAGUE
**Dirty Weekend**
1993 Dir. Michael Winner
**Circus**
2000 Dir. Rob Walker

---

## CARRY ON BRIGHTON
### Carry On Girls
1973 Dir. Gerald Thomas

**The Plot:**
Sid James is on the make as usual, this time as the buttock-slapping Councilor Fiddler who organises a beauty competition, only to be foiled by the sour-faced women's-libber June Whitfield.

Where in Brighton?

It all takes place in the pretend seaside town of Fircombe (oooerrr!!) which is in fact Brighton. The film features shots of the seafront, the West Pier and a fleeting glimpse of Regency Square.

My favourite bit of the film is near the end, when the contest goes awry and Sid James escapes down the West Pier in a go-kart whilst being chased by a crowd of angry men.

Look out for the outrageous gay stereotypes in the movie; there's the camp film director in flowery shirt and mincing walk, and June Whitfield's sidekick, a humourless lesbian who dresses like Hitler and hates men. They just don't make them like they used to.

**Trivia:**

This was the first Carry On film that had to go after the 9pm BBC watershed, as it was considered too saucy.

## Carry On At Your Convenience
1971 Dir. Gerald Thomas

**The Plot:**

Hailed as a Carry-On masterpiece, this tale of industrial strife and romance at WC Boggs toilet factory meant that the lavatorial gags could really let rip (ahem). And of course no Carry-On movie would be complete without Brighton's own Patsy Rowland (as sex-crazy secretary Miss Withering) trying to get into Kenneth Williams trousers as usual. I just don't think you were his type dear.

Starring Kenneth Williams as WC Boggs and Sid James as…Sid. Well, why make life difficult?

Where In Brighton?

The usual suspects take a bus trip down here, head for the Palace Pier and go on all the rides.

**Trivia:**

Alternative title for the film was 'Carry On Ladies Please Be Seated'.

# BRIGHTON AND THE WRITTEN WORD

## As Good As It Gets
Simon Nolan

Trendy novel about a bunch of Twenty-Somethings who find five kilos of coke and decide that they could find a better use for it than the police. Good descriptions of the pub and club culture in Brighton and some funny moments. Think Irvine Welsh on Prozac.

## Beatniks
Toby Litt

Tale of three modern day hippies who move to Brighton to start a magazine called 'Café Bohemia' but all end up in bed together instead. The book tries hard to be hip (but fails) and the descriptions of Brighton are all a bit clichéd. Strangely enough, a Café Bohemia, opened up in Kemptown just as the book was released.

## BOOKS AND MOVIES

### Breakfast in Brighton
Nigel Richardson

Having almost made a legend out of one of the grottiest, least known pubs in Brighton (the Grosvenor) Nigel Richardson has, with this book, weaved a meandering but insightful account of his time spent with the town's motley collection of old actors, fishermen and improbable landladies. The plot may be rather scant but it doesn't really matter, if you love Brighton you'll enjoy the read.

### Queenspark Books

This local publishing company put out a range of books on the theme of local people's stories. Such gems include:
Moulsecoomb Memoirs
Tales from the Fishing Community

### Brighton Rock
Graham Greene

See film guide

### Hangover Square
Patrick Hamilton

Companion to 'Brighton Rock', detailing the sleaze and vitality of London and Brighton of the late 30s.

### The Snowman
Raymond Briggs

Christmas wouldn't be the same without this kids' tale, brought alive every year through the magic of television and the lilting tones of a Welsh eunuch. Written and set locally, next time it's on look out for the flying scene and you should see the snowman and the boy sail over Brighton Pavilion and the Pier.

## BOOKS AND MOVIES

### The Vending Machine of Justice
Simon Nolan

Simon Nolan seems to like writing comedies set around Brighton and here's another one, this time based around Hove crown court and involving a bizarre case and a few local zombies. I confess I haven't read this one but anyone that starts their novel with a quote from Hancock deserves a read.

## LITERARY EVENTS
### Do Tongues

Brighton's longest established spoken word pioneers, have, over the years, put on some remarkable performances by the likes of Ken Campbell, Jah Wobble and Will Self. I think one of my favourite memories of Do Tongues was seeing a guy called Jim Dodge from the States who entertained about 10 of us upstairs in the Mash Tun one night with a story about his dog getting its testicles stuck in the bathtub. It was one of those priceless evenings where you wouldn't be anywhere else for the world. Not as active as they used to be, owing, I believe, to its founder Polly Marshall moving into the world of playwriting. Will it be running for another year? I don't know. Look out for posters or ask Annie in Waterstones, she's always clued up on these kinds of things.

*Both Borders and Waterstones also put on spoken word evenings every month and Borders put out a monthly leaflet with a full list of events including music. Look out for their fliers in the shops or around town.*

### BRIGHTON AUTHORS
**Bertie Marshall**
Queercore Literature
**Helen Zahave**
Dirty Weekend
**Ian Marchant**
In Southern Waters
**Jack Sargent**
Deathtripping
(Cinema Of Transgression)
**Jay Merrick**
Horse Latitude
**Keith Waterhouse**
Billy Liar
Jeffrey Bernard Is Unwell
**Lynne Truss**
Going Loco/ Tennyson's Gift
**Mick Casey**
Kings of the Beach

*And with the recent arrival of the excellent cult writer Jeff Noon to Brighton, it neatly balances having Julie Burchill in our midst. If you don't know his stuff, try Automated Alice, Pollen, or Needle in the Groove, they are all terrific.*

# The Gay Scene

Ever since the 1900s, Brighton has been home to an ever-expanding gay scene. Secretive at first, but now very much integrated into the town, it has grown to become the UK's most celebrated gay community, second only to London.

The town's theatrical history is deemed to be one of the main factors that helped kick-start the scene, as earlier in the century big gay icons like Ivor Novello and Noel Coward lived here for some time, helping make Brighton a magnet for this secretive community. Thanks to this, and to Brighton's already well-established reputation as a fashionable pleasure capital, the scene flourished. Of course, with places like 'Dyke Close' and signs like 'A friendly welcome greets you in the Queen's Arms', it seemed the obvious choice for the gay community to have its headquarters.

From the 60s onwards, the gay community has developed around Kemptown and the Old Steine. This is where the majority of Brighton's gay population now live and socialise. You will find most of the gay bars, clubs, bookshops and saunas here, especially around St. James's Street.

Many of the gay haunts in Kemptown were developed for cruising, but as it's getting so much easier to be out in Brighton now, in recent years the gay population has been branching into other areas. A small, but growing, percentage of the gay population is now integrating into the old Brunswick Town area in Hove, which is fast becoming a new gay hot spot.

There are now believed to be 25,000 gay men and 10-15,000 lesbians living in Brighton, and the scene is growing by over 2000 gay men and women a year.

## THE GAY SCENE

### PUBS AND CLUBS

## FASHIONABLE NEW GAY BARS

### Amsterdam
11-12 Marine Parade (01273) 688825

European-style bar on the seafront, next to the Escape and attracting a large, mixed gay crowd. Arguably, Amsterdam is an important change in Brighton's gay scene, in that it's very up-front and not just for cruising. The huge patio overlooking the sea is a priority spot to sit and watch the chickens on a hot summer's day.

### Charles Street
8-9 Marine Parade, Brighton

Elegant new bar based on their London version (Rupert Street). It wasn't open at time of going to press, but with friendly management (Jimmy) and all the money being thrown at it, this promises to be a very popular hang-out.

### Coopers Cask
Farm Road, Hove

One of a new breed of gay-run, gay-friendly pubs, with a young, integrated, mixed crowd. Always busy, their policy of table service, sweets at the end of the night and caring staff, make 'Coopers' popular among the easy-going gay and straight community. Look out also for their other bars, The Druids and The Hop Poles, for more of the same.
(See Pub Section review).

### Dr Brighton's
16 Kings Road (01273) 328765

One of the coolest gay bars in town and particularly popular at weekends, especially with the pre-club crowd (Revenge, the Zap and The Beach are all within a 5 minutes walk). It is mainly a male gay bar, but straight friendly and welcoming to lesbians. If you think it looks inviting from the outside, you won't be disappointed when you go in, the atmosphere is always lively and warm, even though the sign above the bar says: *'No Camping'!*

## LOCAL GAY BARS

### The Aquarium
6 Steine Street (01273) 605525

Simple but busy back-street bar, with a mixed male oriented gay crowd.

### Bedford Tavern
30 Western Street, Hove (01273) 739495

Tucked away in Hove, and somewhat off the beaten track, this bar has a regular crowd of predominantly older local gay men. The décor leaves a lot to be desired (were brass pistols ever fashionable?) but since last year's review at least someone has cleared out the fish tank. Finding the two microscopic denizens of the deep that live there now, however, is another matter. Tune in next year for another aquatic update.

### The Bulldog
31 St. James's Street
(01273) 684097

One of the most established gay bars, in the heart of Kemptown, though the hip and trendy front is slightly deceiving, since this is mostly an older man's drinking pub. The Bulldog boasts, with good cause, that it has the most Happy Hours in Brighton. On weekends, between 8-11pm, the upstairs becomes a leather heaven night called Dark Angels. Not recommended for vegetarians or animal lovers.

## THE GAY SCENE

### Pink Panther
25 Bristol Gardens
(01273) 299763

The Pink Panther has put in a lot of effort to disassociate itself from the days when it used to be the Clyde Arms, a haven for violence, drugs and poor-quality meat pies. Owner Barry has instead turned it into a thriving new bar, which seems to have enticed some of the lesser-known gay heroes back onto the scene. With entertainment every day, including quality cabaret on the weekends, this comes highly recommended.

### Queens Head
10 Steine Street
(01273) 602939

Recently refurbished, this tricky to find back alley pub is still frequented by the older gay community, and is a well-known Brighton landmark for its fabulous Freddy Mercury pub-sign.

### Regency Tavern
32-34 Russell Square
(01273) 325652

Indisputably the campest pub in town, but not wanting to shout about it. Worth a visit at weekends, just to see the décor and the barman's shirt. (See pub reviews)

### Royal Standard
Queen's Road, Brighton

Located a stone's throw from the station and probably the most central gay friendly pub in Brighton. Great Sunday lunches, and not too cruisy.

### White Horse
Telford Street, Brighton

Not the most exciting venue in town, but it does serve as a useful pre-club bar for all those glamour-pussies on their way to the Zap on a Friday.

# THE GAY SCENE

## CABARET & KARAOKE HEAVEN

### Legends Bar
31-32 Marine Parade
(01273) 624462

Attached to the New Europe Hotel, this place attracts a mature crowd for its regular karaoke and cabaret. On Fridays and Saturdays, downstairs is home to the leather-only Schwartz bar, where there are frequent fisticuffs with the Dark Angels, over the right to hang the 'Home of the Village People' plaque.

### The Oriental
5 Montpelier Road
(01273) 728808

Though this is all that's left of the western end of the gay scene, since the demise of the Beacon Royal Hotel, it's still a popular locals' bar with regular cabaret and plenty of karaoke.

### Queen's Arms
7 George Street (01273) 696873

Traditional pub with more or less constant entertainment. From cabaret to karaoke, no matter when you arrive, there is always something lively about to happen.

## TRANSVESTITE BARS

### Harlequin
(Formerly Ruby's, Marilyns, Charlotte's and Tony's Discount Toolshop)
43 Providence Place (01273) 620630
Late license 2am, Closed Sundays

Hidden behind Woolworths off the London Road, this is (to my knowledge) the only transvestite-friendly bar in Brighton. Started by the king of camp, Danny La Rue, this whole place is a real flashback to the 80s. During the week there is cabaret in the large, glittery bar area upstairs, which sometimes includes some pretty wild drag acts and karaoke. It also attracts quite a few lesbian couples and generally caters for an older crowd, who seem to know each other quite well. Worth a visit, whatever your choice of dress.

## CLUBS

### Club Revenge
32-43 Old Steine (01273) 606064

The biggest gay club on the South coast, open six nights a week with special events, drinks promotions and strip-shows. Sure, you will find the inevitable cliques, but don't be put off, you should still be able to meet new people here. And with all those body beautifuls sweating it out on the upstairs dance-floor, you shouldn't find it hard to get into the contagious party atmosphere. Be nice to the sexy and flirty bar-staff, they are your best port of call to find out everything about the hottest bars and parties.

## Pool Club
(Upstairs from Charles St)
8-9 Marine Parade

This brand new club opened in December 2000 on the sacred ground of Brighton's sadly missed Heavy Metal Valhalla, the Hungry Years. If news doesn't reach the London metal community in time, we can enjoy seeing groups of metal morons coming down for the weekend and discovering a whole new meaning to the notion of having studs on your back.

## Secrets
5 Steine Street
(01273) 609672

Located just behind Scene 22, this place plays a selection of trashy handbag and dance music and attracts a regular young weekend crowd. The club is split into separate levels, so if you don't feel like dancing, you can hang out upstairs with a less deafening soundtrack.

During the week, it is a popular socialising spot for young and old gay men, and their special evenings include cabaret and a snakes and ladders night. Is this a new euphemism I haven't come across yet?

---

# CAN'T FIND WHAT YOU'RE LOOKING FOR?

## TRY CARDOME 2000
47A ST. JAMES'S STREET 'PHONE 01273 692916
(NEXT DOOR TO ROYAL OAK PUB)

Open 10.30 - 18.00 Monday to Saturday

**Adult mags and cards
Hand made cards by local artists
Greeting cards
Glassware and gifts
Candles, insense and much more**

---

# BRIGHTON OASIS SAUNA

2 SAUNAS
STEAM ROOM
12 MAN WHIRLPOOL
EMBALMING ROOM
RELAXATION ROOMS
QUALIFIED MASSEURS
HEATED SWIMMING POOL
RAPID TAN - VERTICAL SUN ROOM
PHARAOH'S FOOD & COFFEE BAR
(Also open to non sauna users)

Opening Hours
Monday to Thursday 12 noon to 10pm
Friday
12 noon to 4am
Saturday 12 noon to 6am
(by public demand)
Breakfast Available
Sunday 12 noon to Midnight

Friday & Saturday
Entry £7 From 1 am
Re-Entry Pass Available Every Day

75-76 Grand Parade
Brighton, BN2 2JA
Tel: 01273 689966
www.oasissauna.com

# THE GAY SCENE

**BRIGHTONS ONLY GAY SHOP & COFFEE BAR**
129 ST James Street, Brighton. Telephone: 01273 626682

### Zanzibar
129 St. James's Street
(01273) 622100
Mon-Sat 7pm-2am, happy hour 7pm-10pm daily

It's small, busy and full of chickens. Great place for drinking Monday-Wednesday when its free to get in. Weekends are very busy, so plan to go early.

## SPECIAL CLUB NIGHTS
### Sunday Sundae
Bar Centro, 2-6 Ship Street
(01273) 206580

Describing itself as 'Brighton's tea dance for gay men and lesbians', this early Sunday club-night kicks off at 6pm, playing up-front club anthems and classic disco, and hosted by the very lovely Miss Marilyn. Loved by many, hated by others, Sunday Sundae seems to have found its place comfortably in between DB's and the Honeyclub on the Sunday night circuit.

### Kinky Booty
Every Friday at the Honeyclub

An evening of Funk, House and Garage, hosted by Miss Bossy Boots and Miss Kinky, with resident DJs Neil Silk Roden and Adam-H. The music gets a littler harder as the night goes on (or is that the audience?). Brought to you by the folks at Wild Fruit.

## CAFES/ FOOD
### Scene 22
St. James's Street (01273) 626682

Scene 22 is a popular first stop for gays and lesbians coming to Brighton, and its owner Freddie is a real charmer, who seems to have endless time for anyone who drops in. It's amusing just to listen to the banter between him and the regular customers, as the saucy double-entendres flow thick and fast. There you go, I'm at it now.

Scene 22 is also a good place to find information on health matters, and pick up free maps and magazines. You can even make hotel bookings, collect tickets for shows, and leave messages on the notice board for anything (or anyone) you fancy.

Don't forget to have a nose around the shop in the back, it sells your usual toys, lubes, vibrators and other goodies, and don't be surprised if Freddie manages to persuade you into buying a kit to make your cock ten times bigger. It's his way of saying that he likes you.

### Fudges
127 Kings Road, Brighton (01273) 205852
First Sunday each month £20
This special event is a late Sunday lunch (6.30pm) in this lovely seafront restaurant with a bevy of cabaret performers to keep away those Monday morning blues.

### Drag Queens
Brighton's most glamorous drag-queen, Lady Laverne, can be found hosting Saturday nights at the Honeyclub, and recommends that the best places to show off your new frock and high heels are still Kinky Booty at the Honeyclub (Fridays), The Pussycat Club at The Zap (Fridays), Vavavoom!, Revenge, and, of course, Wild Fruit.

## CRUISING AREAS

### Duke's Mound
Located 10 min walk east of the pier, overlooking the nudist beach
This area in Brighton is essentially a small hillside of bushes on the seafront, which has become an integral part of the cruising scene. It offers enough privacy for those needing it, yet is risqué enough for you naughty exhibitionists. While it isn't that commonly reported, there are occasional stories of people getting mugged and robbed after being picked up and taken to Dukes Mound, so be careful.

### Nudist Beach
Located 10 min east of the Palace Pier
Brighton's nudist beach is primarily a gay haunt. Straights are welcome but in most cases will feel slightly uneasy, especially if confronted by the old bloke who does windmill impressions with his erection. There is a lot of parading, plenty of stiffies and a whole host of voyeurs.

### Hove Lawns
Opposite Brunswick Square
Increasingly popular cruising area for gay men, especially on Sunday evenings. There is a lot less cover here than at Duke's Mound, but it's a nice place to hang out (ooo...er) especially with the soon-to-be-rebuilt Meeting House Café nearby.

### Shoreham Beach
It seems that every once in a while the 'authorities that be' pick a new area that they earmark as a good place for cruising. This year Shoreham Beach was the suggestion, but to be honest, it's a bit of a hike for what might be just a couple of

## THE GAY SCENE

salty seadogs and a bent accordion player. I do, however, hear that the adventure playground in Hollingbury is a denizen of lonely hunks....

## SAUNAS

*Used as social clubs in Brighton by the gay community, these saunas attract a wide age group and all come with rest room facilities.*

### Brighton Oasis
75-76 Grand Parade (01273) 689966

Opposite the Pavilion and done out in a glorious Egyptian theme, this is one of the newest and nicest saunas in Brighton.

There is a whirlpool, steam room, sun beds, coffee shops and qualified masseurs. During the week it is £11 to get in, although at the weekend it is only £7 (after 1am) and that includes in and out privileges for the day (whey-hey missus!). Get your pass at the door before you leave.

### Amsterdam Hotel
11-12 Marine Parade
(01273) 688825

New sauna offering steam room, showers and many darkrooms. This is open to the public and at £5 a time seems remarkably good value for money. Open until 6am.

## Hanky Panky

*Developed in the days when secrecy was necessary, the coloured hankie in the back pocket is still used in some bars for gay men to express their sexual preferences.*

**Yellow Hankie** Into water-sports
**Red Hankie** Into fist fucking*
**Green Hankie** Into the washing machine it goes for a good clean

### KEY CHAINS
**Worn on the Left** – Active
**Worn on the Right** – Passive
**Hundreds of keys on one key-chain** – Geek

*In the left back pocket means you like taking, right back pocket means you like giving. Or is it the other way around? Oh well, you'll find out one way or another.

## Understanding the Lingo

*Polari, as it is called, stretches back to the 1950s when it was still illegal to be gay (unless involved in theatre, where it was compulsory). This slang language enabled gay folk to get on with matters at hand without fear of persecution. Legend decrees that it started with Julian and Sandy on the radio show 'Round The Horne' and by the 1970s had evolved into such an esoteric and bizarre tongue, that Oliver Postgate used it in the Clangers to send secret messages to many of his gay lovers around the UK.*

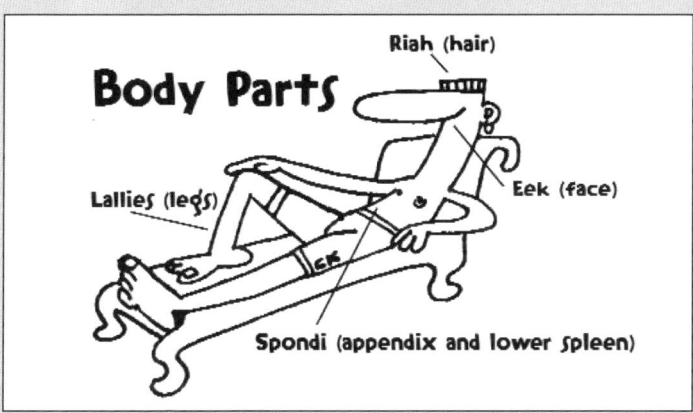

**Body Parts**
- Riah (hair)
- Lallies (legs)
- Eek (face)
- Spondi (appendix and lower spleen)

### Bona palone / homi
Dictionary says – Good looking woman/man
Eg. That bloke from the Cheeky Guide, what a bona homi!

### Chicken
Dictionary says – Hunky young men.
Eg. Check out the chicken outside the Young Conservatives Club.

### Trade
Dictionary says – Your pick-up for the evening.
Eg. Take your trade home and give him something to remember you by.

### Varda
Dictionary says – To check out.
Eg. Varda the legs on him/ her/ that lovely Regency sofa.

### Cruising
Dictionary says – Sail to and fro for protection of shipping, making for no particular place or calling at a series of places.
Hmmm, that just doesn't seem to be what's going on in the bushes.

**THE GAY SCENE**

## THE LESBIAN SCENE

*For years the lesbian scene in Brighton has been almost non-existent, which is strange considering the large numbers who live here. Although in principle most of the gay bars welcome lesbians, few venture in. Recently however, a social scene for gay women has started to develop in Brighton. The first lesbian-run pub, The Marlborough, has been running for three years now, and with several club-nights and the arrival of the Candy Bar, things seem at last to be changing.*

## BARS/CLUB NIGHTS

### Candy Bar
33 St James's Street, Brighton
(01273) 622424
Mon-Sat 11am-11pm, Sun 12-10.30pm

Continuing in the fantastic footsteps of their Soho Bar, the recently opened Candy Bar is what the women of Brighton have been screaming for (well some of them anyway). This local café-bar has two floors for your pleasure: the main floor is bright and airy, and the downstairs is... well.... dark brown.

Other than a good CD player, there are no immediate plans for entertainment, but with fine company, a selection of cocktails and good food, who needs K.D.Lang? Open to anyone during the day, but after 5pm it's generally woman only, although gay males won't be turned away.

### Marlborough
4 Princes Street (01273) 570028

Tucked away behind the Old Steine, this is one of Brighton's main lesbian-friendly bars, and although recently bought out by Zel, they seem to be keeping it pretty much the same. Well-known for its little theatre upstairs, the pub still puts on plays, comedy nights and other events, especially during the festival, and is a good place to pick up gay magazines and information.

There are two bars, a lively one with a pool table and a quieter one at the side. Popular nights are Tuesdays and Thursdays for students, and at the weekend the bar gets very busy with mixed crowds and occasional DJs. Known to be one of Brighton's most haunted pubs, the ghost of Lucy Packham occasionally pops her head round for a quick game of pool, but cheats by dropping her eyes down the corner pockets.

### Fresh
Friday nights at the Royal Pavilion Tavern
Castle Square (01273) 827641

A popular lesbian night in Brighton, though possibly past its prime. It caters for all ages, and still attracts young dressy crowds who have a reputation for knowing how to knock back the booze.

### Shebeen
(Formerly at the Hanbury Arms)
The Sanctuary Café, 51-55 Brunswick Street East (01273) 770002
For dates and details call
(01273) 738712 / 327442

Strictly enforced women-only night 'appealing to sassy, classy gals' every Wednesday, 8pm-late.

The flavour of this successful night seems to change every month. Events have included pop-quizzes, performances, birthday parties, singing, poetry and erotic dancing. It's even known to have the occasional appearance by the only 'out' lesbian belly dancer in the UK. Check G-scene for the latest details.

# Revenge

www.revenge.co.uk

## MONDAY
**MANTRAP**

Two strippers *plus* Alan Thorn plays house & dance

## TUESDAY
**SHAKEDOWN**

Eurodance & Chart *plus* **DRINKS PROMO**

## WEDNESDAY
**fun house!**

Cabaret *plus* Mr Ron plays disco & chart **DRINKS PROMO**

## THURSDAY
**D.I.S.C.O**

Mr Ron plays disco & chart *plus* stripper

## FRIDAY
**LOLLIPOP**

**3** drag hags
**2** DJ's play 70's-90's tunes
**1** hell of a night!

## SATURDAY
**CHOYCE CHOONZ**

Level 1: Nik C plays commercial chart & handbag

Level 2: Dizzy plays house

Monday - Thursday 10:30pm - 2am, Friday & Saturday 10pm - 2am

Regular cabaret — Regina Fong

Lollipop Fridays

Pooh la May — Lollipop Hostess

Regular strippers — Stallion

Angie Brown — Regular cabaret

Lollipop Fridays

Revenge is a club for gays and lesbians

32 -34 Old Steine, Brighton - 01273 606064

Keeping it sweet six nights a week

# THE GAY SCENE

## SPECIAL EVENTS

### Pride
August 11th 2001
Preston Park

Attended by just 100 people when it first started, 'Pride' quickly expanded to become one of the biggest highlights in Brighton's Gay calendar. Gay and straight men and women from all over the country turn up for this annual bash, which includes floats, bands, costumes, cabaret, stalls, shows and more. It's simply fantastic, so don't miss it. The march usually starts at 1pm from the Peace Statue and dances, shouts and parades its way to the Park, stopping only for a sandwich and glass of fizzy pop at the Woolworths café on the way. Look out this year for a great after-show party from Wild fruit.

### Ms Brighton Alternative
Oddly, this didn't happen in 2000, and wasn't confirmed for 2001 at time of going to print, but, along with Pride, this has been an unmissable day in Brighton's gay calendar. Different performers, loads of false boobies, never enough make-up and only one winner. Check with G-Scene to see if it's happening.

## SHOPS

### Cardome
47A St James's Street (01273) 692916
Open 10am-6pm Mon-Sat
cardome@col.com

A wonderful cross between a local craft market, WH Smith and a sex shop, Cardome also proudly lays claim to being Brighton's oldest established gay shop (now in its 16th or 17th year and still going strong). This is a good place to come for greeting cards

# THE GAY SCENE

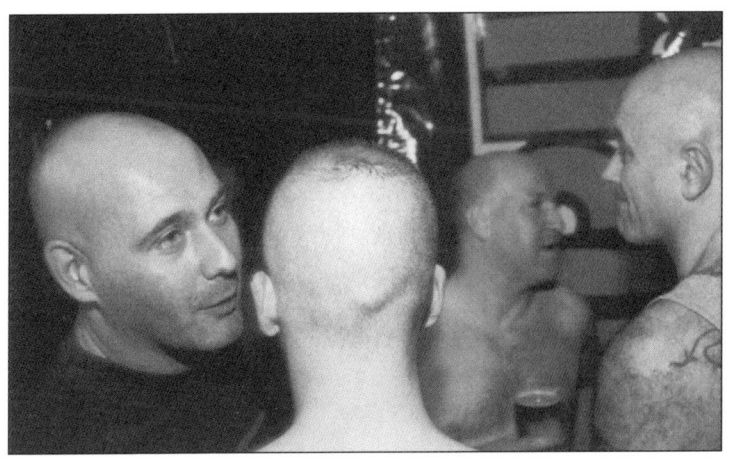

(gay and straight), local hand-made art, jungle juice and much more. In the back room (and soon to be moved to the basement) is a wide range of pornographic magazines. The majority are gay but there's also a wide range of mags for rubber fetishists, TVs, SMs, and even a fair bit of hetro stuff as well. Plans are afoot for other saucy goings on in the basement, and charming owner Mike will fill you on any discreet questions you may have about all aspects of the sex scene in Brighton.

## CloneZone
St James's Street (01273) 626442
Open Mon-Thurs 11am-7pm, Fri-Sat 11am-9pm, Sun 12pm-6pm

Selling a range of toys, videos, fashion, cards and rubber-wear, this is definitely a good place to come and get stocked up for a weekend of unashamed wickedness. They also have a modest selection of music CDs from the likes of Hazel Dean, and a particularly wide range of magazines, including Latin Inches and Euroboy. If only there was 'Pale Northerner Monthly' I might get myself some employment. Never mind.

## OUT!
Dorset Street
Open Mon-Thurs 10am-6pm
Fri-Sat 10am-7pm, Sun 11am-5pm

Quiet little back-street bookshop, offering a fantastic selection of gay literature. If you're after magazines, critical theory or fiction, it's definitely worth seeking out.

## The Pink Pamper
74 St James's Street, Brighton
(01273) 608060
info@thepinkpamper.co.uk

Located on the corner of Rock Gardens and St James's Street, the Pink Pamper sets out to follow its name, and pamper the Pink. Upstairs is a small café, lounging area and hairdressing area, while downstairs is the cross dressing... I mean beauty therapy area. Therapies include; massage, eyelash tinting, aromatherapy, reflexology and Indian head massage. Brighton has been sadly lacking in men-only beauty treatment outlets, and the Pink Pamper fills the void. Facial anyone??

## THE GAY SCENE

**Scene 22** (See café section)
Good collection of magazines from the ever loveable Freddie: '….uh hu honey....uh hu...'

## WEBSITES & MAGAZINES

### www.f-f.org.uk
Locally-based lesbian mail-order website for the 'modern lesbian lifestyle'.

The site is easy to get around and is clear and informative, with plenty to buy, ranging from books, sex toys and videos to leather gear. Although when I had a peep at their bondage site it only had bondage tape for sale, which rather scuppered my plans for a last minute birthday present for a relative. As well as all this, there are some great links to other sites, including several gay Brighton websites and even a lesbian rock band homepage.

### www.gtbrighton.com
Brand new website for the Brighton gay community. Features detailed pub and club listings, forums for chat and plenty of local information. Well-designed, easy to use and plenty of content.

### www.brightonpride.co.uk
Every year Brighton comes alive for this fantastic celebration of gay rights. The festival is certainly one of the main highlights of the Brighton calendar, and should not be missed.

The site is loaded with information with everything you could want to know about the day itself.

### G-Scene Magazine
The gay and lesbian bible for your time in Brighton (along with the Cheeky guide of course) with previews of all the special club nights, up-to-date information, health and community issues, restaurant reviews and personal ads. And amazingly, it's free.

## IMPORTANT INFORMATION

### Safe sex?
Condoms are given free almost everywhere in Brighton, yet still they don't appear to get used. Don't bury your head in the sand, the HIV and AIDS numbers are on the increase again here, yet 'it won't happen to me' is all some guys seem to be thinking. Thankfully most gay prostitutes in Brighton do enforce the condom rule. Just remember, sex is as safe as you're prepared to make it, so wrap up your peckers guys.

### Problems Against Gays Here?
The scene is a big part of the town's life, and most people in Brighton are totally cool and supportive of the gay community. Like anywhere, however, a certain amount of bigotry and homophobia exists.

Violence against gays has been on the increase recently (especially St James's Street at weekends) and although it's sad to have to say it, be careful when you are walking at night. Try and avoid snogging in the middle of West Street at 2am in the morning, and you should be OK.

# BRIGHTON'S EXCITING GAY VENUE

## AMSTERDAM

## Brighton
### BAR · HOTEL · SAUNA

**BRIGHTON'S EXCITING NEW GAY VENUE**
**LARGE PATIO AREA - VIEWS OVER PIER**

## THE HEART OF BRIGHTON'S GAY VILLAGE
**BE THERE**
**EVERYONE ELSE WILL BE**
EVERYONE WELCOME

N.U.S STUDENTS - 1/2 PRICE SAUNA ENTRY

## AMSTERDAM
11 - 12 MARINE PARADE, BRIGHTON
TEL 01273 - 688825 FAX 688828

## GAY ORGANISATIONS

### Gay, Lesbian, Arts, Media (GLAM)
44-46 Old Steine, Brighton
(01273) 707963

GLAM run excellent courses and productions for the gay community. They do everything from Photography to Multimedia design and also perform the occasional stunning play.

Look out this summer for their play 'The Scoobies!', based on the cult cartoon series. The plot goes that while visiting Velma's relatives (Virginia Woolf and Oscar Wilde) the gang get embroiled in a mystery; the ghost haunting the hills of Devil's Dyke.

Having seen the play already, I can vouch that it is a rollercoaster ride of gender-bending, double-entendres and some great comic acting.

Because of its popularity, 'The Scoobies' is taking to the road on a tour throughout the UK in 2001, which will culminate at the Edinburgh Fringe Festival. We wish them well.

### Madison Travel Worldchoice
(Gay Travel)
118 Western Road, Hove (01273) 202532
www.madisontravel.co.uk

Friendly gay travel agent in Hove. Fully bonded and highly recommended.

## SUPPORT GROUPS

### Brighton's Women's Centre
Lettice House, 10 St. George's Mews, off Trafalgar Street (01273) 600526

Offering supportive help and information in a friendly atmosphere. Their services range from accommodation boards, use of photocopier and computer, to free pregnancy tests, creche, counselling and legal advice.

### Speak out
Scene 22 (One Monday per month)
Call Freddie on (01273) 626682 for more details

Good supportive atmosphere for discussing problems going on in the gay community.

## SUPPORT NUMBERS

### Brighton Lesbian and Gay Switchboard
(01273) 204050

Support and information for lesbians and gay men between 6pm-11pm nightly.

### Brighton Lesbian / Gay Community Centre
(01273) 234005

Information centre and informal support on lesbian and gay issues. Mon-Fri 10am-12noon.
Drop in Thursday 12noon-4pm, women only on Friday 12noon-4pm

### Brash
(01273) 293632 or (0973) 873715

Group meetings for young gay and bisexual men.

### Brighton Relate
(01273) 697997

Specialist advice for lesbian and gay relationships.

### HIV Related Support
Open Door
(01273) 605706

Support, referrals, advice, meals, therapies for HIV.
Mon-Fri 10am-4pm.

### Gay Men's Health Matters
(01273) 625222

Information about HIV and sexual health, free condoms given.

**Brighton and Hove HIV Project Bureau**
(01273) 327474
Employment, benefits, money and housing information. By appointment only Tuesday and Thursday 9am-4pm, Wednesday 9am-12.30pm.

**Brighton Body Positive**
(01273) 693266
Complementary therapies, information, support, and counselling for HIV/AIDS.

**Street Outreach Service (SOS)**
(01273) 625577
Mobile AIDS prevention unit, lots of advice, free condoms and lube.

**Claude Nicol Centre**
(01273) 664721
Testing and treatment for HIV (Same day results on Mon-Tue). Free and confidential service.

**Wilde Clinic**
(01273) 664722
Gay and Bisexual men's health clinic offering HIV testing, STI testing and treatment, hepatitis A & B vaccinations.

## Gay Hotels

**Alpha Lodge**
New Stein, Off St James's Street
(01273) 609632

**Amsterdam Hotel**
Marine Parade (01273) 688828

**Avalon**
**Upper Rock Gardens**
(01273) 692344

**Bannings**
(Women) Upper Rock Gardens
(01273) 681403

**Boydens**
St James's Street (01273) 601914

**Catnaps**
Atlingworth Street (01273) 685193

**Cowards**
Upper Rock Gardens
(01273) 692677

**Four Seasons**
(Women) Upper Rock Gardens
(01273) 673574

**Hudsons**
Devonshire Place (01273) 683642

**New Europe**
Marine Parade (01273) 624462

**Nineteen**
Broad Street (01273) 675529

**Roland Rat House**
College Street, Kemptown
(01273) 603693

**White House**
Bedford Street, off Marine Parade
(01273) 626266

# THE NEVER ENDING STORY

Having grown up in the slums of Kensington, Shandy always dreamed of escaping to somewhere exotic. So, when her father got a job teaching colonic irrigation to young offenders in Brighton, she knew this was her chance to really find herself. Within 3 weeks she had enrolled at the Art College, got a part-time job at the Mash Tun and had her labia tattooed. Everything was perfect, except for just one thing... love.

"...Jim just goes clubbing on his own these days, Tasha. He was at the Goth night at the Gloucester yesterday, and he came home raving about the sonic craftsmanship of early Fields of the Nephilim records. I can't understand it."

*That's because he's secretly shagging me you dozy cow.'*

Her parents, Moonbeam and Tizer, were 60s acid-casualties, and a constant source of embarrassment...

One morning...

Shandy darling, I accidentally set the washing machine to 500 degrees and seem to have shrunk all your clothes.

Oh mother you preposterous New Age hag. I hate you, I hate you, I hate you!!

Don't worry darling, there are some lovely charity shops up the London Road, I'll pop out and get you something nice to wear for college.

An hour later...
I bought you this lovely taffeta dress and suede booties, just like those nice girls in the Human League used to wear.
AAAAAAGGGGHHHH!!!!
As the 80s revival was not due for another year in Brighton, Shandy looked a real trollop. Down Sydney Street many attractive, fashionable young people made cruel remarks about her fashion mistakes.
Yeah Dave, hu hu!!
'ere Dave there must be a troglodyte convention at the Brighton Centre today.

At college...
Arts
University of Brighton
You look like a complete dog today Shandy, that's it, you're chucked.
SUDDEN CONVERSION TO GOTH LOOK
See you around Shandy or is it Shitzu??
Woof woof hahaha...
Oh my god, my life has fallen to pieces, if only some handsome pop star would come and whisk me away to his musical paradise.

Still, fat chance of that. I might as well consume this large box of dangerous pills that I just happen to have in my pocket, and end it all now.
Suddenly...
PING!
Who are you?
I'm the Brighton fairy. Many years ago I was lost in Kemptown bushes, when an evil queen took me by surprise from behind and then again about 10 minutes later.
That's as maybe, but how did you come to be trapped in this jar in my pocket??
Well it's a long but fascinating tale...
SCENE MISSING

What an incredible story!
Yes and now I'm free I can give you your heart's desire, and I think I've got just the ticket.
LIMAHL
It's Limahl, my teen idol before I was clouded by the shallow ideals of postmodernism and the inherent irony that goes with it.
Phoooer, cool eighties chick, fancy a bit of that.
Thankyou Brighton Fairy!
THE END

# Sex & Fetish

*Traditionally, Brighton has always been the place where fat London bosses with hairy bums bring their secretaries for more than just a Tele-sales conference. And being a fashionable resort, and the perfect short break from the Big Smoke, are probably the reasons why Brighton has earned its reputation for 'dirty weekends' and countless indiscretions. Even the Prince Regent was at it, having secretly married Mrs. Fitzherbert here. The passageways connecting the Pavilion bedroom to her place were a means of assuring their midnight rendezvous were kept a secret.*

*Brighton's saucy nature today comes more from the liberal nature of its citizens than anything else. It's a good place to live for anyone who wants to come out of the closet and feel relaxed with his or her sexuality. From fetishists to drag queens, you can feel comfortable in the knowledge that in this town there'll always be someone kinkier than you.*

## SHOPPING

### Spanki
33 Sydney Street
(01273) 697475
Open 10am-6pm Mon-Sat
www.spanki.co.uk

Having flitted around Sydney Street and Trafalgar Street for many years and in various guises, owner Martin has finally parked his pipe and slippers in the North Laine with Spanki. Selling everything from alternative club wear, fetish wear and Matrix-style gear to a good selection of kinky boots, this is the kind of shop that separates Brighton from just about every other town in England. They also do their own range of rubber and PVC clothes, hair extensions, Craig Morrison bags, handcuffs and just about anything else you'd need for a pervy night out (or in, for that matter). Friendly staff will also fill you in with information on fetish nights and other related events.

## Manaia
102a North Road (01273) 603056
Open Tues-Sat 11-6pm

Run by New Zealander Garth, (recognisable for his baby ZZ Top beard) Manaia gets my vote as being Brighton's most unusual shop. On entering you are confronted with a rather impressive and forbidding life-size figure (whom I first met at a squat party on the London Road) made entirely out of metal parts and whose job seems to be to guard the shop terrapins. The shop is decorated with skulls, shrunken heads, stretched parchments of skin and bones, and the whole place is an unlikely cross between an anthropological museum of curiosities and a fetish shop. In one corner of the shop is an incredible chair made out of a horse skeleton, while seated in a leather chair opposite is a headless human skeleton.

Garth is a bone-carver by trade, and as well as selling a good selection of fetish rubber-wear and cyber gear, does customised bone, wood and horn carvings. The cabinets displaying body jewellery include everything from bone spikes and flesh tubes to carved tusks and you can even buy shrunken heads for around £100.

The clothes comes from the likes of Cyber Tart, Vera Over, Armoury and Pigalle, and a more extensive range of gear than that on display is available via mail-order. This is another good place to find out about fetish events, and once taken into the staff's confidence, anyone heavily into the scene may learn about very underground parties and special events.

## Cardome
(see shopping section for gay scene)

## Ann Summers
The top of North Street, (opposite the Clock Tower)

Banana dick lip, after dinner nipples, beginners SM kits, willy wash, maids outfits, sexy lingerie, cheap rubber and PVC, dildos and naughty books. It's sex with a smile and a perfect starting point if you're here for a saucy weekend. The clothes are hardly top notch but then you won't necessarily be wearing them out, will you?

## EU Videos
21 Preston Street
Open Mon-Sat 12noon-10pm
Adults only

Stockists of gay and straight videos, most of which you just read about in their catalogues then buy over the counter. And they're only £10 each. Not bad for a quiet night in.

## SEX & FETISH

### Kentucky Woman
www.kentuckywoman.co.uk

Alas Kentucky Woman has now closed, along with its fully equipped dungeon, but all is not lost. Their new website contains everything from corsets, leatherwear, petticoats and bondage gear, to clothing for transvestites. What's more, they offer a specialist fantasy service for men wishing to spend the weekend as French maids, Victorian maids or Sissy boys, in a Regency apartment in Brighton. The two-day stay is with Sir Richard and Lady Elizabeth and costs £300, including accommodation at a nearby hotel.

### Private Shop
11 Surrey Street
Open Mon-Sat 9am-5.30pm
Adults only

The usual collection of dildos, magazines, videos, blow-up dolls and mild fetish toys and clothes. They do seem to have a good selection of foot fetish magazines however, and did I really see a whole collection of mud-wrestling videos there?

### Wildcats
16 Preston Street (01273) 323758
Open Mon-Sat 10am-6pm
Strictly for the over 18s
www.wildcat.co.uk

Not only the largest suppliers of body jewellery in the world but also stockists of tattoo books, fetish mags and some toys for the more adventurous. Their recently-launched new catalogue with over 10,000 products of body-jewellery should be enough to keep the most ardent lovers of body-modification happy.

## TATTOOISTS & PIERCERS

Temple Tatu Design

*In the last few years, Brighton has seen a real boom in tattoo parlours and body piercing studios. The following are only a small selection, but they are the ones I would recommend because either I have been there myself or close friends have had stuff done there.*

*Although tattooing is probably a universal skill, please bear in mind that design and style taste are very individual. So if you're thinking of getting one, I'd recommend that you make an appointment with some of the artists that follow. Go in person to see if you feel comfortable with them, and to see what you think of their work. All good tattooists should carry a portfolio.*

## At Your Pleasure
Downstairs at Penetration
29 Sydney Street (01273) 686369
Open 10am-6pm Mon-Sat
Appointments only

All tattoos here are custom-designed. The idea behind this being that a tattoo should be as individual as the person who wears it.

They specialise in black tattoos, with a lot of influence drawn from Maori, Celtic, Haida and Art Nouveau although, resident tattooist Mickey Clarke also specialises in colourful graffiti-style tattoos. They also do grey shading and cover-up. In short, anything beautiful.

## Perforations
21 Preston Street (01273) 743723
www.perforations.com
email: piercing@perforations.com

A popular and friendly state-of-the-art studio where piercings are more than just skin-deep. Check their website, it's really informative.

## Penetration
29 Sydney Street (01273) 623839
Open Mon-Sat 10.30am-6pm

Piercings here are a totally different experience. While he pierces your tongue, Nick (patron and resident piercer) will tell you all about when he got his willy pierced for the benefit of an Italian TV fashion programme, to which the Pope didn't bat an eyelid.

They totally look after their 'patients' here, to the point that if you're a fainter you get given sweeties. For the more hard-core body-modifications addict, apart from the usual PA and ampallangs (for which you need a consultation to get you…ahem…measured), they also do surgical steel implants and cosmetic dentistry.

The Glitzy Tartz crew get a few discreet tattoos

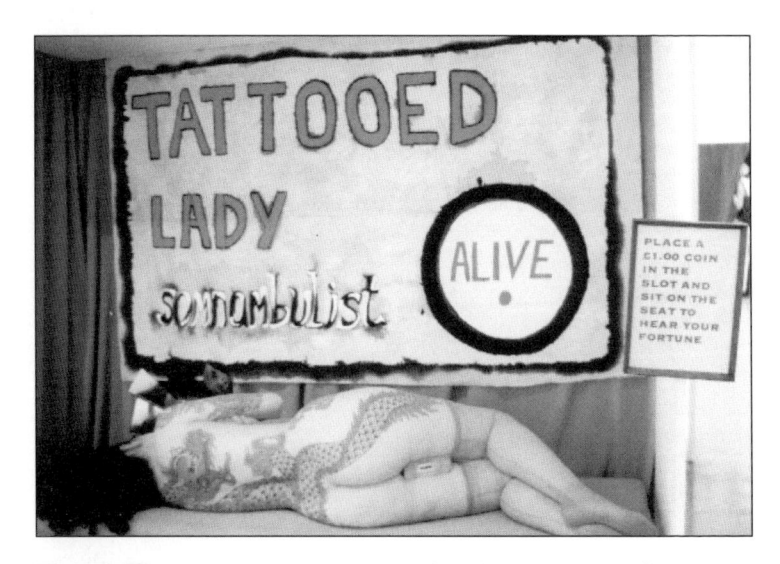

### Temple Tatu
9 Boyces Street
(01273) 208844
Open 12pm-6pm Tues-Sat

This impressive tattoo studio is located just off the busy Duke's Lane. Although they do walk-ins, appointments are encouraged in order to give people the chance to really look into their motivations for getting a tattoo. The three resident artists have a deep knowledge and understanding of the history of tattooing, and make each design individual and unique.

Newcomers are made to feel at ease by discussing over a cup of tea all that the process will involve in the beautiful surroundings. In fact, the reception room at Temple Tatu probably contributes a lot to inspiring you with confidence in these guys' creative skills. From hand-made sequin tiaras to Hindu tiles and stickers, this place has been decorated to welcome you in and make you feel at home.

While here look out for the kitsch-looking alchemical shrine, built by some mad-genius New Zealander, with plastic dolls, driftwood, electric bulbs and old soapboxes inside. You can activate it by inserting a coin and pressing your palms on the designated space. Loads of weird things happen, including stuff whizzing around and the thing talking to you and playing strange music. The shrine is designed to release positive energy, and frankly with the effort and esoteric detail that has gone into these things, I'd happily have one in my lounge if I could afford it.

I can't really tell you what they specialise in, since their portfolio is so varied, (black, tribal, colour, cover up) however, they're quite particular about researching every design, so you can find out what the tattoo you're about to get really means.

## Wizard Of Ink
74 North Road
(01273) 626199 Mobile 0410 471289
Open Mon-Fri 11am-5pm
Sat 10am-6pm Walk in only
www.wizardofink.co.uk

Flash and custom work. This place is probably of the more conventional, no-nonsense, walk in, pick a design off the wall and get-it-done type of parlour. If you're into the philosophical side of tattooing, this place isn't for you. They also have three piercers working full-time (including a girl for the more coy ladies) who will pierce anything above the waist.

## LAPDANCING CLUBS

### The Pussycat Club
The Basement, 176 Church Road, Hove
(01273) 735574/ 709100
£10 compulsory membership
Open 5pm-1am Mon-Thurs £5
Weekends £10, Lap-dance £10

If your idea of fun is having a beautiful girl rubbing her voluptuous breasts in front of you then you may want to pay this place a visit.* The club attracts stag nights, rugby teams and visiting businessmen and there's a friendly feel to the place and everyone seems genuinely eager to please.

Shy voyeurs, be warned, it's quite small down there and not the sort of place you can hide yourself away in. Jeremy had to go down once to chat to the owner about advertising, but auditions were going on all afternoon, so he ended up being the judge. When one of the women said she'd been quite nervous Jeremy unwittingly said, *'it was just as hard for me.'*

*if you don't know the law, you can pay for a personalised topless dance, but no physical contact is allowed

## PROSTITUTION

You'll find a variety of cards and phone numbers in the phone boxes around the Old Steine and Western Road areas. £40 for 30 minutes is a typical price to pay but if you shop around, you might get a student discount. Typically, new laws have been pushed through to stamp out the card system here, which has pushed prostitution back onto the street a bit more. There are also numerous brothels around town but we couldn't possibly tell you where they are, sorry. Here instead are a number of saunas where you can have a nice massage instead.

## SAUNAS

### Ambassador's Sauna & Massage
37 Portland Road, Hove
0870 7409439
Open 12noon-10pm Basic cost £20

This highly rated five-star sauna, with a Jacuzzi, offers a full range of services, including more unusual massages, and photographic portfolios of all the members of staff in various costumes (such as Tarzan's Jane and Miss Santa). Private parties can be catered for, and in summer there's even an outdoor massage facility.

Like Sainsbury's, they have a reward card system, save enough points and you can have a free two-girl Swedish massage or a digital watch.

### Top To Toe
37 Lower Market Street
0870 740 9442
Open 10am-10pm Basic cost £30

Another five-star sauna boasting a sauna, Jacuzzi, uniforms and videos. An international range of lovely ladies await, to tickle your fancy with a sensuous massage.

# Swallows

## Massage and Escort service

Situated in a luxurious Victorian house on the discreet Lewes Road. We have a 5 star McCoys massage guide rating. All rooms are tastefully decorated with showers and videos. These videos may be purchased if required. We offer a wide range of ladies from 18-45 year olds, including Phillipino and Dutch.

Please phone (01273) 818249 / 818250 for the latest info

### Discretion is our key to success

Our receptionists are discreet and will answer any questions you may have. We are always looking for new ladies and can provide accommodation for ladies from out of town while working.

# (01273) 818249 / 818250

# Mind Body Spirit

*From Yoga and Tai Chi classes to Buddhist centres and Homoeopaths, Brighton has them all, and in abundance. Look in the corner of every park and you'll find someone practicing Qi Gong, meditating, or at least reading about it. If you're curious about what day courses are on offer, or if you need somewhere to meditate or practice yoga, your best starting point is to pick up a copy of New Insight from the shops in the Lanes.*

*Since living here I have developed many new interests, most of them illegal, but I probably wouldn't have discovered things like Yoga and Ayurveda without living in a town where anything goes, and where so many different lifestyles co-exist together. Sure there's the usual mystical crap, like places where your cat can have its aura cleansed, but if people believe in it, what's the harm? I love the fact that Brighton people are, on the whole, tolerant and open-minded. After all, why shouldn't you be able to enjoy meditating as well as clubbing? And where else could you indulge your wildest New Age fantasy and learn to sing like Tom Jones, whilst having your bottom cleaned, in Hove's new Welsh Colonic Irrigation Centre?*

## The Jeremy Hardy Sketch
From the Radio 4 series 'Jeremy Hardy Speaks to the Nation'

-Hello, is this where I register for a course?
-Yes love, have you filled in an application form?
-No, not yet.
-Well what area of study are you interested in?
-I want to know more about myself.
-Well, I'm not sure we have a course in **you** specifically. How about Biology?
-No, I just don't believe I can be reduced to bones and atoms.
-Oh, I don't know dear, give me a hammer.
-But don't you think there has to be something more?
-Well let's see.....there's Physics, Art, Literature, Archeologoy, Languages... Medicine?
-Alternative?
-No, dear, **effective**....
-But there's nothing about **me**. I mean the answers I'm looking for must be inside myself.
-Well dear why don't you have a look for them since you've already got your head up there? Tell you what, I'll put you down for gymnastics shall I?

The quote is by kind permission of Jeremy Hardy and Positive Television.

# MIND, BODY, SPIRIT

## SHOPPING

### Neal's Yard
Kensington Gardens
(01273) 601464

Comprehensive stock of herbs, essential oils, homeopathic remedies, vitamins and self-help books. If you're after a free consultation, a Chinese herbalist drops in every Thursday between 3 and 5pm, and a nutritionist comes Fridays 12.30pm-2.30pm. The staff will also give advice on common illnesses and can recommend practitioners for anything more serious. The most usual complaints they deal with are colds and hay fever, but recently some guy came in for herbal hormone replacements for his dog. Typical Brighton.

### Winfalcon's Holistic Shop and Healing Centre
28 Ship Street (01273) 728997
Open Mon-Sat 10(ish)-5.30pm, Sun 12noon-4pm

The usual New Age assortment of crystals, tarots, books and videos that wouldn't look out of place in Glastonbury. For a shop of this nature it seems all the more bizarre (and unintentionally funny) that the bloke who runs it is one of the most miserable and unfriendly shopkeepers I've ever had the misfortune to come across. Now here's a guy in need of a taste of his own medicine...

### The Green Buddha Bookshop
15 Bond Street (01273) 324488

New age bookshop with a good range of titles. Also stocks a modest selection of Dance/Trance/ World-music CDs, together with that obligatory smell of joss sticks.

### Sunsight
4 Little East Street (01273) 724172
Open Tues-Sat 10.30am-5pm,
Sun 12pm-4pm

A small pocket of calm in the Old Lanes selling crystals, Rune Stones, Tarots, candles and a collection of books and CDs. The shop is a useful place to find information on almost all forms of healing and, if you're into Astrology, the Brighton and Hove Astrological Group meet here every second Wednesday (but then you probably predicted that already. Boom, boom!).

## YOGA AND MEDITATION

### The Buddhist Centre
14 Tichborne St (01273) 772090
Open 12-3pm weekdays for visitors

This group is part of 'The Friends of the Western Buddhist Order' and their centre is situated just off the beaten track in the North Laine. It has two stunning meditation and yoga rooms and a library where you can drop in to study, or borrow books and tapes for a nominal fee. Look out for more unusual stuff going on here too, like theatre and lectures. I went to a great talk during the May Festival one year where a Buddhist theatre director talked about the genius of Tommy Cooper and Frankie Howerd. Sunday school was never like this.

### Drop-in meditations
Wednesday 1-2pm and 7.30-9.30pm (donation)

### Drop-in Iyengar Yoga
Mon 6pm-7.15pm, Tues 1pm-2.15pm
Thurs 5.45pm-7.15pm, Fri 7.30pm-8pm
(£4/£3)

### Drop-in Astanga Yoga
Weekdays 1pm-2.15pm (£5/£4)

## The Brighton Natural Health Centre
27 Regent Street (01273) 600010

Parallel to Gardner Street, this centre does a wide range of drop-in classes, in particular different styles of dance, ranging from Jazz and Salsa to contemporary. Along with this comes Yoga with a variety of different tutors, including Brighton's legendary yoga guru Peter Blackaby, who recently appeared on Stars in Your Eyes as Ray Davies from The Kinks.

Phone or drop in for details of times.

## Evolution Arts and Natural Health Centre
2 Sillwood Terrace (01273) 729803

Weekly Iyengar yoga drop-in classes running Tuesday to Saturday at various times. They also do a wide range of one-off workshops from creative writing to mosaics and dramatherapy. Look out for their brochure around town.

## Natural Bodies
28/29 Bond Street
(01273) 711414

This place does about 10 yoga classes a week, most of them drop-in, and at different times of the day. Follow the screams and you'll find the class on the first floor.

I can recommend the yoga classes here as I've been coming for about two or three years now, and my mum doesn't tell me off for slouching any more. The teachers are friendly, clean and sober, and classes are around £4 for one and a half hours. They also do massages, shiatsu, chi kung and feldenkrais.

Lessons take place lunchtimes and most evenings. Phone to check or look in New Insight for details.

# MIND, BODY, SPIRIT

## FLOATATION TANK

### Crescent Clinic
37 Vernon Terrace, Brighton
(01273) 202221
Open 9-5pm Mon-Fri, £20 per session

Initial sessions last one and a half hours and include an introduction from trained members of staff. Newly Feng Shui'ed for your relaxing pleasure, the Crescent Clinic is home to Brighton's only Floatation Tank. Imagine relaxing in a tank of water that deprives you of sound, light and sensation, leaving you to just float in your own little salty glade of heaven. Many people find the experience deeply relaxing, while others talk about it simply making them horny. Make sure to wear the earplugs they supply, or you will be crackling your way through the next two weeks, as the salt water dries out in your ears. If you think you are relaxed, try this. I cannot recommend it enough.

The clinic also offers everything from Acupuncture to Osteopathy.

## ASTROLOGICAL CHARTS

### Tim Burness
35 Guildford Street
(01273) 271469

Astrologer to the stars (well, Chesney Hawkes anyway) Tim is experienced, professional and all-round good egg. All readings are taped, with a personal interpretation. For a sitting you will just be required to know the exact time and place of your birth. (Ask your mum if you can't remember).

## THERAPISTS

*There are literally hundreds of therapists working in Brighton and to list them all would be bonkers. For a full list of what's available, seek out the Alternative Practitioners Handbook from Neal's Yard or simply drink a bottle of scotch and your problems will miraculously disappear.*

*These two fellows below get a special mention because from friends and personal experience, they come highly recommended.*

### Acupuncture with Keith Simpson Lic.Ac. MBAcC
(01273) 622294
£30 Initial Consultation, £24 Subsequent treatments. Some concessions available.

It is comforting to know there are practitioners out there who don't come from the school of tie-dye T-shirts and juggling balls, or even the pipe-smoking, Arran jumper world of 1970s BBC2. Keith is one such person who, instead, is down-to earth, trusty and likeable, and treats his subject with care and passion. Combining Five Element and TCM styles of acupuncture, he can help in the treatment of a wide variety of named complaints such as back pain, piles, IBS, insomnia and depression. For anyone new to acupuncture, it is also excellent for keeping you in good health, helping you feel better in a more general way i.e. increased energy and vitality, better sleep, a more normal appetite and an increased sense of well being. Keith will make you feel completely at ease, gives excellent advice on lifestyle/ health issues and will even wash your car for an extra fiver.

## MIND, BODY, SPIRIT

### Ged Peck
### Bioenergetic Analyst
(01273) 388512
Fees are £35 per hour, but negotiable.

Brighton is full of all kinds of alternative medical practitioners and counsellors, working on body and mind. Bioenergetic Analysis (which has its roots in the work of psychoanalyst Wilhelm Reich) aims to do both of these and consequently can have profound effects, even when other therapies have been tried.

Ged Peck is one of the few accredited Bioenergetic Therapists in Britain, and has been practicing in Brighton for nearly 20 years. His therapy sessions can last from a few weeks to over a number of years, and have been effective with a wide range of problems.

## WHERE TO FIND OUT MORE

### The Alternative Practitioners Directory
This is a comprehensive list of all local practitioners who do everything from acupuncture to past-life regression. It's only about 50p and you'll find it in places like Neal's Yard.

### New Insight
(01273) 245956 www.newinsight.co.uk

Monthly lifestyle magazine that includes a mind-body-spirit section, well-written articles and a comprehensive diary of workshops, events and regular classes around Brighton. A must for anyone looking for a weekend or lifetime in this town that doesn't just revolve around pubs and clubs.

---

**ON-SITE ACUPRESSURE MASSAGE**

OSM is based on the principles of Anma, a traditional Japanese massage. It incorporates over 100 stress release points on the head, neck, shoulders, arms and back leaving the client relaxed and calm, yet energised and alert. It helps to reduce muscle tension in the upper body by concentrating on the areas most affected by stress.

Received fully clothed and seated in an ergonomically designed chair, the treatment takes twenty minutes.

OSM is now widely accepted as an effective form of stress management and is ideal in any environment.

**Claire Miles**
ITEC, Dip AOSM
07779-109933

# WHAT'S ON

## DIARY OF EVENTS

*Isn't it only right that the town that likes to party should be host to the biggest arts festival in England? Not only that, but every month there are always special events going on here, from car rallies and bike rides, to music festivals and a big pagan festival down on the seafront on the shortest day of the year. And where else could you combine the pleasures of a seafront environment with egg-throwing, for the numerous party conferences? Don't you think that William Hague's head was designed for this sport?*

### The Fair at the Level
End of April, into May

Two weeks of flashing lights and projectile vomiting, signifying the beginning of the Festival and letting us know that summer is just around the corner.

### Arts Festival
May

In May this place goes bananas. For four weeks the whole town is packed with theatre, comedy, circuses, all day music events and street performers. It's the largest arts and entertainment festival in England, and if you want to see this town at its most vibrant and colourful, this is the time to visit. Alongside the main festival runs the Fringe, also making use of the countless venues and theatres in town, and providing opportunities for smaller and more unusual performances to take place. Cafés, pubs and clubs transform overnight as you find your favourite seat by the window filled with makeshift stages, movie screens and PAs. Remember, everyone in Brighton is a musician and artist, except in May when they decide to be actors and comedians as well.

Expect everything from guided tours of the gay scene to special club nights, experimental theatre and street parties. And if you do nothing else go see local comedienne Jo Neary.

Two festivals all rolled into one, and a big free fireworks party down on the beach. Miss this at your peril. You know it must be a good event when even Salman Rushdie turns up.

## London to Brighton Bike Race
Middle of June

Every June thousands of people cycle all the way to Brighton from London and then get the train back again. What they don't realise is that a single ticket to London is the same price as a return. So why not take the train both ways and give yourself time to loll about on the beach instead?

## Stanmer Park Music Festival
Usually the last weekend in July

A weekend of big name DJs, popular bands and old-time legends. They even wheeled out James Brown last year but someone forgot to plug him in.

## Gay Pride
Middle of the second week in August at Preston Park (See gay section)

## Lewes Fireworks
5th November

Still upset about a bunch of Protestant martyrs, who were burned here centuries ago by the wicked Catholics, Lewes remembers them by the biggest and most phenomenal bonfire night celebration in the UK.

Along with small carnival style floats, the people of Lewes all dress up in Freddie Kruger jumpers and march down the street holding big torches and throwing bangers at the crowd's feet. Around 8pm the crowds head off to bonfires in different corners of the town, where some loonies stand on scaffolding, dressed as cardinals, and encourage the audience to hurl abuse (and fireworks) at them. A few effigies of the Pope and political figures are then ceremoniously blown up for good measure, followed by huge firework displays.

The whole thing has a very dark, anarchic feel to it and there are definite hints of the Wicker Man in there too. It's only a short train ride from Brighton but you must get there no later than 7pm or you'll miss the street processions. And it's best not to bring any pets.

**WHAT'S ON**

## Veteran car Rally
First Sunday in November

Not being one who gets particularly excited by cars I never take much notice of this. They all seem to congregate down at Madeira drive, share notes on the pros and cons of tungsten drive-cam-shafts and then disappear back to their stately mansions. The only way I could enjoy it would be if I dressed up as Terry Thomas and let down a few tyres. I'm just a terrible cad at heart.

## Burning of the Clocks
Winter Solstace or December 31st

While most seaside towns go into hibernation for the winter, Brighton celebrates the shortest day with this pagan procession along the seafront, culminating in a fireworks display. Expect hundreds of strange and beautiful designs around the theme of time, and lots and lots of candles. It all has that perfect, dark wintery spirit to it, mixed with the excitement of knowing that Christmas is just around the corner. One of my favourite events in the Brighton calendar.

Street theatre during the May Festival

## Poseidon's Day
December 28th

Once a year, 23 Brighton councillors gather on the nudist beach to offer blessings and sacrifices to this venerable sea-god. Hosted by Simon Fanshaw the dancing, nudity and orgies normally go on until the small hours, weather permitting.

## LOCAL PRESS

*In this town people sell their own grandmothers just to get good wall space in a café for their poster. The problem in Brighton is not so much finding information as how to avoid spending the weekend sifting through thousands of fliers, posters and magazines trying to find a club that plays Def Leppard. In our continuing efforts to cull all forms of freethinking, listed below are some of the best papers and magazines for finding out what's on.*

*The following publications can be found in most newsagents, cafés and bars around town.*

## THE ARGUS

Our infamous daily rag features everything from local news to the usual Nazi rants in the letters page. Very readable and indispensable for keeping up with local issues, every now and again the Argus likes to surprise us in a Richard Madeley does Ali G sort-of-way, with bizarre and funny stories. Personal highlights in recent years have included:

### 'CHRIS EUBANK IMMORTALISED IN MOULD'

The Argus did this now-legendary feature a couple of years back about a model who discovered Eubank's apparition on a mould stain on her living room wall.
Freddie Star eat your heart out.

### 'I FOUND JESUS IN MY PANCAKE'

Following on the success of mouldy Chris came this similar theme. '....*the 29-year old couldn't believe his eyes when the outline of a beard, nose, eyes and hair appeared among the burn marks in the batter..."I suppose if it is a sign, there's no reason why it shouldn't be on a pancake," he said.*' (but how did he know it was Jesus and not any old beardy bloke?)

Artist's impression of the pancake

### 'OVER AND SPROUT'

A Beano-style tale about a policeman who slipped on a sprout while chasing a flasher outside the fruit and veg market. 'The detective, who enjoys flying, came crashing to the ground like a sack of spuds.....he said he was in a lot of pain but the accident has not put him off sprouts.'

### 'LIMPETS MUNCHING AWAY AT COASTLINE'

I can only deduce that this was a four-in-the-morning job after the full effects of the hash cakes had kicked in.

**WHAT'S ON**

## WHAT'S ON

**Impact** Free Monthly Magazine
Re-launched in October 2000, Impact aims itself at the 18-40s club/pre-club market, and carries a comprehensive special pull-out 8-page listings, compiled by 'What's On Guide.'

**G-scene** (See gay section)

**The Latest** 50p Monthly Magazine
Comprehensive listings and features, not only for Brighton but also the surrounding areas. Especially good coverage of theatre and cinema, plenty of interesting features and the Perv's legendary and hilarious column.

**The Source** Free monthly magazine
Colourful, glossy mag with a saucy style. Everything you'd want on the local club scene from what's hot and what's not, to good features on pubs and restaurants and the odd bit of gossip.

**New Insight** Free Monthly Magazine
Set up as a kind of antithesis to the local club/pub culture magazines, New Insight initially slanted heavily towards features on alternative lifestyles and health in Brighton with listings of relevant workshops and special events. Over the years, however, it has branched out and now covers most local events, including the comedy scene and gay scene, and features well-written articles.

### What's On Guide
Free monthly poster
www.whatsonguide.co.uk

Found in over 800 shops, bars, hotels and notice boards, this monthly listings poster is especially useful for those last minute plans when you're in town and want to know what's cooking that evening. For those of you who like to plan ahead, check out their website for regularly updated listings.

### Tonight
0901 201 2222 Calls cost less than £1
Updated daily, this handy number will keep you informed of club nights, live music, theatre, comedy, arts events and more, for the day.

# WEBSITES

### www.brighton.co.uk
They own just about every domain name that even comes close to the word Brighton, so you are going to find them even if you don't want to. There are listings for everything from clubs and pubs, to hotels, cinemas and local weather, but there are better sites if you want more specific information and something less corporate looking.

### www.brightonforever.co.uk
Another local information page, full of restaurants, pubs, clubs and other goings on. Unlike many of the other pages, 'brightonforever' does seem to keep its listing and news pages up to date. Loads quite quickly due to its basic nature, but with its name, I struggle to take it seriously.

### www.brightonlife.com
Excellent site, full of information on pretty much all that is Brighton. Possibly the best local site in terms of usability and style.

### www.brightononline.co.uk
Highly searchable site, not entirely easy to navigate, but seems to keep up to date with listings and job boards. Doesn't really have a strong Brighton feel to it though.

### www.totallybrighon.co.uk
Fun-filled site with lots of useful information and silly graphics. Now I could easily say that it has excellent reviews, good humour, and a solid representation of all that is Brighton, but then I would because I wrote all the text for it. Its weaknesses, however, are a lack of reliable listings and some problems with the database. But, at the time of going to print, it was being bought by The Source magazine, so, fingers crossed, it should be on the ball by now.

### www.seelife.brighton.co.uk
Fairly fast-loading site with lots of Brighton news and information. The site is colourful and full of pictures, but is seriously out of date in its content. The daily news and weather pages hadn't been updated since the 19th of August 2000 when we looked at it, and while this makes Brighton's winters appear luxurious, I assure you that they are not.

### www.whatsonguide.co.uk
From a design perspective, this site is excellent; is easy to use, fairly fast loading, and has a good balance of technology and common sense. The best part of the site is the fact that its information is actually useful and up to date. The first time I went to the page, I couldn't find the search button so make sure to let the pages fully load before making your searches, as the search button is one of the last items to load.

# Places to Sleep

*Brighton literally has hundreds of places to sleep, from hotels and B&Bs to guesthouses and hostels, and to be honest most of them are pretty similar. Despite this, in our efforts to bring you an intriguing slice of what's out there, we've tried to cover a range, from the most expensive to the cheapest, the friendliest to the rudest, and the simplest to the most outrageous.*

## DEAD POSH
### The Grand
Kings Road
(01273) 321188
Singles £155, Doubles £220 (add £65 if you want a sea view or save your cash and walk the 9.4 feet to the door and look from there)

The most famous hotel in Brighton and at £1350 per night for the Presidential suite, by far and away the most expensive. This may seem a bit steep but when you take into account that Ronald Reagan and JF Kennedy flossed their teeth in that very room, it almost makes it worth the money.

The over-the-top grandeur of this white palace is only matched by its facilities, which include pool, health spa, hair salon and full sized indoor go-karting track, which was said to be a favourite of Ronnie's.
**Dress code** – Armani, Hugo Boss etc. No jeans unless you're royalty.

### Stakis Metropole
Kings Road
(01273) 775432
Rooms with Dinner/Bed/Breakfast from £75 Most expensive room £480

Another grand affair situated right on the seafront between the two piers. It looks impressive enough and again caters for the more affluent ladies and gentlemen.

There is a small heated swimming pool (if you don't want to get greased up for swimming in the channel) three restaurants and a nightclub, which is not even worthy of the phrase 'tacky hell-hole'.

## Thistle Hotel
Kings Road
(01273) 206700
Rooms range from very expensive to extremely expensive

From the outside the Thistle is not a vision to behold, but once you make your way inside, the lobby opens up into a rather huge expanse of err…yet more lobby. The prices here rival both the Grand and the Metropole, yet it doesn't quite have the same air of snobbery. Notable guests include Van Morrison, Tom Jones, and many of the Eastenders brigade. Rumour has it that David Soul was asked to leave after refusing to re-enact the opening scenes of Starsky and Hutch, in which he bursts through the revolving doors, and rolls four times across the floor and shouts: *'Freeze'*. Well recommended.

## QUITE POSH WITH A HINT OF BOHEMIAN
**Cavalaire House**
34 Upper Rock Gardens
(01273) 696899
Single £30-40, Double £49-75, Triple £80, Extra cot bed £15

My favorite hotel on Upper Rock Gardens, the Cavalaire offers a rather unusual tropical breakfast, with mango, kiwi fruit and a whole host of other goodies (but if you prefer, you can opt for the fry-up instead). The rooms are pleasant and bright, the bathrooms are clean, and they offer Internet access, fancy soaps, and four-poster beds. Make sure to bring a camera, as late night sightings of naked women walking the halls are not unheard of. Quote 'luvvies' for a special deal.

## Montpelier Hall
Montpelier Terrace
(01273) 203599
Singles from £25, Doubles from £50

More the kind of guesthouse you'd expect to find in some exotic English village than the centre of Brighton. For the Percy Thrower types it has some lavish gardens, is host to some of the rarest plants in the world and the garden furniture is made from bits of HMS Ganges. The building is also reputedly haunted by a female ghost, and the king of pantomime, John Morley, clocked up quite a bill when he wrote his encyclopædia here. It's a phenomenal place if you care for detail.

## VERY BOHEMIAN
### The Oriental Hotel
9 Oriental Place
(01273) 205050
Singles £25-30, Doubles £54-69

Leave behind the world of floral carpets and gaudy wallpaper and enter the stylish surroundings of this hotel. Done out in lively colours, and with themed rooms, spattered with art, pine furniture and loads of plants, this place shines a light for all visitors to Brighton who want somewhere 'fab and groovy' to stay. Popular with all ages, and of course the odd famous novel has been scribbled here too. Gets top marks from the ever-critical eyes of the Cheeky team.

### Hotel Pelirocco
10 Regency Square
(01273) 327055
Singles £45, Doubles £85-£105
(Rates set to increase by 10-15% shortly) All rooms include Playstations

Located just off the seafront in Regency Square, the Hotel Pelirocco is everything that a hotel normally isn't. Artistic heroes have transformed each room into individual pockets of creativity. With rooms named 'Sputnik', 'Bettie's Boudoir', 'Modrophenia', 'Pussy' and 'Lenny Beige's Love Palace', it is easy to see why the Pelirocco created such a media phenomenon earlier in the year. Despite the fact that Jane gets asked daily to show the rooms, like an exhibition, she was happy to take me for a tour around the place, and I was suitably impressed. The Pussy room, the Karen Savage room, and Sugar Glider's Abstract Art room are truly stunning. The only downside to the place is that with sponsorship overload from the likes of Playstation, Smint and Absolut Vodka, you can't even take a shower without being reminded to get drunk and keep your breath fresh. That aside, this is a very stylish hotel, that will especially appeal to the hip, media types. Highly recommended.

# FOR BED FETISHISTS
## Adelaide Hotel
51 Regency Square
(01273) 205286
Singles from £41 and doubles from £65
Prices drop if you stay more than one night

Twelve good-sized rooms, all with en-suite bathrooms. If you really want the fancy stuff then go for the Regency room, which has a fabulous four poster bed.

## The Lanes Hotel
70 Marine Parade
(01273) 674231
Singles from £25 Doubles from £66
Four-Posters from £66

Located on the Brighton seafront, this typical hotel offers good views of the Palace Pier and the beach, and has eight rooms with four-poster beds. 'Room of the week' award goes to 118 for its fabulous waterbed. Not advisable if you get seasick.

## 21st Century Hotel
21 Charlotte Street (01273) 686450
Singles from £40, Doubles from £45

This highly acclaimed guesthouse can be found on the little street in Kemptown, immortalised by the once-famous Lloyd Cole song. The rooms are individually named (Oak, Golden, Champagne) and each have different characters. Kind of like The Chelsea Hotel, but Victorian style. It's all a bit gaudy and over the top for me, but the rooms are spotless and refreshingly different from most of the other stuff I've seen. The brass and four poster beds in some rooms might interest those of you planning a saucy weekend.

Pussy room at Hotel Pelirocco

## NICE AND EASY DOES IT
### Avalon
7 Upper Rock Gardens (01273) 692344
Singles £20-25, Doubles £35-45,
Family £45-65

Recently taken over by Bernie and Bob (call him Graham, he really likes that) the Avalon is a class example of how to run a bed and breakfast. Everything is spotless, the quality of the rooms is excellent, and Bernie seems to be one of the nicest people you could ever meet. There are CD players in most rooms, sun kissed sweeties everywhere, and even a four-poster bed. If you want a little more wood in your life, then may I suggest room 6. They do target the gay community, but everyone is welcome.

### Bannings Guest House
14 Upper Rock Gardens (01273) 681403
No single rooms, Doubles £40-47,
Triples £22 pp
(Women only at Weekends)

After eleven and a half years of suffering, Steven the owner has decided that he wishes to attract a predominantly gay female clientele. Put simply, *'Women are less hassle than blokes'*, except in the instance of the woman who asked him to call Buckingham Palace to complain that Princess Anne had broken into her room, stolen her purse, and left her with only £10.

Friendly and clean (and the rooms aren't bad either. Boom, Boom!).

### Colson House Hotel
Upper Rock Gardens, Kemptown
(01273) 694922 Single £30-35,
Doubles £30-35pp, Triples £25-30pp

Owned by the ever-energetic Jane from the Pink Pamper, the Colson house is one of the brighter B&Bs in Kemptown. The rooms are large, spacious and spotless, and the hardwood floors in the bathrooms give it a modern feel. Good quality beds and a quiet location make it a good choice to rest a weary head or two.

### Funchal
17 Madeira Place (01273) 603975
Twin / Doubles from £30-36
No singles

One of the best B&Bs on the street. The owners seem to like the stories of old, when B&Bs used to be awful, and you would get beaten with bread rollers if you didn't finish your breakfast.

Incidentally, does anyone know what the Capital of Madeira has anything to do with Brighton??

### Grapevine
29-30 North Road (01273) 703985
www.grapevinewebsite.co.uk
Dorm £12-15, Single £18, Double £30,
No en-suite rooms

If you're young and want to be right in the thick of things, then this is an excellent place to sleep. Located right in the North Laine, you can't stay in a more central area. The rooms, while not spectacular, are certainly pleasant enough for the young traveller types that frequent Brighton. The dorm room is a little dark for my liking, so try to avoid it but room 12 is nice and bright, and through the large windows you can peer down onto North Road. The Mexican restaurant downstairs is also a good place to lounge around and meet like-minded souls.

## Keehans Hotel
Regency Square
(01273) 327879
Single room and breakfast £30
Doubles vary all the way to £85 for the top room

This family owned guesthouse is vehemently non-smoking, and they would rather gnaw their own arms off than let you in with a fag.
If you feel the same way about tobacco, owners John and Nancy will welcome you in, tell you all about their grandson (who plays for Aston Villa) and let their floppy old dog lick your arms. Famous guests include Shredded Wheat fanatic Brian Clough.

They've also got indoor parking for bikes, which is pretty useful, and yes it's on the seafront.

## Kelvin
Madeira Place (01273) 603735
Singles £18-20, Doubles £36-40

Promising to give better breakfast than anyone else on the street, Kelvin offers rooms, prices and services all on par with the rest of the street.

## Strawberry Fields
6-7 New Steine, Brighton
(01273) 681576 Prices from £28pp

Now I know what you're thinking, what were John Lennon and Brian Epstein doing alone in this Kemptown B&B, and where did they hide the body of the real Paul McCartney? Unfortunately to find that out, you need to check in at the 'Paul Is Dead' guesthouse next door, as this friendly place has no Beatles connections, other than its name.

Located in a seafront garden square and run by Barry and Lynn, there is a nice energetic feel to the place. Clean rooms, good views, good location and very reasonable pricing.

Four-poster at the Avalon

PLACES TO SLEEP

The wonders of hi-tech advertising

## THE CHEAPEST IN TOWN
### Abbey Hotel
Norfolk Street (01273) 778771
Rooms on floors 1-3 start at £50 per week Rooms on the fourth floor are all quite nice and start at £155 per week

Probably the cheapest weekly rental hotel in Brighton. The cheap self-catering rooms are on the first 3 floors and on the whole are small and pretty hairy and if it's really all you can afford, I'd rather you came and slept on my floor. The rooms on the 4th floor, however, are pleasant, with clean bathrooms, and start at about £155 for the week. Tony Benn always stays here when he's in town.

Last year some American guy totally pissed off the manageress by plonking a pair of shoes on the counter and saying in an arrogant voice, *'Have these cleaned by the morning.'*

She's still angry so if you're afflicted with the accent, tell them you're Canadian.

### Aquarium Hotel
13 Madeira Place
(01273) 605761
Singles from £12, Doubles from £16 per person if you're willing to haggle

In the heart of Kemptown and a stone's throw from the Palace Pier, this little B&B stands out as it has negotiable pricing based on what you can afford. They do a veggie breakfast on request and the rooms are clean, if a little squashed.

### Madeira House
14 Madeira Place
(01273) 681115
Rates change daily

One friendly owner whose claim to fame is that he got in the Guinness book of records for gargling non-stop for 14 hours. Trivia aside, the rooms that I saw were generally a little better than most of the others in the same street.

## B&B & GUESTHOUSE STRIPS

*If you don't have any luck with the ones listed, or you fancy going it alone you will find countless B&Bs and guesthouses in the following places. In the most traditional B&B areas, like Madeira Place, prices change daily and sometimes in accordance to what they think you'll pay. So be terribly polite but dress down for the occasion when you show up. Rooms come with TV, coffee and tea-making facilities, and breakfast is normally included in the price.*

### Madeira Place, Lower Rock Gardens & New Steine

Located close to the seafront but without a proper sea view. Fairly cheap, plentiful and close to just about everything.

### Grand Parade

Right in the town centre, ten minutes walk from the sea and close to the North Laine area.

### Regency Square & Bedford Square

These squares are found just past the West Pier and the rooms overlook the sea (unless of course you get one at the back with a view of the gasworks).

## Various Others

### Aegean Hotel
5 New Steine
(01273) 686547

### Ainsley House
28 New Steine
(01273) 605310
Single £24-£30, Double £42-£70

### Alvia Hotel
36 Upper Rock Gardens
(01273) 682939

### Amalfi
44 Marine Parade
(01273) 607956

### Ambassador Hotel
22 New Steine
(01273) 676869
£23-£33 pp sharing, also has good weekly rates available

### Barringtons
76 Grand Parade
(01273) 604182

### Brighton Marina House Hotel
8 Charlotte Street
(01273) 605349
Single £20-£35, Double £45-£70

### New Steine Hotel
12a New Steine
(01273) 681546

### The Quality Hotel
West Street
(01273) 220033
Single £ 56-£97, Double £66-£120

**PLACES TO SLEEP**

**PLACES TO SLEEP**

# The George Hamilton V Award

*Every year we will be awarding the coveted George Hamilton V Award to the hotel that was most insulting to us in the process of doing our reviews. The usual criteria of arrogance, belligerence and downright rudeness must be attained.*

How it all began....

### George Hamilton V
27 Lower Rock Gardens

I incorrectly thought this place was named after the Scottish Country and Western singer and thought it might be interesting. When the door opened, a rather unshaven man emerged, smelling of booze…

**Me:** *Hello.*
**Him:** What do you want?
**Me:** *I am writing a guide book on Brighton and…*
**Him:** I'm not interested. (shuts the door)

**The end.**

## This Year's Award Goes To...
# The Old Ship Hotel

Kings Road, Brighton

**PLACES TO SLEEP**

**Cheeky:** Good afternoon
*The desk clerk sees that I'm carrying what appears to be potentially threatening advertising packs, and rolls her eyes.*
**Desk clerk:** We don't advertise in any publications.
**Cheeky:** That's OK, I am not here to get advertising, I am here from the Cheeky Guide to Brighton, we're updating the guide and I was wondering if you could show me around.
*Once again the desk clerk rolls her eyes, but this time decides to throw in a heavy sigh for good measure.*
**Desk clerk:** We don't have any time for this sort of thing.
**Cheeky:** Well, our guidebook has sold well in Brighton, and besides… it is free advertising for you.
*More eye rolling, repeated heavy sighs, a bored flick of the hair out of her face, followed by another heavy sigh.*
**Desk Clerk:** Hold On.
*She disappears behind the counter to talk to someone, and then after about 15 seconds returns with the sort of grin on her face that you would never get fed up punching.*
**Desk clerk:** I have spoken with my manager, and she says we don't want to be in the book.
**Cheeky:** Would it be possible for me to speak with them please?
*Desk clerk now combines sighs, eye rolling and hair flick in one perfect movement and with a face of thunder walks back to the manager. After a moment or two she once again returns with the same annoyed face.*
**Desk clerk:** She doesn't wish to be disturbed, doesn't wish to see you, and doesn't wish to be in the book. Goodbye.

*And everybody lived happily ever after.*

## PLACES TO SLEEP

## HOSTELS
### Baggies Backpackers
33 Oriental Place
(01273) 733740
Fax No. (01273) 733740
Dorm rooms are £10 pp and doubles are £25 (£12.50pp) Laundry machines on site, free soap powder provided, and if you ask nicely enough Homeopathy and foot massages are provided too.

Close to the West Pier, Baggies is one of the best hostels in Brighton, and while at first glance it may not seem as lively as some of the others, it does get going at night.

The rooms all have built-in sinks and are always clean and fresh, as are the showers and bathrooms. There are two lounging-about rooms, the upstairs one has TVs and videos, while the downstairs one is for listening to music and general hanging about. Unlike most hostels where the owner is never there and the desk clerk is caned out of his box, owners Jem and Val are ever-present and take an active roll in making everything flow smoothly. If you are looking to stay in a hostel, then look no further.

### Friese Green Backpackers Rest
20 Middle Street
(01273) 747551
www.friesegreen.demon.co.uk
There are 9 dorms and only one double room Prices are £10 pp for the dorms and £15pp for the double

Friese Green is just up from the Sumo bar in the club area of Brighton. This isn't the cleanest hostel in the world but it does seem to be a friendly and fun place to hang out. There are kitchen facilities provided for your own cooking, but it didn't look all that clean to me at the time, and if I were you I'd rather eat out or go on a fast for a while.

### A Cheeky Tale
I'd just been to the Arts club with my girlfriend, to see a band, and out of sheer laziness we had driven into town and parked outside Friese Green Backpackers. At the end of the night we were getting into the car to go home when I noticed a guy slumped on the pavement. He was out cold and his feet were dangling into the road. It was early March and still freezing, so I went over to see if I could wake him up. After a lot of gentle poking and shaking he came to and I asked him how he was.

'I'm alright I guess,' he slurred, 'I must have just fallen asleep on my way home', and he got to his feet.

'Can I drive you home?' I asked.

'Naaaaa,' he said, 'I only live there.' And he pointed to the Friese Green hostel, three metres across the road, and staggered inside.

---

## You do your thing. We'll do the rest.

PREMIER LODGE

From **£46** per room

Whatever the reason for your visit to Brighton; the famous pier or shopping in 'The Lanes'. Premier Lodge has everything you need for a good night's sleep.

**Brighton Central** 144 North Street
**Tel: 0870 700 1334**

**PREMIER LODGE**
THE BEST. REST ASSURED.

## Brighton Backpackers
75-76 Middle Street
(01273) 777717
Fax (01273) 887778
www.brightonbackpackers.com
Dorm Roomss £10 pp and
£25 for a double room

Brighton Backpackers is the typical hostel that you find in most cities around the world; loads of fun, full of colourful people, and with enough Reggae to keep even the most ardent Rasta happy.

The rooms aren't particularly tidy, but I can't blame the staff for this as they do clean the rooms, it just seems like everyone throws their junk, tapes, towels and general shit all over the floor. Come on guys, you might have travelled India by dingo but clear away those smelly socks!

The rooms are all painted different colours and most doors in the older building have Disney characters on them. You can get some discounts if you feel like a spot of painting.

Despite the odd mess, it's a lot of fun staying here and there's a good chance you'll meet some cool people who know how to party.

## Walkabout Hostel
78-81 West Street, Brighton
(01273) 770232
www.walkaboutinn.co.uk
Dorms £10 daily, £55 weekly,
Doubles £12 daily, £70 weekly,
Triples £11 daily, £60 weekly

The hostel is part of a chain of Ozzie bars that cater mainly for the young traveller. While the Brighton branch is the only one with accommodation attached to it, they plan to open more in the future.

They offer a belly-busting £3 meal for the hostel residents, and all things considered it is a pretty good deal. The hostel rooms are clean(ish), and if you need some privacy for a little saucy fun, then rumour has it that the laundry room cupboard is getting some pretty heavy use.

---

# CAMPING
## Sheep Cote Valley
Behind the Marina off Wilson Ave  (01273) 626546

Costs vary according to the season but it's around £3.90 per person per tent plus £3.50 if you've arrived by car. By foot it's only an extra £2 per night.

This is the only campsite in Brighton and living in the town centre, I've never had cause to stay here, so can only really tell you what's in their blurb.

They don't like all-male groups and it's not exactly walking distance from town but it may be one of your cheapest ways of staying here, aside from sleeping under the pier.

Directions for getting there are a bit complicated, so it's best to ring.

# Outside Brighton

## Beachy Head

Celebrated suicide spot, which featured in Quadrophenia and several Python sketches. It gets pretty windy up there so be careful near the edge but if you're feeling brave look for the spooky old burned-out car half way down the cliffs, I think it's still there. It takes about forty-five minutes to reach Beachy Head from Brighton and there's not much else around, but it's definitely worth a visit, especially if your morbid curiosity is aroused or you're a die-hard Mod.

## Lewes

(15 minutes drive from Brighton)

Generally speaking this is a cosy little town where you could take your parents for the afternoon (and I have) for a stroll round the castle and a sniff through some old bookshops. It is most notorious, however, for being host to the largest fireworks event in the UK (see diary of events). Below the surface the town has more than its share of occultists, witches and eccentrics, but whether you get any feel of this from an afternoon visit is another matter.

The best pub here, without a doubt, is the Lewes Arms, a wonderful little place tucked away down one of the many side streets. Host to a number a bizarre games, including an annual Pea Throwing Competition (the rules of which are very amusing), it's probably your best port of call for a real taste of Lewes, and a chance to meet some of the town's fruitier characters.

## Stanmer Park

(10 minutes drive from Brighton)

Go out of Brighton on the A27 towards Lewes and you'll find it just before Sussex University. There's ample room for big footie games and

Frisbee throwing, or you could go lose yourselves in the woods. There's an organic farm and the usual teashop, which is next to a stable full of cows, and always smells of shit, but we love it because it's good old-fashioned country shit. It's the closest place to Brighton I know where you can forget the crowds, especially if you take the walk past the village and up the hill. Look out for the tree trunk carved into animals.

### Devils Dyke

So the story goes that the devil started to dig a deep chasm here to let the sea in to drown all the pious villagers of the Weald. But an old lady on hearing the noise lit a candle and tricked the devil into believing it to be the rising sun. So the devil left his terrible work unfinished, a 300ft valley in the heart of the Downs.

Now I know there are several flaws in this local myth (like why didn't the devil come back the next night?) but we'll let it pass as it's a good story. This is a popular beauty spot with plenty of walks. There's a good one down the hill to the pub in Fulkin if you can face the journey back again.

The Dyke is a twenty-minute drive out of Brighton and in summer you can usually catch an open-top bus there. Expect crowds at the weekend.

### Ditchling

Your typically 'nice' country village, with an amazing cake shop (huge treacle tarts for about a quid). Beyond the pond there's a walk I really like because you get a great view of The Downs. To find where it starts, look for the sign that says:

*'Public right of way, except for 21st December when for legal reasons this is not open to the public'.* I'd love to know why. Go up the hill, take a picnic and enjoy the view. Expect to share the field with a few friendly cows.

**OUTSIDE BRIGHTON**

# Useful Info

## LATE NIGHT CHEMISTS

### BRIGHTON
**Ashtons**
98 Dyke Road, Seven Dials 9am-10pm
(01273) 325020

**Westons**
6 Coombe Terrace 9am-10pm
(01273) 605354

**Moss Chemists**
(Asda, Brighton Marina)
Open until 8pm (01273) 688019

**Sharps Pharmacy**
26 Coombe Road 9am-7pm
(01273) 604384

**Sainsburys**
(01273) 688105
Lewes Road 8.30am-8pm

### HOVE
**Codex Chemist**
314 Portland Road
Open until 6.30pm (01273) 418129

**Moss Chemists**
4 Parade Hangleton (01273) 733718
Open until 6.30pm

**Co-op**
Neville Road Open until 8pm

## POLICE
For Brighton, Hove and more or less everywhere in East Sussex
(0845) 6070999

## HOSPITALS
**Brighton General**
Elm Grove, Brighton
(01273) 696 011

**Royal Sussex County**
Eastern Road (01273) 696955

**Family Planning**
Morning after pill etc (01273) 242091

### Tourist Information
10 Bartholomew Square
0906 7112255 (50p per minute, what a rip off!) Open Mon-Fri 9am-5pm
Sat 10am-5pm, Sun 10am-4pm
www.tourism.brighton.co.uk

Located near the sea front, close to the bus depot and behind the Thistle Hotel. By a strange twist of fate most of the staff here are ex-circus performers. Ask them about their days in the big top and they'll be happy to share a few stories. If it's information you're after they can also sort out on-the-day bookings for B&Bs and hotels, as well as for National Express coaches and day trips. You'll also find all the usual gubbins about local tours, museums and places to visit here.

## OTHER CONTACTS

### Samaritans
(01273) 772277

### Brighton And Hove Council
(01273) 290000

### Latest Postal Collection
North Road Sorting Office has a late collection at 8pm.

## CRIME

The usual stuff about being vigilant for pickpockets applies here as much as anywhere really. I don't have much extra advice on this except that if you hang around on West Street at the weekend for long enough, you will be robbed by junkies, stripped naked by drunken loose women and beaten up by lager louts.

## DRUGS

### Add Action
(01273) 321000

Because drug-use is widespread in Brighton, the clubs are very strict with their policies. You will see countless clubs whose advertising features PVC-clad models smoking huge reefers and the club night is called 'Dope-tastic!' or something. The reality is that all they really want to do is sell you expensive gassy lager. One whiff of grass and you'll be chucked out. If you want to purchase legal highs check out the review for Hocus Pocus.

## INTERNET @CCESS

*Need to find a web-site for the best donkey-ride in Brighton or maybe your mum needs to e-mail you some clean socks? Here's where it all happens.*

### Foobar / Internet
(aka The Arena aka Vyrus, aka Molly's Palace of Bondage) 36 Preston Road (01273) 710730 Open daily 12noon-10pm

At the time of going to press last year, the café owners were in intense squabbles over the name. At the time of going to press this year they are still fighting... nothing has changed at all (except the name of course). Pretty cool little place. Price is £3.50 per hour or 5p per minute.

### H And C
109 Western Road (01273) 772882
(20% off internet price if you show up with this book)
30 min for £1.50 or an hour for £2.50

This is a small computer shop along Western Road, with the upstairs converted for internet access. This is probably the cheapest access in town.

### Sumo Bar
Middle Street (01273) 749465
Prices undecided when going to press

At the time of going to press, Sumo had decided to scrap the main bar, and change pretty much the whole place back into an Internet café. So assuming that they complete the plan, Sumo will become Brighton's main Internet café with a booze license. Drunken computer geeks of the world unite. On Thursdays – Saturdays, the downstairs bar will still be open until 1.30 for drinks and music.

### Curve Internet
44-47 Gardner Street, Brighton
(01273) 603031 £3.65 per hour,
£2.75 per hour after 6pm

Located upstairs in the Komedia Café, this place is tastefully designed, and, unlike many other internet cafés, isn't a haven for all types of advertising. Adequate connection speeds and 12 terminals to choose from.

USEFUL INFORMATION

# INDEX

124 Queen's Road bookshop 67
Acme Art 78
Acupuncture 224
Adaptatrap 73
Adventure Activities 51
Adventures Unlimited 50
Akademia theatre 149
Alf Resco cafe 90
Alforno cafe 105
Alfresco cafe 105
Alicats bar 117
Anatolia 68
Ann Summers (naughty shop) 215
Arkham (creepy shop) 78
Arts Festival 226
Aum Thong 110
Backpackers Rest 242
Badger baiting 275
Baggies Backpackers 242
Bali Brasserie 112
Bankers chippy 113
Bardsley's chippy 113
Basketmakers pub 126
Battle Of Trafalgar pub 126
Beach 135
Beachy Head 244
Becky's Café 95
Bedford Tavern 192
Big Green Bagel 27
Billies cafe 90
Black Chapati restaurant 104
Blackout 70
Blind Lemon Alley restaurant 100

BN1 Club 135
Bombay Aloo restaurant 104, 111
Bookmarks 64
Booth Museum 37
Borders bookshop 64
Brighton Backpackers 243
Brighton Bystander 86
Brighton Centre 156
BRIGHTON IN THE MOVIES AND BOOKS 186
Brighton Museum 37
Brighton National Spiritualist Church 52
Brighton Natural Health Centre 223
Brighton Oasis 198
Brighton Pottery Workshop 70
Brighton Rock 186, 189
Brunswick Square Gardens 33
Buddhist Centre 222
Bugle pub 122
Burning of the Clocks 228
Cajun & American restaurants 100
Camden Traders 76
Candy Bar 200
Casablanca club 135
Catfish Club 136
Charlie's Orbit 60
Cheese Shop 87
Cheung's Restaurant 101
China Garden 100
Chinese restaurants 100
Chinese Take-Away 114
ChoccyWoccy DooDah 79

Cinematheque 146
Circe's Island 76
City Books 65
Club Revenge 194
Colonnade bar 122
Concorde 2 136, 156
Coopers Cask pub 117, 192
Core Club 137
Country and Western Weekends 50
Crepe Dentelle restaurant 103
Crescent Clinic 224
Cricketer's pub 126
Cripes Creperie restaurant 102
Cuba club 137
Cushy B 76
Cutie 76
D & K Rosen Clothiers 55
Dance 2 Records 159
Dave's Cafe 98
David's Comic Shop 67
Debbie McGee completely starkers! 267
Deb's Deli 88
Devils Dyke 245
Disastronaut (mad Jeff) 158
DISCOTHEQUES 134
Ditchling 245
Divall's Cafe 97
Do Tongues 190
Dolphin Derby 51
Donatello 105
Dr Brighton's pub 192
Duke Of York's cinema 146
Duke's Mound 197

# INDEX

Dumb Waiter cafe 91
Dyke Road
 Cemetery 33
Edgeworld record
 shop 61, 159, 162
EM-Space 70
English restaurants 102
English's Oyster Bar 102
Enigma club 137
ENTERTAINMENT 146
Escape club 138
Essential Music 61
Evening Argus 229
Evening Star 122
Event 2 139
Fabrica gallery 39
Fair at the Level 226
Famous Moe's
 Pizzas 114
Fish and Seafood
 restaurants 102
FOOD 86
Food for Friends
 cafe 91, 111
Fortune of War 118
Fossil 2000 71
Free Butt 156
French restaurants 102
Friese Green
backpackers 242
Fruit and Veg
 Market 82
G-Scene Magazine 204
Gardner Arts
 Centre 148, 156
GAY SCENE 191
Gay Pride 227
Gay, Lesbian, Arts,
Media (GLAM) 206
Geese pub 126
Gingerman

restaurant 104
Glitzy Tartz 74
Gloucester club 139
GoodBean
 Coffee shop 91
Great Eastern pub 127
Green Buddha
 Bookshop 222
Greyhound Track 154
Greys pub 123
Grosvenor
 Casino 154, 130
Grubbs take-away 86
Guitar and Amp
 Shop 73, 162
Hand In Hand 123
Harry's restaurant 102
Havana restaurant 108
HD2 61
Heart and Hand 124
HERE, THERE, AND
 EVERYWHERE 18
Hive 67
HMV 159
Hocus Pocus 79
Honeyclub 139
Hop Poles 118
Hove Lagoon 49
Hove Lawns 197
Hove Museum 38
How to build a time
 machine 281
Hungry Monk
 restaurant 112
Impact Magazine 230
Indian/Jazz
 restaurants 104
Infinity Café 91
Infinity Foods 89
International Casino
 Club 154

INTRODUCTION 8
Iron Duke pub 124
Italian restaurants 105
Italian Shop 88
Jamaican 107
Japanese
 restaurants 106
Jazz Place
 nightclub 140
Joint club 140
Jump The Gun 74
Junk Television 150
Kambi's 108, 114
Kappa 55
Kebab Express 87
Kemptown Flea
 Market 84
Kensingtons Cafe 91
Kentucky Woman 216
King Alfred Centre 49
King and I
 restaurant 110
Kinky Booty 196
Kitchen Cafe 99
Komedia 148
Krater Comedy
 Club 151
L Mexicano Ltd 108
La Fourchette
 restaurant 103
Lanes Armoury 80
Lanes Patisserie 89
Latest Magazine 230
Latest Postal
 Collection 241
Lebanese
 restaurants 108
Level, the 32
Lewes 244
Lewes Fireworks 227
Lift club 156

249

# INDEX

Little Gems
  record stall  62
Llama Trekking  50
LOCAL HEROES AND
  ECCENTRICS  170
London Unity  124
Lunar Bar  92
Mamba  74
Mambo  75
Manaia  215
MAP  254
Marina Breakwater  44
Market Diner  86
Marlborough pub  200
Masquerade  84
Meeting Place cafe  92
Melting Vinyl
  promoters  157
Mexican
  restaurants  108
MIND, BODY AND
  SPIRIT  221
Mock Turtle cafe  92
Modern Continental
  restaurants  108
Moons cafe  92
Moshi Moshi
  restaurant  106
Moulsecoomb museum
  of corkscrews  268
Movie Mania  68
Mrs Hudson's  98
Ms Brighton
  Alternative  202
MUSIC  156
Nan Tuck's Tavern  128
Natural Bodies  223
Natural Health
  Centre  223
Neal's Yard  222
New Hong Kong
  restaurant  114

New Insight
  magazine  225, 230
New Venture
  Theatre  149
New Whytes
  Restaurant  109
Nia Cafe  93
Nishat Tandoori  114
North Laine
  Market  82
Nude pictures of
  the author  277
Nudist Beach  197
Ocean Rooms
  club  140
Office pub  118
Old Orleans
  restaurant  100
Old Postcard Shop  72
Olde Rock Shop  80
Open-Topped Bus
  Tour  15
Organic Matters  89
Oriental Market  87
OUTSIDE
  BRIGHTON  244
Palmers Bar  119
Paradox club  141
Pasta Shop  88
Pat's Place cafe  89
Pavilion Gardens  33
Pavilion Theatre  157
Pavilion, Brighton  36
Pells Pool At
  Lewes  48
Penetration  217
Penny Lane Gallery  81
Perforations  217
Peter Pavement and
  Slab-O-Concrete
  Publications  170
Phoenix Gallery  39

Pickwicks Café  93
Pink Pamper  203
PLACES TO
  SLEEP  232
Pool Club  195
Portslade Sports
  Centre  49
Pound Shop  80
PRACTICAL STUFF  3
Practical Books  65
Pressure Point
  club  141
Preston Park  32
Pulse Station
  (Rollerblading)  49
Pure cafe-bar  93
Pussy (Home
  Boutique)  68
Pussycat Club  144
Pussycat Club  219
Pyramid  68
Quadrant pub  128
Queen's buttocks  295
Queen's Head  193
Queen's Arms  194
Queen's Park  32
Queenspark
  Books  189
Rabbit Roundabout  51
Rainbow Books  65
Ray Tindle
  Centre  157
Record Album  62
Recordland  62
Regency Tavern  124
Regency Tavern  193
Revamp  84
Rikki Tik cafe-bar  94
Rin*Tin*Tin  69
Rock pub  128
Rockpooling  47

# INDEX

Rokit  77
Rounder Records  63, 159
Route One  75
Ryelight Chinese Supermarket  88
Sada Thai Cuisine  110
Sallis Benney  149
Saltdean Lido  48
Sanctuary cafe-bar  94
Scene 22  196, 203
Sealife Centre  47
Secrets  195
SEX AND FETISH  214
Shakespeare's Head  120
SHOPPING  59
Shoreham Beach  197
Sidewinder  120
Silverado  72
Sir Ian Helliwell  158
Snoopers Paradise  83
Source magazine  230
Southern FM  159
Southover Wine Shop  116
Spaghetti Junction  88
Spanki  214
spunky cavern pub 286
St Peter's Bar  119
St. Ann's Well Gardens  32
St. Bartholomew's Church  38
Stanmer Park  227, 244
Star Of Brunswick  129
Sumo bar  129, 241
Sunday Market  82
Sunday Sundae  196
Surf FM  159

Sussex Stationers  64
TAB  69
Taj Mahal Stores, Delicatessen and Food Stores  88
Tall Storeys Bookshop  66
Tamarind Tree restaurant  107
Tavern Club  141
Taylor's (Tobacconist)  81
Temple Tatu  218
Terre A Terre restaurant  111
Thai restaurants  110
The Artists' Quarters  26, 39
Theatre Royal  149
Tiger Bar and Canteen  94
Tin Drum cafe-bar  95
To Be Worn Again  77
Tony Young Autographs  55
Top To Toe  219
Tourist Information  246
Trogs Organic Vegetarian Restaurant and Cafe Bar  111
Two Way Books  66
UGC Cinema  146
Urban Records  63
USEFUL INFORMATION  246
Vavavavoom! clubnight  143
Vegetarian restaurants  111
Veggie/Vegan sandwiches  89
Veteran car Rally  228

Victorian Penny Arcades  26
Volks Tavern club  142
Wai Kika Moo Kau cafe  95
Wallis Macfarlane  72
Walmer Castle pub  120
Watch This Space  68
WATERING HOLES  117
Waterstones bookshop  64
Wax Factor  63, 66
WEIRD AND WONDERFUL  36
West Pier  27
West Pier Books  67
West Pier Market  83
Western Front pub  121
WHAT'S ON  226
What's On Guide  230
Wild Fruit clubnight  144
Wildcats  216
X To Z  75
Yamama  75
Yum-Yum Noodle Bar  101
Zanzibar club  196
Zap club  142

# INDEX OF STREETS

Albert Rd  F5
Albion Hill  K4
Albion St  K4
Alfred Rd  F5
Ashton Rise  K5
Bath St  F3
Bedford Place  D8
Bedford Square  D9
Belgrave St  L4
Blaker St  M7
Bond St  I7
Borough St  C7
Boyces St  H9
Broad St  L9
Brunswick Pl  B7
Brunswick Rd  B7
Brunswick Sq  B9
Brunswick St East  B9
Brunswick St West  A9
Buckingham St  G5
Buckingham Place  F4
Buckingham Rd  G5
Cambridge Rd  B7
Camford  L9
Cannon Place  F9
Carlton Hill  L6
Castle St  E8
Cavendish St  D9
Chapel St  M8
Charles St  K9
Cheltenham  J6
Church St  I7
Churchill Square  G8
Circus St  K6
Clarence Square  F8
Clifton Hill  E6
Clifton Pl  E7
Clifton Rd  E5
Clifton Terrace  F7
Coleman St  L2
Davigdor Road  B4
Dean St  F7
Devonshire Pl  M8
Dorset Gdns  L8
Duke Street  H8
Dyke Road  D3

East St  J9
Edward St  L7
Egremont Place  M7
Elm Grove  L1
Ewart St  M3
Farm Road  A7
Finsbury Rd  M4
Foundry St  I6
Frederick Pl  H5
Frederick St  H6
Freshfield Rd  O7
Furze Hill  B6
Gardner St  I7
George St  K8
Gloucester St  J5
Gloucester Rd  H5
Grafton St  N9
Grand Parade  J6
Grove Hill  K4
Grove St  L4
Guilford Rd  G5
Guilford St  G5
Hanover St  L2
Hanover Terr  L2
Hereford St  N8
Holland Street  L4
Hove Lawns  B9
Islingword Rd  N2
Islingword St  M3
Ivory Place  K5
Jersey St  L4
John St  L5
Kemp St  H5
Kensington Gdns  I6
Kensington Place  I5
Kensington Street  I6
Kings Road  E10
Kingsway  A10
Kingswood  K7
Lanes  I8
Lansdowne Place  A7
Lansdowne Road  A7
Lavender St  N8
Leopold  F6
Lewes Road  K3
Lewes St  K4

Lincoln St  L3
Lion St  I9
Little Preston St  E9
London Rd  I2
Lower Rock Gdns  M9
Madeira  L9
Madeira Drive  L10
Manchester Rd  K9
Margaret Street  L9
Marine Parade  M9
Marlbr  F7
Middle St  H9
Montpel. St  E7
Montpel. Vil  E7
Montpelier Place  C7
Montpelier Rd  D7
Montreal Rd  M4
Mt Pleas St  M7
New England Rd  F3
New Rd  I7
New Steine  M9
Newark Pl  L4
Newhaven St  K3
Norfolk Rd  C7
Norfolk Sq  C8
Norfolk St  C9
Norfolk Terrace  C6
North Gdns  G6
North Rd  I6
North Street  I8
Old Steine  K8
Oriental Pl  D9
Over St  H5
Palace Pier  K11
Pavilion Gdns  J8
Pool Valley  J9
Portland Road  H7
Powis Grv  F6
Powis Rd  E6
Powis Vil  E6
Preston St  E9
Prince Albert St  I9
Princes St  K8
Quebec St  M4
Queens Gdns  I6
Queens Park  N5

# INDEX OF STREETS

| | | |
|---|---|---|
| Queen's Park Rd   M6 | St James Ave   M8 | Vernon Terrace   E5 |
| Queen's Road   H7 | St Jame's St   L8 | Viaduct Rd   I1 |
| Regency Square   E9 | St Michael's   E6 | Victoria Rd   E6 |
| Regent Pl   F7 | St Nicholas Rd   G6 | Victoria St   E7 |
| Regent St   I7 | Steine St   K9 | Vine Place   F6 |
| Richmond St   L5 | Sussex St   L6 | Vine St   J6 |
| Robert St   J6 | Sydney St   I5 | Washington St   L3 |
| Rock Pl   M9 | Temple St   D7 | Waterloo St   C9 |
| Russell Rd   G9 | Terminus Road   G4 | West Hill Rd   F5 |
| Russell Sq   F9 | The Level   K2 | West Pier   E11 |
| Scotland St   M4 | The Station   H4 | West Street   H9 |
| Ship St   I9 | Tidy St   I5 | Western Road   D8 |
| Silwood Rd   D9 | Titchborne   I7 | Western St   C9 |
| Silwood Street   D9 | Toronto Terr   M4 | White St   L7 |
| South   H9 | Trafalgar La   I5 | Windlesham Gdns   D5 |
| Southampton St   M3 | Trafalgar St   I4 | Windlesham Rd   D6 |
| Southover St   L3 | Upp. Bedford   O8 | Windsor St   H7 |
| Spring Gdns   H6 | Upp. Gloucester   G5 | Wyndhm   N9 |
| Spring St   E7 | Upp. Rock Gdns   M8 | York Avenue   C6 |
| St Annes Wells Pk   B5 | Upper Gdnr   I6 | York Rd   C7 |
| St Georges Road   P8 | Upper North St   F7 | |

Thoroughly researched and packed with anecdotes and humour, the *Cheeky Guide to Oxford* will take you on a rollercoaster ride through this world-famous city. Featuring the usual Cheeky trademarks, the book provides information on the city's famous music scene, its vast array of drinking establishments, restaurants, shops, museums and shoddy selection of nightclubs.

Peppered with cartoons and illustrations by local artists, this guide really does give an insider's perspective on Oxford and even includes information on famous movie locations and a spotters guide to local celebrities and eccentrics.

Of course Oxford wouldn't be the same without the students, and the Cheeky Guide includes an A-Z of the many ridiculous University traditions, from tortoise races to hitting Marks and Spencers with sticks, as well as providing detailed information, fruity stories and maps to some of the city's most celebrated colleges. Whether you're staying in Oxford for a weekend, three years or a lifetime, this book is a must. **£5.95 • ISBN 0953611019**

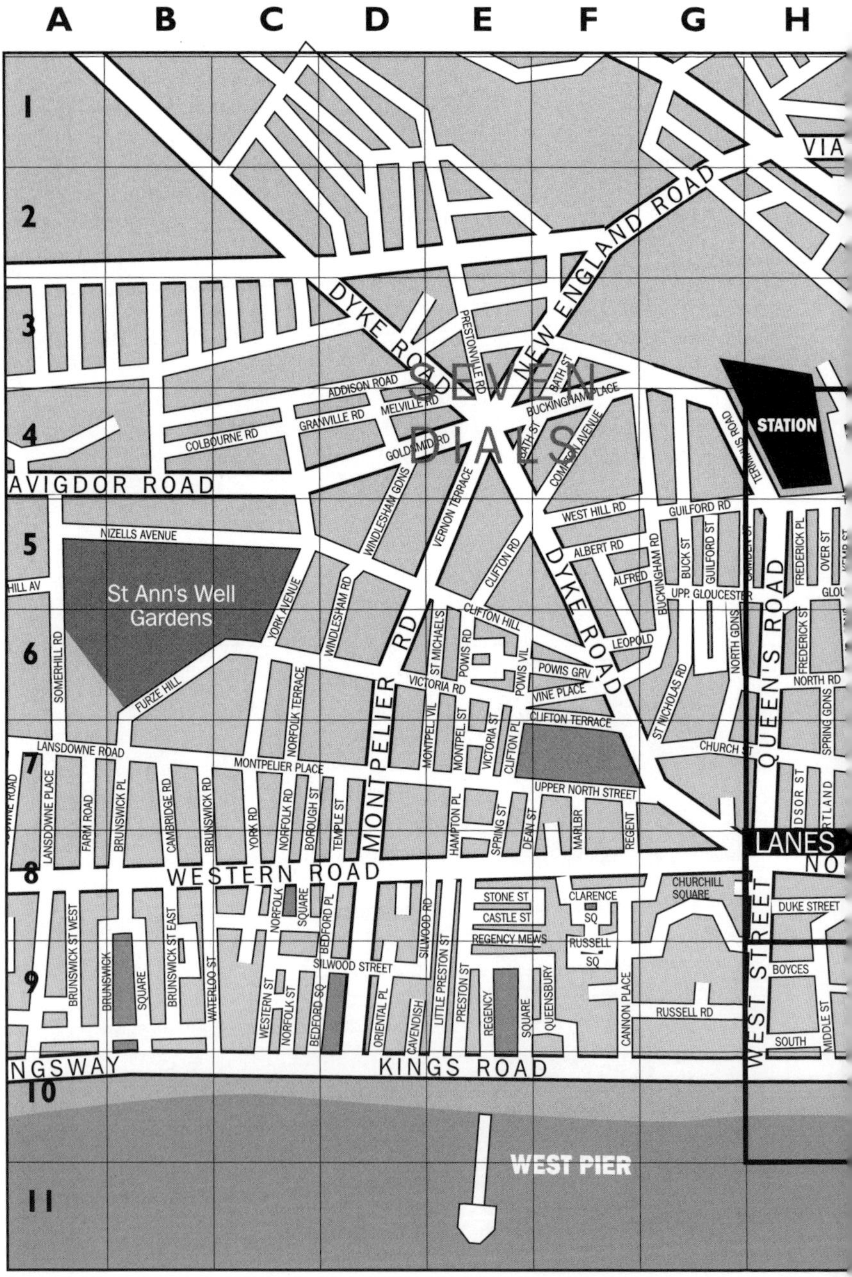
A
B
C
D
E
F
G
H
1
2
3
4
5
6
7
8
9
10
11
VIA
NEW ENGLAND ROAD
DYKE ROAD
SEVEN DIALS
PRESTONVILLE RD
BATH ST
BUCKINGHAM PLACE
ADDISON ROAD
MELVILLE RD
GRANVILLE RD
COLBOURNE RD
GOLDSMID RD
BATH ST
COMPTON AVENUE
STATION
TERMINUS ROAD
AVIGDOR ROAD
WINDLESHAM GDNS
VERNON TERRACE
WEST HILL RD
GUILFORD RD
NIZELLS AVENUE
CLIFTON RD
DYKE ROAD
ALBERT RD
BUCKINGHAM RD
BUCK ST
GUILFORD ST
FREDERICK PL
OVER ST
HILL AV
St Ann's Well Gardens
YORK AVENUE
WINDLESHAM RD
ALFRED
UPP. GLOUCESTER
QUEEN'S ROAD
CLIFTON HILL
LEOPOLD
NORTH GDNS
FREDERICK ST
SOMERHILL RD
MONTPELIER RD
ST MICHAEL'S
POWIS RD
POWIS VIL
POWIS GRV
ST NICHOLAS RD
NORTH RD
FURZE HILL
NORFOLK TERRACE
VICTORIA RD
VINE PLACE
SPRING GDNS
CLIFTON TERRACE
MONTPEL. VIL
MONTPEL. ST
VICTORIA ST
CLIFTON PL
CHURCH ST
LANSDOWNE ROAD
MONTPELIER PLACE
UPPER NORTH STREET
LANSDOWNE PLACE
FARM ROAD
BRUNSWICK PL
CAMBRIDGE RD
BRUNSWICK RD
YORK RD
NORFOLK RD
BOROUGH ST
TEMPLE ST
HAMPTON PL
SPRING ST
DEAN ST
MARLBR
REGENT
LANES
WESTERN ROAD
NORFOLK SQUARE
STONE ST
CLARENCE SQ
CHURCHILL SQUARE
CASTLE ST
DUKE STREET
REGENCY MEWS
RUSSELL SQ
WEST STREET
BRUNSWICK ST WEST
BRUNSWICK SQUARE
BRUNSWICK ST EAST
WATERLOO ST
BEDFORD PL
SILWOOD RD
SILWOOD STREET
LITTLE PRESTON ST
PRESTON ST
BOYCES
WESTERN ST
NORFOLK ST
BEDFORD SQ
ORIENTAL PL
CAVENDISH
REGENCY SQUARE
QUEENSBURY
CANNON PLACE
RUSSELL RD
MIDDLE ST
SOUTH
NGSWAY
KINGS ROAD
WEST PIER

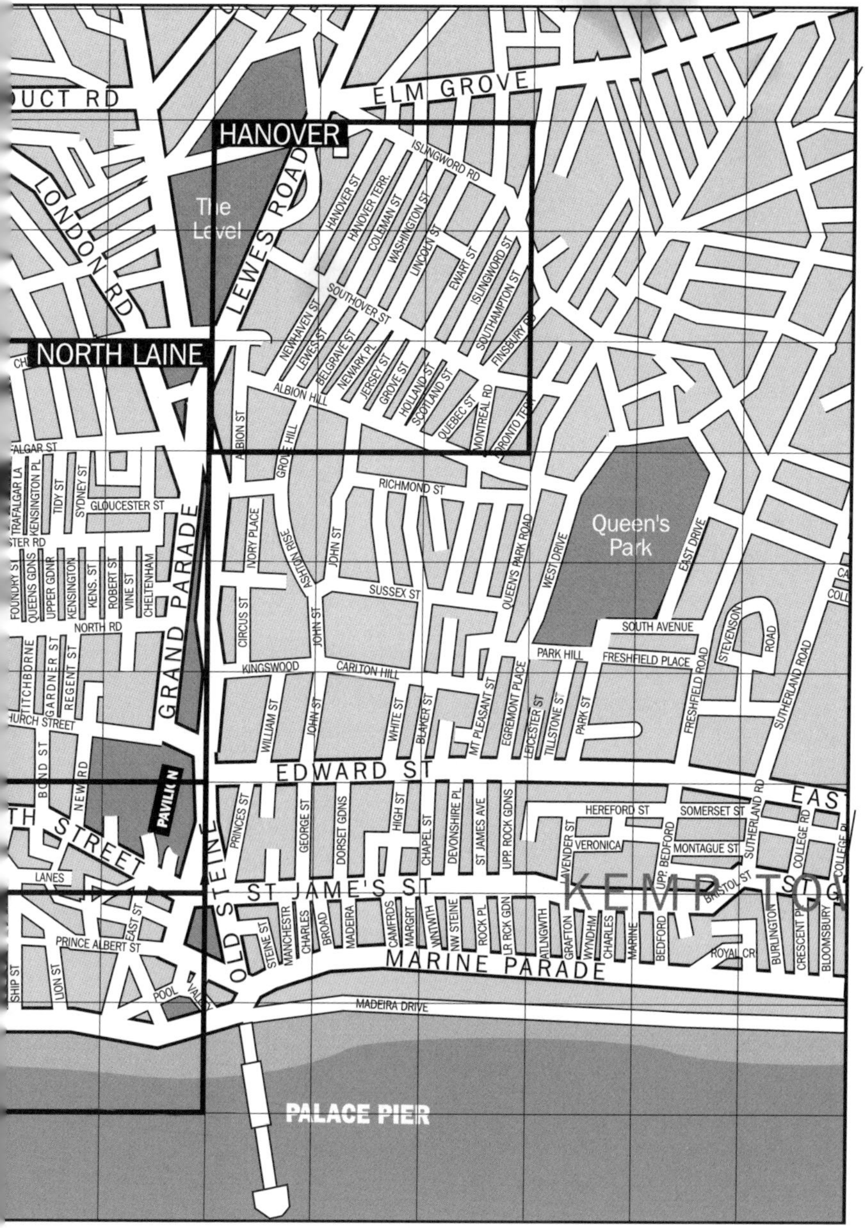

I J K L M N O P
ELM GROVE
HANOVER
The Level
LEWES ROAD
LONDON RD
NORTH LAINE
ISLINGWORD RD
HANOVER ST
HANOVER TERR.
COLEMAN ST
WASHINGTON ST
LINCOLN ST
EWART ST
ISLINGWORD ST
SOUTHAMPTON ST
SOUTHOVER ST
NEWHAVEN ST
LEWES ST
BELGRAVE ST
NEWARK PL
JERSEY ST
GROVE ST
HOLLAND ST
SCOTLAND ST
QUEBEC ST
MONTREAL RD
ALBION HILL
ALBION ST
GROVE HILL
RICHMOND ST
GLOUCESTER ST
TIDY ST
SYDNEY ST
KENSINGTON PL
TRAFALGAR LA
IVORY PLACE
ASHTON RISE
JOHN ST
QUEEN'S PARK ROAD
WEST DRIVE
Queen's Park
EAST DRIVE
GRAND PARADE
SUSSEX ST
FOUNDRY ST
QUEENS GDNS
UPPER GDNR
KENSINGTON
KENS. ST
ROBERT ST
VINE ST
CHELTENHAM
NORTH RD
CIRCUS ST
SOUTH AVENUE
PARK HILL
FRESHFIELD PLACE
STEVENSON
ROAD
FRESHFIELD ROAD
SUTHERLAND ROAD
KINGSWOOD
CARLTON HILL
TITCHBORNE
GARDNER ST
REGENT ST
WILLIAM ST
WHITE ST
BLAKER ST
MT PLEASANT ST
EGREMONT PLACE
LEICESTER ST
TILLSTONE ST
PARK ST
BOND ST
NEW RD
EDWARD ST
PAVILION
PRINCES ST
GEORGE ST
DORSET GDNS
HIGH ST
CHAPEL ST
DEVONSHIRE PL
ST JAMES AVE
UPP. ROCK GDNS
HEREFORD ST
SOMERSET ST
SUTHERLAND RD
VERONICA
UPP. BEDFORD
MONTAGUE ST
COLLEGE RD
BRISTOL ST
LANES
ST JAMES'S ST
KEMP TOWN
OLD STEINE
EAST ST
PRINCE ALBERT ST
STEINE ST
MANCHESTR
CHARLES
BROAD
MADEIRA
CAMFRDS
MARGRT
WNTWTH
NW STEINE
ROCK PL
LR RCK GDN
ATLNGWTH
GRAFTON
WYNDHM
CHARLES
MARINE
BEDFORD
ROYAL CR
BURLINGTON
BLOOMSBURY
MARINE PARADE
SHIP ST
LION ST
POOL VALLEY
MADEIRA DRIVE
PALACE PIER

# Directory Adverts

## Liquid Lounge
2 Brighton Square, The Old Lanes
(01273) 207774
Mon-Fri 9.30am-5.00pm,
Sat 10am-6pm, Sun 10am-4pm
Brighton's new juice and soup bar with a growing reputation for good healthy food with the emphasis on alternative. Wheatgrass has become a cult amongst its customers who claim miraculous effects despite it tasting like hmmm grass! They also now deliver, so you have no excuse not to get healthy.

## Greys Pub
15 YEARS DOWN THE DRAIN!! BACK-STREET SHOE-BOX PUB. ONLY THREE CHEFS IN ALL THAT TIME - AA AND EGON RONAY REC. TWICE A WEEK THE PUB CONVERTS ITSELF TO A 75 PEOPLE VENUE WITH STAGE, LIGHTS, P.A., EVEN ADAT RECORDING.
GET MONTHLY LISTINGS AND MENUS FROM:
*mike@greyspub.com*
*www.greyspub.com*

## Lumen
Lumen is Brighton's premier production house offering the best in 16 and 24 track digital recording, programming & production in an easy going, comfortable atmosphere. Our friendly, creative team have an impressive track record of major and independent productions so bring your music to the cutting edge at Lumen studio.
(01273) 690149
*info@lumenstudio.co.uk*

## Gaff
Contemporary rugs. Over 200 designs in stock, inspirational designs for people who want something different! Buy 'off the peg' or design your own. Borrow our designs and put it in your choice of colours to match your interior! We are
**'Great art for floors'**
66 Trafalgar Street, Brighton
(01273) 819202

## Honeyclub
Centrally located in the seafronts picturesque artistes quarter, the redesigned Honeyclub is now the largest and most luxurious of the seafront clubs. Now widely regarded as Brighton's trendiest club, the Honeyclub has overtaken all competition as the very best that Brighton has to offer. Open 7 nights a week.

## Blackwell's
Academic specialists, most customer orders fulfilled within 48 hours, open all year round. Knowledgeable, friendly and funky staff.
Blackwell's University Bookshop, University of Brighton, Cockcroft Building, Moulsecoomb, Brighton, BN2 4GJ, Tel: (01273) 571974
*brighton@blackwellsbookshops.co.uk*

## Cardome
Can't find what you're looking for ? Cardome 2000: From Adult mags to Jungle Juice plus loads more; humour cards, art cards, candles, incense, gifts. Mon-Sat 10am-6pm 47a St James's Street, (01273) 692916 (Next to the Royal Oak Pub

## Brighton Oasis Sauna
75-76 Grand Parade, Brighton, BN2 2JA, England(01273) 68996
The finest men only sauna in th heart of the UK's friendliest Ga village. Re-entry passes available every day Mon-Thu 12noon-10pm, Fri 12 noon-4am, Sat 12noon-6am, Sun 12noon-midnight
*www.oasissauna.com*

## Green Buddha
'Brighton's newest bookshop offers a wide range of Mind, Body, and Spirit books, many at reduced prices. They also stock music, crystals, incense and artwork. Special orders can be taken and a mail order service available. So go and see Carl, Lucy and Nick for friendly advic on all aspects of your spiritual journey.

## Adaptatrap
26 Trafalgar Street, Brighton, BN1 4ED (01273) 672 722
Large selection of world percussion instruments: Conga's, Bongo's, Djembes, Tablas, Sanzas, Bells, Reqq, Digeridoos, Shamen-Bowls, Gongs, Bodhrans, Bendirs, Rattles, Koras, Guiros, Time, Tapes, Books, Repairs, Advice, Maintenance, Workshops, Humans, Falookas